Terrorism, Trauma, and Tragedies

A Counselor's Guide to Preparing and Responding

Third Edition

Edited by Jane Webber and J. Barry Mascari

American Counseling Association Foundation

Alexandria, Virginia

Terrorism, Trauma, and Tragedies: A Counselor's Guide to Preparing and Responding
Third Edition

10   9   8   7   6   5   4   3   2   1

American Counseling Association Foundation
5999 Stevenson Avenue
Alexandria, VA 22304

Editorial Assistant
Julia Runte

Copy Editor/Production Manager
Debra Bass

Cover design by Matthew Mascari

Library of Congress Cataloging-in-Publication Data

Terrorism, trauma, and tragedies : a counselor's guide to preparing and responding/edited by
Jane Webber and J. Barry Mascari.—3rd ed.
    p. cm.
    Includes bibliographical references.
    ISBN 978-1-55620-308-4 (alk. paper)
    1. September 11 Terrorist Attacks, 2001—Psychological aspects. 2. Terrorism—United States—
Psychological aspects. 3. Victims of terrorism—Counseling of—United States. 4. Crisis intervention
(Mental health services)—United States. I. Webber, Jane. II. Mascari, Barry.

HV6432.T472 2010
362.2'04251—dc22   2010007454

For Hart and Sherry Webber, who taught us that life is lived in bringing joy to others.
We miss your music, your meals, and your love.
For Joe and Doris Mascari whose tenacity keeps us going.
For our grandparents who taught us what it was like to be strangers in a strange land.

Contents

The American Counseling Association Foundation was honored and pleased to welcome Barry Mascari as co-editor of this new edition of *Terrorism, Trauma and Tragedies: A Counselor's Guide to Preparing and Responding.* He joins lead editor Jane Webber who took the second edition to the next level of excellence after the book was first launched following the September 11 terrorist attacks. Together they have assembled an impressive team of 51 contributing authors—each of whom has a unique perspective and specific expertise to share.

This third edition represents an extensive revision over the first two editions and again brings new attention to the field of disaster mental health. With the dramatic increase of tragic events around the world, this book is more timely than ever. The scope has broadened even further than that of the second edition to include the shocking Virginia Tech shooting, the devastating hurricanes in New Orleans and the Gulf Coast region, as well as the ongoing wars in Afghanistan and Iraq and the effects on soldiers and their families.

And, as the manuscript was in the final stages of production, the earthquake in Haiti struck—yet another reminder of the need for resources and training in this field. ACA Foundation Chair Howard Smith, EdD, LPC, was part of a response team of the International Services Department of the American Red Cross that went to Haiti on a special assignment to provide services to American responders who were already in Haiti and those who went immediately after the disaster.

The goal of this edition, like the previous two sold-out editions, remains the same: to share practical strategies and lessons learned from those on the front lines of terrorism, trauma, and tragedies. The sharing of experiences will help to ensure that counseling professionals are well-prepared for the inevitable events that lie ahead.

The ACA Foundation is grateful to Editors Jane Webber and Barry Mascari and all of the contributors who volunteered their time, shared their stories and insights, and opened up their hearts to help those who were in need.

PREFACE TO THE FIRST EDITION

Every book begins with an idea, a thought, or a commitment to communicate something that will be of interest or importance to the reader. This publication, *Terrorism, Trauma and Tragedies: A Counselor's Guide to Preparing and Responding*, is no exception.

Conceived as a resource for counselors, teachers, administrators, parents and others, this is a hands-on, practical book that provides useful information and guidance on strategies, techniques, and plans that have worked well. It was not developed as a theoretical or formal text on the root causes of terrorism or tragedy, so much as something that caregivers can pick up and use immediately in their practice with children, adolescents, teens, and adults of all ages who are experiencing the trauma of a tragic event.

This book is a collection of original material, news stories, handouts, and even adaptations of recent conference presentation. As such it includes a variety of writing styles and approaches. In Section 1, for example, you will read straight-from-the-heart moving, personal accounts of counselors who were on the front lines on September 11 and afterward. It is important to hear their stories in their own words.

The Trustees of the American Counseling Association Foundation formulated the idea for this publication shortly after the terrorist attacks. While they had contemplated some type of resource in the wake of school shootings and other tragedies over the past few years, the events of September 11 dictated that the book move into an accelerated production schedule. This is the first book published by the Foundation.

It is the hope of the ACA Foundation that this book will be a resource to helping professionals as they grapple with how best to work with persons who are facing tragic and traumatic events in their lives, indeed in today's world. Terrorism has become a fact of life in recent months.

The American Counseling Association Foundation (2001-2002)

Jane Webber, Chair
William Cox, Immediate Past Chair
Quincy Moore, Chair-Elect
James Henderson, Trustee
Clemmie Solomon, Trustee-Designate
Jane Goodman, ACA President
David Kaplan, ACA President-Elect
Richard Yep, Secretary/Treasurer

ACKNOWLEDGMENTS

This third edition has been the collaborative effort of 51 authors, and we thank all our colleagues who have contributed to this book. We are grateful to those pioneers whose work guided our journey, especially Tom Query, Steve Crimando, Mike Dubi, Charles Figley, Eric Gentry, Eliana Gil, and Bessel van der Kolk.

Our projects have always been a family experience and we are indebted to our children, Julia Runte, manuscript editor; Matthew Mascari, for the cover design; and Janine Mascari and Chris Runte for their assistance and encouragement to keep doing what we love. We are especially appreciative of continued support from Carol Gernat and Tassie and Don Livingston.

We have been privileged to work with Debra Bass of the American Counseling Association whose skill and wit have kept us on track as this volume evolved through three editions. This book would not be possible without the vision and commitment of the American Counseling Association Foundation to respond to the needs of counselors after September 11.

To our graduate students whom we have the honor and privilege of teaching and whose trauma stories have informed our development as trauma counselors, we are deeply grateful.

Section One

Strategies and Techniques for Disaster Response

ADVANCES IN DISASTER AND TRAUMA COUNSELING

1

J. Barry Mascari and Jane Webber

The evolution of this book from the first to the third edition reflects the rapidly developing field of disaster and trauma response. In the second edition (2005), we cautioned, "...many counselors were not educated about the risks of trauma work..." (Webber & Mascari, 2005, p. 22). Critical issues identified were preparing professionals for disaster response and self care; providing a clearinghouse for rapidly deploying volunteers; understanding what treatments work in the field; and promoting coordination among federal, state, and local agencies and professional groups. Each edition has contributed to the growing body of evidence-informed practice for helping people who have experienced traumatic events.

The September 11 attacks in 2001 and the devastating hurricanes of 2005 led to government allocation of billions of dollars for research and projects to improve disaster and trauma response. Professional associations found a common cause and a voice with the government in developing federal and state codes (Uniform Emergency Volunteer Health Practitioners Act (UEVHPA) and the Emergency Management Assistance Compact (EMAC) (see Chapter 41) to facilitate the deployment of credentialed counselors in future disasters. Advances in interventions led to a common cross-disciplinary language used by responders that did not exist 8 years ago (e.g., psychological first aid, combat stress injury, compassion fatigue, posttraumatic growth, and natural capacities for healing).

Military campaigns in Iraq and Afghanistan that were launched in response to the September 11 attacks have lasted longer than any in American history. This has led to a growing number of veterans diagnosed with posttraumatic stress disorder (PTSD) and a suicide epidemic attributable to multiple combat deployments (Mueller & Dinges, 2009). A 2006 Stanford University research project found that 35% of veterans from these two wars suffered PTSD compared to 19% of Vietnam veterans (Mueller & Dinges, 2009). Boscarino (2007) reported that Vietnam era military veterans with long-term PTSD had an increased risk of death from multiple causes. This likely will be the case with veterans of the Iraq and Afghanistan as well. As returning veterans fill VA hospitals, trained mental health professionals in community agencies and private practice will be called upon to treat both veterans and their families.

Credentialing

The September 11 aftermath in New York City demonstrated that well-meaning professionals hoping to "do therapy" with victims often were not helpful. As a result, the federal government set minimum training standards for individuals providing disaster response through the Federal Emergency Management Agency's National Incident Management System. Trauma-related professional organizations, notably the American Red Cross, the American Academy of Experts in Traumatic Stress, Green Cross Academy of Traumatology, and the Association of Traumatic Stress Specialists established credentials for disaster and trauma counselors; however, a single national credential for disaster mental health responders has yet to emerge.

In 2007, New Jersey implemented the first state-sanctioned credentialing process for professionals who serve on county and state disaster mental health teams. The New Jersey Disaster Response Crisis Counselor certification is a trend among states that will strengthen efforts to professionalize the field and standardize training. For example, the Multi-State Disaster Behavioral Health Consortium, currently made up of 21 states, was established in 2009 to coordinate resources.

The counseling profession has taken a major step to ensure that counselors are prepared for disasters and traumatic events. The 2009 Standards, adopted by its accrediting body, the Council for Accreditation of Counseling and Related Education Programs (CACREP), require disaster and trauma training throughout master's and doctoral program curricula. Webber and Mascari (2009) noted, "These [CACREP] standards represent a major shift from basic counselor training requirements to an infusion of disaster and trauma competencies across counselor preparation" (p.126). How the various professional associations and disaster and trauma organizations will ensure that practicing mental health professionals also receive state-of-the-art disaster and trauma skills remains to be addressed.

Trauma Research

Trauma counseling has emerged as a specialty across the mental health fields, whereas early practice models were based on field research and observation. Many pioneers have expanded our knowledge and practice dramatically in recent years, including: van der Kolk (biological aspects of traumatic memory), Figley (compassion fatigue and combat stress), Shapiro (EMDR and brain hemisphere integration), Grand (Brainspotting to identify the location of trauma in the brain), Pittman (neurobiology and the role of adrenaline in re-traumatizing memory), Ford (the brain's processing of emotions after trauma), and Courtois (healing sexual trauma). Responses to Hurricanes Katrina and Rita raised questions about long-term disaster recovery procedures, and, coupled with the recent economic disaster and pandemic threats, expanded areas for trauma research and the development of new treatment models. We now recognize that different kinds of traumatic events may require subtly different responses. Turner, McFarlane, and van der Kolk (1996) noted:

> Therapists who treat traumatized individuals need to have a range of therapeutic options at their disposal, and to be able to tailor these to the needs of individual patients. These therapists must specifically take into account such issues as avoidance and outreach, acceptance and tolerance, cultural appropriateness, safety and security, and instillation of hope. (p. 545)

New discoveries emerge so quickly that professional associations and journals are morally committed to speed this information to the practice field. For example, in his research in 2007–2008, Pittman concluded that traumatized individuals only had a 48–72 hour window for medical intervention. However, only a year later Pittman (2009) found:

> The traumatization doesn't occur all at once… People rehearse in their minds over and over again the traumatic events in the days and weeks following the trauma, and each time they do that, they may further release adrenaline, which further consolidates the memory. If that's the case, you may have a much longer window of opportunity.

The Internet has become the fastest way to deliver this rapidly expanding knowledge base of disaster and trauma practice, especially with online professional journals gaining mainstream acceptance. Even before appearing in books or journals, Grand's Brainspotting approach, an extension of EMDR, has been found on several online sites (Heart, 2010).

OVERVIEW OF THE THIRD EDITION

This third edition *of Terrorism, Trauma and Tragedies: A Counselor's Guide to Preparing and Responding* is organized into seven sections and 42 chapters, with each section focusing on themes and events addressing specific areas of disaster response and trauma counseling.

Section I. Strategies and Techniques for Disaster Response highlights advances in the field for counseling clients with acute stress disorder and PTSD after traumatic events. Sand therapy and EMDR models are examined in two new chapters. New chapters also address cultural issues with disaster survivors and preparation for international disaster deployment.

Section II. Lessons Learned from Hurricane Katrina and Other Disasters is a new section that records the experiences of survivors and responders in the aftermath of the hurricanes, describes the dual roles of disaster responder and victim, and shares authors' trauma stories of recovery and return to professional practice.

Section III. Support for Returning Veterans and Their Families speaks to the US military culture and experiences of personnel and their families when deploying, as well as the school counselor's role in supporting students with deployed parents. Three new chapters describe issues specific to treating returning veterans and their families, and post-deployment counseling for National Guard and Reserve families.

Section IV. Virginia Tech and Other University Trag-

edies is a new section with the reflective experiences of Virginia Tech and Northern Illinois communities responding to the shootings and living through the grief and healing process. Two chapters provide suggestions for preparing non-counseling faculty to assist students after a tragedy, as well as the development of public education resources and resiliency workshops.

Section V: Responding to School Crises and Tragedies addresses planning for a crisis to a school's response to war, Katrina, and school shootings. Chapters provide questions and answers for counselors about responding to death and sudden loss, and a family debriefing model for students after terrorist acts.

Section VI: Helping Children Cope with Tragedy presents practical strategies to use after traumatic events including a structured 12-step intervention process, play therapy, and interventions in China following the 2008 earthquake. Updated chapters address violence toward children in the nation's capitol and counseling the children of first responders after September 11.

Section VII. Self Care for Counselors and First Responders records the experiences of counselors after acts of terrorism and natural disasters, and provides models for peer supervision and compassion fatigue recovery. New chapters address CISD and self care for disaster mental health responders.

Section VIII. Current Issues in Disaster Mental Health examines international disaster counseling, domestic pandemic planning and response, and the recent financial crisis. Chapters also present standards for disaster response, legislation for volunteer credentials and deployment, and emerging practices.

THE TRAGEDY IN HAITI

While the emerging disaster and trauma specialty has brought real hope and resolution for victims, we have learned over the years that preparing for those tragedies we wish will never happen is an essential part of counselor preparation and practice.

In the final moments before publication, the world witnessed such a devastating tragedy: the enormous suffering of Haitians after the earthquake in January 2010, and the heroic attempts of rescuers and doctors to save lives. The impact of the earthquake on Haitian-Americans remains to be examined as the response moves from rescue and recovery to reestablishing social order. We hope to include in the next edition lessons learned and experience gained from the earthquake in Haiti.

The third edition, with its emphasis on disaster mental health, cultural competence, and international collaboration, is our modest contribution to this growing specialty and our hope for the recovery of Haiti.

J. Barry Mascari, EdD, LPC, LCADC, is chair of the Counselor Education Department at Kean University, Union, New Jersey and holds New Jersey Disaster Response Crisis Counselor certification (NJDRCC).

Jane Webber, PhD, LPC, is associate professor and coordinator of the Counseling Program at New Jersey City University. She is a counselor in private practice and holds New Jersey Disaster Response Crisis Counselor certification (NJDRCC).

REFERENCES

Boscarino, W. (2007). The mortality impact of combat stress 30 years after exposure: Implications for prevention, treatment, and research. In C. Figley & W. P. Nash (Eds.), *Combat stress injury: Theory, research, & management* (pp. 97–117). New York: Routledge.

Dinges, T., & Mueller, M. (2009). Military suicides: Cases of post-traumatic stress mount at an alarming rate. Retrieved from http://www.nj.com/news/index.ssf/2009/11/military_suicides_soldiers_ira.html

Heart, K. (2010). An "inside view" of brainspotting and mental health recovery. Retrieved from http://www.brainspotting.pro/files/BSP-and-Mental-Health-Recovery.pdf

Pittman, R. (2002). Can beta blockers prevent PTSD: A first look. *Neuropsychiatry Reviews, 3*(2). Retrieved from www.neuropsychiatryreviews.com/march02/ptsd.html

Turner, S. W., McFarlane, A. C., & van der Kolk, B. A. (1996). The therapeutic environment and new explorations in the treatment of posttraumatic stress disorder. In B. A. van der Kolk, A. C. McFarlane, & L. Weisaeth (Eds.). *Traumatic stress: The effects of overwhelming experience on mind, body, and society* (pp. 537-558). New York: Guilford.

Webber, J., & Mascari, J. B. (2005). 9/11: Lessons learned. In J. Webber, D. Bass, & R. Yep (Eds.), *Terrorism, trauma and tragedies: A counselor's guide to preparing and* responding (2nd ed.) (pp. 21–26). Alexandria, VA: American Counseling Association Foundation.

Webber, J., & Mascari, J. B. (2009). Critical issues in implementing the new CACREP Standards for disaster, trauma, and crisis counseling. In G. R. Waltz, J. C. Bleuer, & R. K. Yep (Eds.). *Compelling counseling images: The best of VISTAS 2009* (pp. 125–138). Alexandria, VA: American Counseling Association.

UNDERSTANDING AND WORKING WITH ACUTE STRESS DISORDER

2

Michael Dubi and Samuel Sanabria

It is unlikely that any of us can go through life without experiencing at least one traumatic event. For most of us, extreme physical, emotional, cognitive, and behavioral reactions are a natural part of responding to these events. It is important to keep in mind that many of the extreme responses to trauma are, in fact, normal reactions to abnormal events such as tsunamis, hurricanes, combat, physical and sexual abuse, events witnessed on TV, or vicarious trauma. However, there may be instances in which the individual responses are not normal, making it difficult to predict how those individuals will react.

In August 2005, the entire world watched as thousands of people huddled in a collapsing football stadium or stood stranded and desperate on the roofs of buildings surrounded by rising floodwaters. Those individuals who found a safe place to stay during and after the storm, who received adequate food, water, and medical care, who were able to contact family and friends, and who were informed as to what was being done to help them were able to cope better. However, for several days after Hurricane Katrina had left the area, residents of the Louisiana and Mississippi coasts were in a daze. Those individuals were probably experiencing Acute Stress Disorder (ASD).

UNDERSTANDING ASD

ASD is an anxiety disorder that develops within 2 days after a severe traumatic experience and lasts up to 1 month. It can affect anyone at any age and can develop into posttraumatic stress disorder (PTSD). Some of the common symptoms of ASD—which differentiate it from PTSD—include numbing, depersonalization, derealization or dissociative amnesia, and reduced awareness of one's surroundings. Individuals suffering from ASD seem to be in a daze and will avoid any reminder of the traumatic incident. If this occurs, they should seek professional mental health services. Professionals who are interested in crisis work should be trained to assess and treat traumatic stress disorders (Bryant & Harvey, 2000).

Physiological reactions. Individuals may display a range of physiological responses to trauma that include fatigue, rapid heartbeat, elevated blood pressure, and hyperventilation. These are normal responses to abnormal events. Physiological behaviors that may require immediate medical attention include difficulty breathing, chest pains, cardiac palpitations, and shock symptoms.

Emotional reactions. Individuals with ASD may display a variety of emotional responses ranging from shock to dissociation. They also may be in denial or unable to acknowledge that the event has occurred. Other emotional responses include anxiety, panic, fear, depression, irritability, guilt, emptiness, horror, and depression.

Cognitive reactions. Individuals with ASD often have difficulty concentrating or making decisions. Other cognitive reactions include confusion, disorientation, short attention span, forgetfulness, self-blame, blaming others, hypervigilance, lowered self-efficacy, and perseverative thoughts of the traumatic event.

Behavioral reactions. Individuals who have experienced a traumatic event may exhibit withdrawal, noncommunication, changes in speech patterns, regressive behaviors, erratic movements, impulsivity, a reluctance to abandon property, seemingly aimless walking, pacing, inability to sit still, exaggerated startled response, and antisocial behavior (Lerner & Shelton, 2005).

WORKING WITH ASD

The following interventions provide a brief guide for the helping professional:

- Identify those who have been exposed to the traumatic event

- Assess for danger to self and others and seek assistance if possible

- Assess the level and type of injury and seek appropriate medical help

- Assess the responsiveness of the victim: alert, unresponsive, intoxicated, etc.

- Connect with the individual by introducing yourself

- Move from the stressful situation when appropriate and begin to develop rapport

- Let the individual "tell his/her story"

- Be supportive and empathetic

- Normalize the individual's response

- Prepare for the future and provide case management

SPECIFIC INTERVENTIONS

Individuals who have been exposed to severe traumatic events may react in a variety of ways including wandering about in a state of shock. Lerner and Shelton (2005) suggested techniques to help connect with persons having a difficult reaction to reconnect cognitively and relate to the counselor.

Distraction aims to refocus the individual. Use caring comments that are powerful enough to divert the individual's attention back to the counselor, such as offering water. These comments should not be flippant or show a lack of concern. This intervention works well with children.

Disruption is an intervention that can be implemented quickly. For example, you may move to the individual's level and make eye contact. Calmly ask the individual to take a deep breath (several commands may be necessary) or ask a question that will disrupt the emotional reaction such as "What is your phone number?"

Diffusion of the emotional state is a third technique. With someone who is anxious or agitated, you may begin speaking by matching. Then, gradually, begin to slow the pace and volume until you can provide support and direction. As the individual begins to slow down, you also should gradually begin to slow things down. If the individual is depressed, begin at a similar rate and then start to increase the pace until he or she becomes more energetic and involved. This intervention will take more time than the other two.

Many individuals who experience ASD benefit from receiving professional counseling. Considerable research suggests using interventions such as eye movement desensitization reprocessing (EMDR) and cognitive-behavioral therapy. In fact, exposure therapy, in general, has a strong evidence base for working with traumatic stress victims. After individuals receive such treatment, emotional distress often is relieved significantly, negative physiological arousal is reduced, and dysfunctional beliefs are reformulated (Friedman, 2006).

COUNSELOR ISSUES

Working with trauma victims can be a challenge to remain therapeutically neutral while listening to stories about murder, torture, rape, child abuse, war, and natural disasters. It is common for such stories to stimulate powerful emotions in the counselor. These vicarious experiences can produce intrusive thoughts and feelings as well as nightmares. Counselors may feel guilty and powerless for not being protective enough of their clients leading to boundary violations and attempts to control the client. Trauma workers are at risk for compassion fatigue and should practice self care including their own individual or group counseling.

Michael Dubi, EdD, LMHC, is associate professor, and is certified in acute traumatic stress management and in compassion fatigue.

Samuel Sanabria, PhD, LMHC, is assistant professor and program chair.

Both are in the School of Psychology and Behavioral Sciences at Argosy University, Sarasota, Florida.

REFERENCES

Bryant, R. A., & Harvey, A. G. (2000). *Acute stress disorder: A handbook of theory, assessment and treatment.* Washington, DC: American Psychological Association.

Friedman, M. J. (2006). *Post-traumatic and acute stress disorder: The latest assessment and treatment strategies.* Kansas City, MO: Compact Clinicals.

Lerner, M. D., & Shelton, R. D. (2005). *Comprehensive acute traumatic stress management.* New York: The American Academy of Experts in Traumatic Stress.

EMDR: RESOLVING TRAUMATIC MEMORY

3

Michael Dubi and Mindi Raggi

Eye Movement Desensitization and Reprocessing (EMDR) was developed serendipitously and popularized by Francine Shapiro in the 1990s. This powerful method of psychotherapy has an extensive research base and is an effective intervention for traumatic stress. It has been accepted for the treatment of posttraumatic stress disorder (PTSD) by the American Psychological Association, the American Psychiatric Association, the Department of Defense, the Department of Veterans Affairs, and the International Society of Traumatic Stress Studies.

EMDR is an information processing intervention that uses an eight-phase approach to explore past experiences that set the groundwork for pathology. This is accomplished by connecting what was experienced at the time of the traumatic event to a bilateral pattern of eye movements. The approach works with current situations that trigger dysfunctional emotions, beliefs, and sensations, as well as installing new, more adaptive positive experiences needed to enhance future behaviors and mental health (EMDR Institute, 2009).

Studies have suggested that EMDR has a positive effect on clients with a diagnosis of PTSD, an anxiety disorder that typically occurs after an individual has experienced a traumatic event that involved the threat of injury or death (Datta & Wallace, 1996; Greenwald, 1998; Lee, Gavriel, Drummond, Richards, & Greenwald, 2002). Research also suggests that these results occur in from three to seven sessions and that treatment effects are long lasting. EMDR has been recognized as an efficacious treatment for PTSD (EMDR Institute, 2009; van der Kolk et al., 2007).

With EMDR, clients can rapidly recall and process memories of traumatic events. These memories frequently begin with bits and fragments of the original experience in the form of visual images, physical sensations, emotions, and/or cognitions. As the client is processing, the therapist provides bilateral stimulation; this can involve eye movements, tones, or taps. During the bilateral stimulation phase, the client usually experiences therapeutic insights, new memories, more adaptive cognitions, and reduced physiological arousal. It is also during bilateral stimulation that clients experience and learn to incorporate feelings and cognitions more functionally and adaptively to help resolve the negative effects of their traumatic experiences (EMDR Institute, 2009).

Traumatic memories, in fact all memories, are stored in the nervous system. These memories are accessed through thoughts, images, emotions, and sensations using bilateral stimulation, and they help create new associations with already stored material—this is how learning occurs. Shapiro (2001) explained that information processing may be incomplete when traumatic events occur, which may be due to the powerful emotions associated with them. Through bilateral stimulation, emotional arousal is reduced and clients can complete processing of the event.

EIGHT PHASES OF EMDR

EMDR is divided into eight sequential phases (EMDR Institute, 2009).

Phase One

History taking occurs and readiness for EMDR is assessed. Possible targets for treatment are discussed.

Phase Two

The therapist helps the client develop adequate methods of handling emotional distress and coping skills and determines that the client is in a relatively stable state.

Phases Three Through Six

The target is identified and processed. During these phases, the client is asked to identify the most vivid visual image related to the memory, a negative belief about self, related emotions, and body sensations. The client also is asked to identify a positive belief. During this part of the protocol, the client is asked to rate the validity of the positive belief and the intensity of the negative emotions. Then, during bilateral stimulation, the client focuses on the image, negative thought, and body sensations for approximately 30 seconds. The therapist instructs the client to be aware of what happens and then to let his or her mind go blank and to notice the thought, feeling, or sensation experienced. The client continues to process; this part of the procedure is repeated many times throughout the session. After several sets, clients usually report increased confidence in the positive belief. If negative sensations remain, they are processed and if there are positive sensations, they continue to be enhanced.

Phase Seven

This is the closure phase and the therapist asks that the client keep a journal during the week to record new material and to remind the client to use coping techniques learned in Phase Two.

Phase Eight

Progress since the last session is explored in order to provide both the most effective treatment and client stability. "EMDR treatment ensures processing of all related historical events, current incidents that elicit distress, and future scenarios that will require different responses" (EMDR Institute, 2009).

Commonly after EMDR treatment, clients report that emotional distress related to the trauma memory has ceased or been greatly decreased, which is related to more positive behavioral and personal changes. EMDR has been an effective treatment with both adults and children.

COUNSELING CLIENTS WITH TRAUMA

Sara

Sara is a 71-year-old widow whose husband had died of cancer less than 2 weeks before Hurricane Katrina hit her home. She was alone in her living room when Katrina tore the roof off her home. She huddled in a corner for several hours, too frightened to move and thinking she was about to die. She was rescued and moved to a shelter the following day. Several weeks later, a shelter worker referred her to a counselor who was providing pro bono services for survivors of Katrina. Almost immediately in the first session, she began to process memories and feelings of her intense experiences during Katrina. In just three sessions, she was able to eliminate the intrusive thoughts and feelings of panic she re-experienced daily. Sara and her therapist decided to continue treatment for a few sessions to allow her to process her grief over the loss of her husband and to develop a plan to get her life in order.

Wendy

Wendy is a mental health practitioner, well versed in the symptoms and treatment of PTSD. In an effort to "give back" to her community, she was providing pro bono counseling services to women seeking safe housing after escaping abusive situations. The women and staff in the shelter were reminded frequently never to answer the phone with the name of the church in which they were confidentially housed. One evening, this rule was inadvertently breached, and one of the women's batterers appeared at the site. He was angry and threatening. Wishing to shield the woman and her children from further trauma, and believing she could talk calmly to the man, Wendy left the building. In a matter of minutes, she was beaten and raped by the batterer whose anger had been fueled by crack and cocaine.

Wendy eventually returned to work and felt healed with the help of her supportive family. A full 3 years after the event, Wendy found herself suffering a nightmarishly real flashback of the event accompanied by a full throttle panic reaction. She recalls feelings of derealization and disassociation accompanied by the physiological symptoms commonly seen in panic disorder: sweating, dizziness, and difficulty breathing. Often, the specific trigger that precedes the onset of symptoms remains a mystery. However, through EMDR, the nightmares stopped and Wendy began to manage the symptoms of PTSD, which were accompanied by strong feelings of guilt and self-blame with regard to the incident.

This reaction is common in victims of sexual trauma, and is additionally often seen in younger victims of trauma. EMDR helps complete the trauma narrative through the process of bilateral integration, which is essential in reducing the PTSD symptoms.

Caroline

Caroline, a 44-year-old female, came to therapy following an episode of "hysteria and out of control anger, and a feeling of not belonging in my own body." The episode had occurred in the days following the arrival of Caroline's 6-year-old granddaughter, who had been removed from her mother's home (Caroline's own daughter) due to her mother's substance abuse and parental neglect.

Initially, Caroline expressed anger at her daughter, and her own feelings of guilt at "not showing her how to be a better mom." As the therapeutic relationship grew, Caroline began to discuss her continuing physical symptoms of nausea, emotional symptoms of fear and shame, and her bewildering feeling of anger at her granddaughter. It was during an EMDR session in which Caroline recalled an early memory from her own childhood—she was sexually abused at age 6. She had not shared this piece of her own traumatic childhood with either her spouse of 22 years or her children. The sexual abuse occurred at the hands of Caroline's stepfather who then left the home. Caroline had not seen nor spoken to her stepfather in the past 38 years.

EMDR was successful in resolving her traumatic memories and distress and assisting her in developing mechanisms that helped her to accept a belief in her own ability to be an adequate and loving caregiver for her granddaughter and to lead a more proactive life.

BENEFITS OF EMDR

Considerable research over the last 15 years suggests that EMDR is an effective and efficacious intervention for use with victims of trauma (Bradley, Greene, Russ, Dutra, & Wesson, 2005; van der Kolk et al., 2007). The short-term benefits of EMDR are immediate relief of emotional distress and elimination of the debilitating effects of unresolved past trauma. The longer-term benefits include restoration of the client's optimal state of emotional functioning, including a greater sense of personal power, more enriching relationships, and a more peaceful and productive life. Furthermore, EMDR has encouraged the development of other bilateral methods such as Brainspotting (Grand, n.d.).

Because this is a highly specialized method that requires supervised training for therapeutic effectiveness and client safety, only licensed mental health professionals can be qualified to use EMDR with clients.

Trauma therapists throughout the world are using EMDR as an intervention in the treatment of PTSD. It is particularly useful in working with PTSD and other anxiety disorders by facilitating the rapid processing and desensitization of disturbing cognitions, feelings, and memories, and the rapid reprocessing and development of more adaptive cognitions and behaviors.

Michael Dubi, EdD, LMHC, is an associate professor in the School of Psychology and Behavioral Sciences at Argosy University, Sarasota, Florida. He is trained in Brainspotting and is a certified EMDR therapist.

Mindi Raggi, EdD, LCSW, is a licensed clinical social worker in private practice in Pennsylvania specializing in rape trauma and sexual assault. She is affiliated with the Penn Foundation for Behavioral Health.

REFERENCES

Bradley, R., Greene, J., Russ, L., Dutra, L, & Wesson, D. (2005). A multidimensional meta-analysis of psychotherapy for PTSD. *American Journal of Psychiatry, 162,* 214–227.

Dutra, I., & Wallace, J. (1996). *Enhancement of victim empathy along with reduction in anxiety and increase of positive cognition of sex offenders after treatment with EMDR.* Presented at the annual conference of the EMDR International Association, Denver.

EMDR Institute, Inc. (2009). *A brief description of EMDR.* Retrieved from http://www.emdr.com.

Grand, D. (n.d.). *What is Brainspotting?* Retrieved from http://www.brainspotting.pro/page/what-brainspotting.

Greenwald, R. (1998). Eye movement desensitization and reprocessing (EMDR): New hope for children suffering from trauma and loss. *Clinical Child Psychology and Psychiatry, 3,* 279–287.

Lee, C., Gavriel, H., Drummond, P., Richards, J., & Greenwald, R. (2002). Treatment of posttraumatic stress disorder: A comparison of stress inoculation training with prolonged exposure and eye movement desensitizing and reprocessing. *Journal of Clinical Psychology, 58,* 1071-1089.

Shapiro, F. (2001). *Eye movement desensitization and reprocessing: Basic principles, protocols and procedures (2nd ed.).* New York: Guilford Press.

van der Kolk, B. A., Spinazzola, J., Blaustein, M. E., Hopper, E. K., Koran, D. L., & Simpson, W. B. (2007). A randomized clinical trial of eye movement desensitization and reprocessing (EMDR), fluoxitine, and pill placebo in the treatment of posttraumatic stress disorder: Treatment effects and long-term maintenance. *The Journal of Clinical Psychiatry, 68*(1), 37–46.

Unlocking Traumatic Memory Through Sand Therapy

4

Jane Webber, J. Barry Mascari, and Julia Runte

In the fictional film, *Reign Over Me* (Binder & Rotenberg, 2007), Charlie Fineman struggles with the debilitating impact of posttraumatic stress disorder (PTSD). Intrusive memories and visual images of his family haunt him several years after his wife and children were killed on the plane from Boston on September 11. Charlie lives a shattered life playing the same video game and repeatedly remodeling his kitchen—stuck in this repetitive task after his last communication with his wife was an argument about kitchen plans. By chance, Charlie's college roommate reconnects with him, and eventually Alan Johnson brings Charlie to a therapist. Week after week, the therapist tries to engage Charlie who, unable to cope with his emotional and physical distress, puts on his earphones and turns the volume up so that rock music shuts everything out. In the first minutes of each session, Charlie asks if the session is over. Each week the therapist replies, "It is if you want it to be." Knowing that the process is not working, she tells Charlie that he needs to share his story with someone, even if it is not with her.

The danger of retraumatization increases when a therapist asks the client to let the story out but is not skilled in helping the client integrate traumatic memories safely. Ogden, Minton, and Pain (2006) observed that "The body, for a host of reasons, has been left out of the 'talking cure'" (p. xxvii). Clients with trauma fear that if they get the story out, it cannot be put away again. Baranowsky, Gentry, and Schultz (2009) suggested that a different approach is needed for clients who are unable to complete their narratives with the therapist. "We believe that a courageous, optimistic, and non-anxious approach, tempered with safety and pacing, to be the keys to rapid amelioration of traumatic stress symptoms" (p. 2). We have found that sand therapy is an effective and powerful approach to trauma recovery that jumpstarts the therapeutic process without the threat of retraumatization.

The Power of Sand Therapy

Van der Kolk, van der Hart, and Marmar (1996) showed that "a traumatic memory cannot be adequately processed if its affective and sensory-motor elements remain isolated from the rest of the memory" (p. 322). Fragments of memories (sounds, smells, images) are embedded in the right hemisphere, separated from the words of the trauma event in the left hemisphere (Gil, 1996; van der Kolk et al., 1996). Gil described these fragments as a "...mirror that has re-

Figure 1. The Perpetrator, a sand tray in the reintegration stage of trauma recovery

ceived a single jolt and is shattered into small pieces" (p. 141) unable to be reconstructed.

Expressive therapies such as art, play, and sand therapy provide an alternative modality that reduces emotional and physiological distress, provides a safe environment to restore control, and accesses fragments of traumatic memories. The kinesthetic experience of placing and moving figures in sand promotes safety, control, therapeutic disclosure, and expression. When fragments of traumatic memories are integrated, intrusive thoughts disappear and "...a release of emotion and a change of perception frequently occur" (Boik & Goodwin, 2000, p. 15). The client can continue the healing process without debilitating physical and emotional distress. Thus, scenes in sand give voice to their trauma stories when verbal expression is not possible.

Individuals often are surprised by the depth of their emotional connection to the world they have spontaneously created in the tray. Many report that they did not plan to make a scene, but felt drawn to certain figures that held personal meaning. In numerous case studies, Gil (2006) documented the power of sand therapy for abused children that can "bring out hidden concerns whether they intend to reveal them or not" (p. 77). Simply choosing certain miniatures provided a bridge to accessing the traumatic event, resulting in therapeutic release and calming (Webber, 2009; Webber & Mascari, 2008).

The Perpetrator

Carol explained her world in the tray. On one side of the fence, Carol pointed to a tall woman sitting on a large couch—both miniatures were much larger than others in the tray. On the other side of the fence was a tiny figure.

> The perpetrator attacked and raped me, taking away my life with my family. Here I am over on this side, now confident and strong. These are my children and their sports games I missed trying to deal with it. The hourglass and the timeline over here—that's the time I lost with my family. The perpetrator—he's out of my life.

As she completed her story, Carol turned the perpetrator upside down and buried him in the sand. She successfully reconstructed the trauma narrative. Carol moved from victim to victor with an empowering ending and reconnected with her family (Webber, Mascari, & Dubi, 2008).

Sand Therapy: Not Only for Children

Although many consider sand therapy a tool for children, case studies have shown that it is a highly effective modality for adolescents and adults who experienced individual trauma or large-scale disasters. To help distraught students on September 11, a sand therapist brought miniatures and trays to their high school close to Manhattan. Several students spontaneously created scenes with metaphors of "a fallen lighthouse toppled over into the sand, surrounded by superheroes who dropped like stones from the sky"—unaware that several other students created similar scenes. Winter (as cited in Sullivan, 2003, p. 2) explained that the twin towers had been symbols of strength and direction for the community—"we oriented ourselves by the twin towers…when you saw them you always knew you were looking east, you knew where you were."

Experience with veterans has revealed that PTSD and combat stress frequently remain untreated. Fragments of traumatic memories are intensely sensory bits: the sound, image, smell, and taste of war. When traditional therapy is not working, the kinesthetic elements of sand therapy provide a sensorimotor channel to access memories safely. For many veterans returning from Iraq with physical and emotional trauma, sand therapy may be an effective alternative and adjunct to talk therapy.

The Bridge

John was a highly respected teacher who served with the National Guard in New York City after September 11 and was later deployed to Afghanistan and Iraq. When John returned home from Iraq, he was different—quieter and more somber. John frequently missed classes to attend therapy sessions at a veteran's hospital. One day, he left class suddenly and did not return. He was found sobbing and cowering in a corner of the men's room.

John began to visit the counselor's room and was attracted to the military figures in her miniature collection. He created chaotic battle scenes in which everyone died, burying the figures in sand. John later orchestrated complicated battles, focusing on detailed scenes of the armies and the landscape. Sometimes John broke miniature vehicles and soldiers into pieces and placed the bits in the tray. One day he gathered all the medical items, over-filling the tray with an ambulance, stethoscope, hypodermic needle, stretcher, wheelchair, bandages, and Red Cross trucks. Months later, John created a tray with six objects: a lone soldier facing a mother and three children on the other side of a bridge. He stared at the scene for a long time, and said, "Now I can talk" (Webber & Mascari, 2008, p. 2).

Moon (2006) also documented the power of sand therapy in the treatment of a posttraumatic Iraq veteran who was unable to speak and was not responding to talk therapy. When their sessions were at a therapeutic impasse, Moon shifted to sand therapy and "the mood of the session changed instantly...had he not had the tray to express himself, I doubt that we would have moved forward in his treatment." (p. 64)

THE SAND THERAPY EXPERIENCE

As individuals externalize events and feelings in the world of the tray, they gain needed physical, verbal, and emotional distance between the event and themselves. Clients can rearrange the figures to reconstruct the event as well as its outcome, increasing their personal power and mastery over their world. The unique sensory characteristics of each element–sand, water, tray and miniature figures—are integrated into the experience to promote concrete, realistic grounding as well as symbolic meaning.

Sand provides the foundation for creating the client's world. In both Eastern and Western culture and religion, sand is valued in rituals for its cleansing and purifying qualities; most clients find playing with sand comforting and self-soothing. Therapists often provide two trays, one with moist sand. Water provides form and substance to shifting sand so that individuals can create buildings, caves, mountains, rivers, and lakes needed for their story. Clients often search the collection for miniature figures with specific gender, ethnic, and racial features. Integrative therapists provide a wide range of human figures so that clients can connect and identify with a figure that represents them. Clients might also look for specific objects e.g., military or emergency response vehicles, medical personnel, or hospital equipment needed to recreate the traumatic event.

Traditional sandplay therapists (Kalff, 2003) use large, shallow, standard size rectangular wooden trays. To promote free choice and expression, De Domenico (2002) and other integrative therapists (Webber et al., 2008) provide trays in various sizes and shapes so the tray can "contain" the trauma experience safely. In the early stages of trauma treatment, clients may not feel safe or powerful enough to be directly in the scene and often place themselves outside the tray, with more physical distance from the event.

The Deathbed

Jose, a trauma therapist for veterans and their families, was overwhelmed with grief after the tragic death of his colleague. He felt that the vast space in the tray was too large to hold his sorrow fearing it would "spill out all over," until he noticed a small 6-inch square container. In this tiny space, Jose created a scene in which his friend lay dying and he placed a second figure representing himself outside the tray looking in. Jose disclosed, "I needed a very small space to contain and hold my overpowering sorrow...this is the first time I have risked letting it out" (Webber, 2009).

The Therapeutic Process

The process begins when the therapist invites the client to make a scene in the tray, and then silently witnesses the construction. It is important that the event or narrative is held safely within the physical boundaries of the tray as well as within a trusting therapeutic relationship. The story unfolds naturally when the individual feels safe, although the client may create many trays over several weeks before being able to speak. De Domenico (2002) emphasized that "both silence and verbalization are essential: wisdom and compassionate understanding let us know which to apply at a given moment in time" (p. 9). As the client guides the therapist on a tour of the world, the client becomes the author of a new narrative often reconstructing the story's end.

Sand therapy is easily integrated into several trauma counseling approaches. The process of building and rebuilding the world in the tray becomes a constructivist therapy experience. This frees the victim to deconstruct outcomes imposed by others and reconstruct the story, empowering the survivor to control and transform reactions to the traumatic event. As author and narrator of the narrative, the survivor can safely change roles from victim to victor, protagonist, and hero.

The September Birthday Party

The third phase of trauma recovery involves reconnecting with the community and "redefining oneself in the context of meaningful relationships" (Webber, Mascari, Dubi, & Gentry, 2006, p. 18). To restore relationships, the story is reconstructed in a way that frees the client to move forward. Often this process involves group sand therapy with family members and children transforming the traumatic loss into a meaningful and manageable remembrance.

Kara attended a family therapy program with her mother and brother after her father died in the World Trade Center attack of September 11. Kara liked working with figures in sand. She initially selected tiny inanimate objects, rocks, and shells and grouped them in one corner, leaving the rest of the tray empty. Later she added trees and animals. Four years later, around the anniversary of September 11 and her father's birthday, Kara selected an umbrella, a picnic table, and barbeque placing her family—and her father for the first time— around the table. Then she formed a cake and candles from clay. "Dad misses his birthday party. We can't have it at home, because Mom cries so much. Happy birthday, daddy" (Webber & Mascari, 2008, p. 3). Kara eagerly agreed to invite her family to the sand therapy room. They took turns making scenes and, when they felt safe, Kara's mother and brother shared stories with similar themes of grief and loss. The process helped them to rebuild their lives by reestablishing family rituals with new remembrances.

INTEGRATING SAND THERAPY INTO TRAUMA COUNSELING

Many treatment approaches facilitate trauma recovery, including pharmacological, cognitive behavioral, emotionally focused, contextual, and sensorimotor interventions; however, few theories use multisensory modalities in addition to language. Ogden et al. (2006) shared our concern that "therapists of all disciplines are often puzzled and frustrated by the limitations of existing treatment modalities to resolve the symptoms of trauma in their clients" (pp. xxix–xxx). McFarlane and van der Kolk (1996) are optimistic about the benefits of nonverbal techniques in facilitating the integration of traumatic memories, and remind us "different treatments are needed at different stages of posttraumatic adaptation" (p. 572).

Sand therapy has been integrated successfully into traditional treatment approaches in each phase of Her-man's (1992) trauma recovery model. It is an effective adjunct to trauma recovery models as well as an alternative modality that safely achieves the desired outcomes of trauma recovery: (a) establish and regain safety (reduce physiological symptoms and distress and increase emotional tolerance and self-reflection); (b) come to terms with the trauma story (regain self-mastery and control over memories and restore emotional and relational regulation after trauma processing); and (c) restore relationships and connections (redefine the existential life as worth living and restore self-efficacy and spiritual meaning in reengagement with others) (Baranowsky et al., 2009; Courtois, Ford, & Cloitre, 2009; Herman, 1992; Ogden et al., 2006: Webber et al., 2006).

In the film *Reign Over Me*, Charlie Fineman relived his trauma every day and night for years. Sand therapy's multisensory process could have helped to prevent retraumatization, eliminate the debilitating symptoms of PTSD, and open pathways to resolve the trauma narrative so that Charlie could reconnect with his world.

Jane Webber, PhD, LPC, is associate professor and coordinator of the Counseling Program at New Jersey City University. She is a counselor in private practice and holds New Jersey Disaster Response Crisis Counselor certification (NJDRCC).

J. Barry Mascari, EdD, LPC, LCADC, is chair of the Counselor Education Department at Kean University, Union, New Jersey and holds New Jersey Disaster Response Crisis Counselor certification (NJDRCC).

Julia Runte is a graduate student in the Multicultural Education Department at New Jersey City University.

REFERENCES

Baranowsky, A. B., Gentry, J. E., & Schultz, D. F. (2010). *Trauma practice: Tools for stabilization and recovery* (2nd ed.). Cambridge, MA: Hogrefe & Huber.

Binder, J., & Rotenberg, M. (Producers), & Binder, M., (Writer/Director). (2007). *Reign over me* [Motion picture]. United States: Columbia Pictures Industries.

Boik, B. L., & Goodwin, E. A. (2000). *Sand tray therapy: A step-by-step manual for psychotherapists of diverse orientations.* New York: W.W. Norton.

Courtois, C., Ford, J. D., & Cloitre, M. (2009). Best practices in psychotherapy for adults. In C. Courtois & J. Ford (Eds.). *Treating complex traumatic stress disorders: An evidence-based guide* (pp. 82–103). New York: Guilford Press.

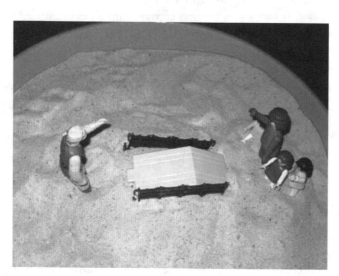

The bridge in Iraq: Traumatic memories.

De Domenico, G. S. (2002). Sandtray-worldplay: A psycho-therapeutic and transformational sandplay technique for individuals, couples, families, and groups. *The California Therapist*, 55–61.

Gil, E. (1996). *Treating abused adolescents*. New York: Guilford Press.

Gil, E. (2006). *Helping abused and traumatized children: Integrating directive and nondirective approaches*. New York: Guilford.

Herman, J. (1992). *Trauma and recovery: The aftermath of violence--from domestic abuse to political terror*. New York: Basic.

Kalff, D. M. (2003). *Sand tray: A psychotherapeutic approach in the psyche*. Cloverdale, CA: Temenos Press. (Original work published 1980).

McFarlane, A. C., & van der Kolk, B. (1996). Conclusions and future directions. In B. A.van der Kolk, A. C. McFarlane, & L. Weisaeth (Eds.), *Traumatic stress: The effects of overwhelming experience on mind, body, and society* (pp. 559–576). New York: Guilford Press.

Moon, P. (2006). Sand play therapy with U.S. soldiers diagnosed with PTSD and their families. In G. Walz, J. Bleuer, & R. Yep (Eds.), *VISTAS: Compelling perspectives on counseling 2006* (pp. 63–66). Alexandria, VA: American Counseling Association.

Ogden, P., Minton, K., & Pain, C. (2006). *Trauma and the body: A sensorimotor approach to psychotherapy*. New York: W. W. Norton.

Sullivan, M. G. (2003, January). Sandplay therapy used to help teens heal. *Clinical Psychiatry News. 31*(1), 62. Retrieved from http://www.clinicalpsychiatrynews.com/

Turner, S. W., McFarlane, A. C., & van der Kolk, B. A. (1996). The therapeutic environment and new explorations in the treatment of posttraumatic stress disorder. In B.A. van der Kolk, A. C. McFarlane, & L. Weisaeth (Eds.), *Traumatic stress: The effects of overwhelming experience on mind, body, and society* (pp. 537–558). New York: Guilford Press.

van der Kolk, B.A., van der Hart, O., & Marmar, C.R. (1996). Dissociation and information processing in posttraumatic stress disorder. In B. van der Kolk, A. McFarlane, & L. Weisaeth (Eds.), *Traumatic stress: The effects of overwhelming experience on mind, body, and society* (pp. 303–327). New York: Guilford Press.

Webber, J. (2009). [Sand tray session]. Unpublished raw data.

Webber, J., & Mascari, J. B. (2008). Sand tray therapy and the healing process in trauma and grief counseling. In G. Walz, J. C. Bleuer, & R. Yep (Eds.), *VISTAS 2008* (pp. 1–6). Alexandria, VA: American Counseling Association. Retrieved from http://www.counselingoutfitters.org

Webber, J., Mascari, J. B., & Dubi, M. (2008, February). *The power of sand tray therapy*. Paper presented at the meeting of the Fourth Annual Trauma Symposium: Responding to Tragedy, Trauma, and Crisis. Argosy University, Sarasota, FL.

Webber, J., Mascari, J. B., Dubi, M., & Gentry, J. E. (2006). Moving forward: Issues in trauma response and treatment. In G. Walz, J. C. Bleuer, & R. Yep (Eds.), *VISTAS: Compelling perspectives in counseling 2006* (pp. 17–66). Alexandria, VA: American Counseling Association.

Providing Disaster Services to Culturally Diverse Survivors

5

Carlos Zalaquett, Iraida Carrion, and Herbert Exum

A common thread throughout different types of disasters is the element of human suffering that unites all people affected by such events. This universal experience has an impact on both individuals and families regardless of their worldview, culture, or language. Utilizing multicultural competencies is critical when working with victims of disasters or trauma. Counselors must understand the needs of different cultural groups and how survivors make decisions, especially after a disaster.

The negative emotional impact of a flood, an earthquake, or a hurricane upon the survivors is referred to as primary traumatization and it generally begins immediately after the disaster, though delayed reactions do occur (Norris, Friedman, & Watson, 2002). The disaster also may affect significant people in the survivor's life who did not experience the event. Secondary traumatization tends to occur in many immigrant families who maintain multiple linkages to their homeland although they are firmly rooted in their new country. Typically, they have ongoing communication with family members in their country of origin. Therefore, when a disaster such as a volcanic explosion or flood occurs in South America, Central America, or in Asia, family members—especially college students who reside in the United States—may experience secondary trauma. Similarly, family members living abroad may experience secondary traumatization when their relatives are victims of disasters in the U.S. Behaviors associated with this trauma-induced stress include sleep disturbance, emotional instability, and impaired concentration (Foa, Davidson, & Frances, 1999).

For some ethnic groups, these symptoms may be viewed as a physical condition, but in Asian or Hispanic/Latino communities, they may be considered a punishment from their ancestors or God. Victims of

diverse backgrounds may hold strong religious interpretations of the reasons for disasters. For example, when counseling a woman from Honduras who traveled to Florida to be with family members during Katrina, she responded, "God was angry and needed to get our attention." Clients' religious interpretations of their ordeals may conflict with counselors' interpretation of the situation. Nonetheless, counselors may need to help survivors process feelings of guilt and responsibility and challenge clients' deep religious beliefs. The counselor can ask, "Is there something about your religion that I need to know in order to provide you with better care?"

Historical and political stressors of a cultural group must be considered in the counseling process. Individuals who have experienced political persecutions and have fled oppressive countries such as El Salvador, Cambodia, and Russia will respond differently to disasters while in the U.S. After September 11, 2001, some felt unsafe and manifested symptoms of anxiety or posttraumatic stress disorder (PTSD); thus, counseling interventions can focus beyond the individual victim to include family support systems and other social networks. Providing information brochures in the victims' primary language while being cognizant of their literacy levels will facilitate communication with relief agencies.

PTSD

Although PTSD generates symptoms thought to be the same for everyone, regardless of the specific events they suffered, these symptoms may be described differently by various cultural groups (Survivors International (SI), 2004). In some cultural groups, disturbing symptoms are attributed to being punished by one's ancestors; in other groups they may be considered self-imposed. Although PTSD may manifest itself differently in various cultures, several common symptoms are likely to emerge.

Many emotional and cognitive processes become more intense while, paradoxically, others are deadened (Zalaquett & Exum, 2005). Individuals who have their lives suddenly and drastically changed by destructive events experience more than they can integrate, particularly because their feelings of personal control, competence, security, and safety are greatly diminished. This problem is intensified for individuals who face linguistic and cultural barriers in communicating with mental health providers, which can lead to misdiagnoses, frustration with services, premature service termination, and underutilization of services.

Individuals whose second language is English may prefer to express their thoughts and emotions about the disaster in their primary language. This was evident when an elderly couple who, despite being successful business owners in New York City for many years, requested a translator when seeking assistance after the September 11 terrorist attacks. Therefore, it is vital for counselors to assess language preferences, levels of literacy, and also attitudes and beliefs regarding the seeking of mental health services. Respect for values unlike our own is key to being effective with diverse populations (Boss, Beaulieu, Wieling, Turner, & LaCruz, 2003), including the importance of the age of the survivors and prescribed gender roles within families at the time of a disaster. In some cultural groups, it is expected that priority and preferences be given to the elderly, women, and children rather than to men, regardless of their age. Beliefs about religion, mental health, prior experience with treatment, and the degree of openness in discussing a diagnosis and a prognosis also have an impact on treatment decisions.

BEHAVIORAL RESPONSE TO DISASTERS

Individuals who previously have experienced traumatic events are at a higher risk of developing PTSD when exposed to a disaster. The disaster may trigger dormant thoughts, feelings, and memories. This is the case for immigrants and refugees who have fled disasters such as volcanic eruptions in Ecuador, mudslides in Guatemala, and earthquakes in China only to encounter hurricanes and tornadoes in their new country. With individuals in this situation, counselors are very likely to encounter intense emotions and reactivity, numbness, forgetfulness,

flashbacks, intrusive thoughts, and nightmares, especially in the early phases of the disaster. These victims feel intense pain, terror, shame, horror, grief, rage, and shock.

The four-phase "biopsychosocial response pattern" typically follows natural disasters and clearly shows that recovery is not a short-term process and it is not automatic (SAMHSA, 2009). The Heroic Phase occurs during the first 72 hours of the disaster when energy is high, neighbors work together, and local and state resources are marshaled to respond. The Honeymoon Phase, also known as the Early Post-Impact Phase, begins as early as the second day after the disaster and is characterized by optimism, sharing, and giving thanks. There is still a great deal of media coverage and some of the euphoria of the Heroic Phase still persists. Hopes for a speedy recovery and community cohesion are both high. The Disillusionment Phase occurs when the full implications of the disaster are felt or when individuals come to grips with the extent of their losses. Involvement with survivors of natural disasters is most likely to occur during the Heroic and Honeymoon phases of the natural disaster response and, unfortunately, ends about the time they need it most.

Traumatized individuals report difficulty in performing regular duties and forgetting to keep appointments. This may be due to cultural factors related to perceptions of their disorder, attitudes toward mental illness, and perspectives about the origin of the problem, its course, and cure. Their personal views about what is important in one's life along with their decisions about mental health treatment can influence their willingness to seek, continue, or complete treatment. They respond to events that remind them of the trauma with all the feelings that belonged to the traumatic event. Flood victims, for example, may demonstrate very strong emotional responses to rain, storm clouds, the sound of running water, or the sight or smell of mud (Dahlen, 1999). It is imperative for counselors to explore how hope is negotiated within families. Ethnocentric assumptions and styles may hinder the counselor's ability to help victims. For example, if a family believes that God punished them, hope is diminished (Cavaiola & Colford, 2006). Counselors may at times need to use religious leaders, family members, and language translators in interpreting the relevance of cultural dimensions.

SOMATIC AND EMOTIONAL REACTIONS OF SURVIVORS

Since somatization is one method individuals use to express emotional distress, disaster survivors may have physical complaints of headaches, backaches or stomachaches, sudden sweating and/or heart palpitations, constipation, or diarrhea (SI, 2004; Shen & Sink, 2002). Changes in sleep patterns, appetite, greater susceptibility to colds and other illnesses, and being easily startled by an unexpected touch are also common. (For information regarding children, see Chapters 25, 27, 28, 30.)

Other more overt or direct expressions of emotional distress include shock and disbelief, fear or anxiety, grief, and disorientation. Denial, hypervigilance, irritability and/or restlessness, outbursts of anger or rage, uncontrolled crying and laughing, feelings of panic, or feeling out of control are also common. Many also report the tendency to isolate themselves, along with increased use of alcohol or drugs and/or overeating; other typical reactions include difficulty trusting and/or feeling betrayed, depression, guilt, and anger directed at God. These emotions are intensified if individuals have experienced violent crimes, homicides, and disasters as a result of living in cities or countries that experienced wars or civil unrest.

EMOTIONAL AND PSYCHOLOGICAL NEEDS OF SURVIVORS

Many people think that highly specialized medical or psychological skills are necessary in order to help traumatized individuals. Although there are specific treatment strategies for PTSD and this type of training is quite useful, the most important aspect of any treatment approach is personal involvement and commitment.

Counselors as Translators

Bilingual counselors often will be asked to function as translators for survivors, which provides an opportunity to engage with them and provide additional services. To illustrate, a Cuban woman in the U.S. who experienced a disastrous flood asked for a translator. A bilingual counselor agreed to serve as a translator; shortly thereafter, the woman began to discuss her fears of fleeing the flooded area because it reminded her of when she had to flee from Cuba. "I had to leave everything that I worked so hard for behind in Cuba and now for a second time in my life, I have lost everything." She discussed her feelings of sadness, loss, and uncertainties about the future. The counselor provided her with emotional and psychological support, which would not have been possible without first functioning as a translator.

Often it is the responder's caring presence and practical assistance, rather than actual training, that comforts the traumatized individual in the aftermath of a disaster.

This is true even when the counselor needs a translator to provide counseling and trauma training (Jordan, 2006). Survivors benefit from knowing that responders have left the comfort of their own surroundings to help people that they do not know and that they did it because they care about them, want to understand their experience, and want to provide help.

Survivor's Guilt

Effective counselors respect the right of disaster survivors to end a session if it becomes too uncomfortable. Sometimes traumatized individuals are not ready or willing to face what has happened to them and need to be alone for more personal reflection. They may judge themselves very harshly (Shelby & Tredinnick, 1995; SI, 2004), or experience survivor's guilt (Why am I alive while so many others perished?) Survivor's guilt was observed when providing counseling to a Honduran couple after Hurricane Katrina. After waiting several hours to speak to the counselor, this couple let other people go ahead of them in line stating, "We can wait to talk to you, we have each other, some of the people here are all alone." Traumatized individuals need a certain amount of detachment from counselors. Many events that counselors see and learn about after a disaster may elicit very strong feelings. Counselors need to remember that the survivor's feelings are the focus of the session.

COUNSELING INTERVENTIONS

The first step in the recovery process is helping survivors understand that their feelings are real, normal, and acceptable. Normalcy may not return immediately—the emotional recovery process alone may take weeks or months. New or unprepared responders may mistakenly believe that they are to provide mental health counseling immediately after a disaster. However, providing immediate counseling to disaster victims has unintended negative effects (Sijbrandij, Olff, Reitsma, Carlier, & Gersons, 2006). Extreme reactions to a disaster are not usually a sign of a mental disorder. Most people recover after a disaster despite their intense psychological and somatic initial reactions. These distressing but normal reactions to overwhelming events subside within weeks or months, either on their own or with the use of helping networks and resources in the family and community. Early intervention for disaster victims emphasizes helping the victims to connect with families, neighborhood support networks, and community resources as this has been shown to enhance post disaster functioning, return individuals more quickly to pre-disaster routines, and reduce the likelihood of chronic PTSD (Robbins, 2002). Culturally sensitive counseling and appropriate mental health treatments are indicated for those who are unable to overcome the trauma without assistance.

Counselors begin by introducing themselves and letting the survivor know they are there to listen. The primary counseling goal is to establish rapport in a culturally and racially respectful manner and provide a safe environment for the survivor. As the survivor begins to talk about whatever he or she decides, the counselor should be prepared to ask questions to elicit deeper reflection to increase understanding of the client's feelings, strengths, and needs. When uncertain about what an individual wants to talk about or if the approach used is inconsistent with the survivor's worldviews and cultural values, the best approach is to ask the client, and trust the client's process.

CARE FOR THE CAREGIVERS

As counselors provide therapy and other support to disaster victims, they too may experience mood disturbances, traumatic dreams, and other signs of personal distress indicating more than sleep deprivation or burnout. Vicarious traumatization (Perlman & Saakvitne, 1995) and compassion fatigue (Figley, 2002) refer to a negative transformation in the therapist's inner experience that results from exposure to the client's trauma story.

Group debriefing gives counselors and other caregivers an opportunity to share what they have experienced during the crisis and how it has affected them. In these groups, practitioners may disclose any significant feelings, reactions, and thoughts with others who may be experiencing the same emotions. This decreases the potential for social isolation and often provides the first contact for further service. There is little systematic examination of the critical features of effective prevention of traumatic stress reactions, so the design and provision of interventions for counselors should take into account the atmosphere and social processes that emerge relative to the incident (Raphael, Wilson, Meldrum, & McFarlane, 1996). Interventions should also be culturally sensitive and consider the counselor's worldviews and cultural values.

RECOMMENDATIONS FOR COMMUNITY CARE

With the diversification of the U.S. population, encountering survivors with worldviews and values different from the counselor's is now commonplace. Recognizing traumatic stress symptoms and cultural factors about the survivors is key to developing appropriate therapeutic interventions. Providing appropriate and effective culturally competent counseling interventions requires collaboration among all members of the community. Family and group counseling extends and multiplies the effectiveness of a counselor, and will increase the rate of social integration among survivors, especially among those who place a strong value in familial relationships. Teachers and parents should receive training in the principles of culturally sensitive psychological first aid in order to help their children and themselves in the event of disasters. Ethnocentric assumptions and styles may hinder the helping families after a disaster.

Most of the recovery will take place at home and within schools so it is very important that teachers, counselors, and parents become aware of the symptoms and the possible remedies for traumatic stress. Counselors may help by using empathy, offering parents information about children's responses to disaster, helping them become more receptive to their children's needs, and educating them about normal developmental patterns (Juhnke, 1997). Counselors may need to prepare to work at a realistic pace and make arrangements for their own emotional rejuvenation to provide the most effective interventions to the diverse populations they will serve.

Carlos P. Zalaquett, PhD, LMHC, is associate professor and coordinator of the Mental Health Counseling program in the Department of Psychological and Social Foundations of Education.

Iraida V. Carrion, PhD, is assistant professor in the School of Social Work.

Herbert A. Exum, PhD, is professor and chair of the Department of Psychological and Social Foundations.

All are at the University of South Florida in Tampa.

REFERENCES

Boss, P., Beaulieu, L., Wieling, E., Turner, W., & LaCruz S. (2003). A community-based intervention with families of union workers missing after the 9/11 attack in New York City. *Journal of Marital and Family Therapy, 29*, 455–467.

Cavaiola, A. A., & Colford, J. E. (2006). *A practical guide to crisis intervention*. New York: Houghton Mifflin.

Dahlen, P. (1999). Follow-up of counseling after disaster: Working with traumatic dreams toward healing. *Traumatology, 5*, 3. Retrieved from http://www.fsu.edu/~trauma/a4v5i3.html

Figley, C. R. (2002). *Treating compassion fatigue*. New York: Brunner/Mazel.

Foa, E. B., Davidson, J. R. T., & Frances, A. (1999). Expert consensus guideline series: Treatment of posttraumatic stress disorder. *The Journal of Clinical Psychiatry, 60 (Supplement 16)*, 1–31.

Jordan, K. (2006). A case study: How a disaster mental health volunteer provided spiritually, culturally and historically sensitive trauma training to teacher-counselors and other mental health professionals in Sri Lanka, four weeks after the tsunami. *Brief Treatment and Crisis Intervention, 6*, 316–325.

Juhnke, C. A. (1997). After school violence: An adapted critical incident stress debriefing model for student survivors and their parents. *Elementary School Guidance & Counseling, 31*, 163–170.

Norris, F. H., Friedman, M. J., & Watson, P. (2002). 60,000 disaster victims speak: Part II. Summary and implications of the disaster mental health research. *Psychiatry, 65*, 240-260.

Perlman, K. W., & Saakvitne, L. A. (1995). *Trauma and the therapist*. New York: Norton.

Raphael, B., Wilson, J., Meldrum, L., & McFarlane, A. (1996). Acute preventive interventions. In B. van der Kolk, A. McFarlane, & L. Weisaeth (Eds.), *Traumatic stress: The effects of overwhelming experience on mind, body, and society* (pp. 463–479). New York: Guilford Press.

Robbins, S. (2002). The rush to counsel: Lessons of caution in the aftermath of disaster. *Families in Society, 83*, 113–116.

SAMHSA. (2009). *Training manual for mental health and human service workers in major disasters. Section 2. Responses to disaster.* Retrieved from http://mentalhealth.samhsa.gov/publications/allpubs/adm90-538/tmsection2.asp

Schmookler, E. L. (2001). *Trauma treatment manual.* Berkeley, CA. Retrieved from http://www.trauma-pages.com/schmookler-manual.htm

Shear, K. M., Frank, E., Foa, E., Cherry, C., Reynolds III, C. F., Bilt, J. V., & Masters, S. (2001). Traumatic grief treatment: A pilot study. *American Journal of Psychiatry, 158*, 1506–1508.

Shelby, J. S., & Tredinnick, M. G. (1995). Crisis intervention with survivors of natural disaster: Lessons from Hurricane Andrew. *Journal of Counseling & Development, 73*, 491–505.

Shen, Y., J., & Sink, C. A. (2002). Helping elementary-age children cope with disasters. *Professional School Counseling, 5*, 322–330.

Sijbrandij, M., Olff, M., Reitsma, J. B., Carlier, I. V. E., & Gersons, B. P. R. (2006). Emotional or educational debriefing after psychological trauma. Randomised controlled trial. *British Journal of Psychiatry, 18*, 150–155.

Survivors International. (2004). *SI Community Training Manual.* Retrieved from http://www.survivorsintl.org/fmd/files/FullSICommunityTrainingManual.pdf

Zalaquett, C., & Exum, H. (2005). Disaster survivors counseling: Issues and strategies. *Journal for the Professional Counselor, 19*, 5–18.

The Counselor's Role in International Disaster Response

Joseph D. Wehrman

6

A significant awakening in disaster response is occurring following extensive media coverage of disasters such as September 11, the Indian Ocean tsunami, Hurricane Katrina, and genocide in Darfur. This has created a heightened interest for counselors to seek training and participate in international crisis and disaster response. According to Rogers (2007), "Psychological intervention provided within days to the first few weeks following mass disasters is qualitatively different from the services mental health counselors provide in their day to day professional work" (p. 2). Counselors need to enhance or develop a different skill set along with different procedural expectations in order to be effective in crisis and disaster response. This chapter presents practical tips and strategies for volunteers, based on the author's experiences providing medical and mental health services following Hurricane Katrina and in Honduras, Kuwait, Iraq, and Sri Lanka.

Getting Started

How do volunteers get started or become involved? The first step is becoming knowledgeable about current best practice guidelines for counseling services in response to crisis or disaster. Some starting points include the National Center for Posttraumatic Stress Disorder, The National Child Traumatic Stress Network, and Centers for Disease Control and Prevention, as well as networking in the counselor's local community. Crisis or disaster response may be linked to school districts, fire departments, law enforcement, or local chapters of organizations such as the Red Cross. (The American Counseling Association usually offers the American Red Cross Foundations of Disaster Mental Health Training course at no cost during its annual conference.) After obtaining local experience, counselors can branch out and seek state, national, or inter-national opportunities (the International Federation of Red Cross and Red Crescent Societies). Nongovernmental agencies (NGOs) providing international humanitarian service may seek mental health experts trained in culturally responsive service delivery to augment their services.

Preparing for Deployment

Utilize Technology to Prepare

Whether the counselor is being deployed as an individual or with an identified group of professionals, technology can provide the initial structure for collaboration and communication. Success in providing crisis and disaster response is anchored to the individual's preparation. Details regarding initial training, logistics, and the types of interventions that will be utilized can be addressed efficiently utilizing email and websites. Online tutorials prior to deployment could outline regional customs such as social greetings, gender, and religious norms.

Create a Checklist of Needed Gear

Counselors will be working and living in conditions that often lack typical amenities. The area may have limited or non-functioning electricity, shortages of potable water, and unconventional accommodations (living in tents, or the basement of a church or community center). The time of year and regional climate are factors to consider. One of the most valuable tools packed for travelling to Sri Lanka was a bug net for use while sleeping. Team members stayed in a part of an orphanage that provided only overhead cover and therefore they were exposed to the elements. The bug net allowed for peaceful nights of sleep without the distraction of mosquito bites. Although this may seem minor, mosquito bites can have a great impact on the quality of services provided because the distraction results in focusing on one's own needs rather than the needs of those being served.

Get Immunizations and Medications

Vaccinations and medications for malaria or other tropical diseases are often required prior to travel. Crisis response volunteers need to keep current with vaccinations and medical care to maintain a level of readiness, ensuring that sufficient medications are packed to exceed the expected time frame of travel and stay. It is imperative for counselors to self-assess regarding physical or medical concerns that would affect deployment.

Be Invited and Have Proper Clearance

Counselors should be sponsored by the appropriate government or NGO to avoid duplication of services and to ensure that services are tailored to the host culture. It is important for the host government or region to have administrative control over the relief operations group.

Identify and Access Team Members' Talents and Expertise

To optimize services, pre-deployment preparations should include identifying each team member's strengths, weaknesses, and expertise. A crisis or disaster is often unconventional and unpredictable; therefore, knowing who the experts are in everything from sexual assault to play therapy to de-escalation skills will come in handy.

DURING THE DEPLOYMENT

Knowledge and understanding about culture-specific norms, customs, and values (Chandra, Pandav, & Bhugra, 2006), as well as the geopolitical climate and history, helps counselors avoid operating from a model that does not fit the situation and environment. Skepticism of intervention by outsiders is expected and is a natural method of protection for individuals who are highly vulnerable as a result of the crisis or disaster.

Emphasize the Use of Core Counseling Skills and Relational Development

Providing crisis or disaster response services requires that counselors intervene differently than they do in their day-to-day work with clients. The primary focus is on connecting with and conveying compassion for another human being who has experienced great tragedy (Goodman & West-Olatunji, 2008). Emphasis is placed on resiliency and helping individuals enhance or foster

greater adaptive coping skills. In conducting cross-cultural work, incorporate the norms and customs of the host culture such as how to meet, greet, and interact.

Understand How to Work with a Translator

When working with a translator, consider how this dynamic may affect the way in which services are provided. "What is important for translation is the notion that what [a translator] says may be a representation of what someone else meant...." (Boase-Beier, 2004, p. 277). Counselors using a translator should maintain culturally appropriate eye contact with the client rather than the translator and should encourage the client to take breaks to allow time for accurate translation. The translator should not obstruct the appropriate interpersonal space between the counselor and client (Santiago-Rivera, Arredondo, & Gallardo-Cooper, 2002) and should sit behind or adjacent to the counselor.

Utilize Approaches That Fit for the Host Culture

Beware of classic pitfalls when providing cross-cultural services. Some counselors rush to pathologize behaviors based on a Western idea of mental illness when, in reality, individuals are going through normal and natural states of grieving. Operating solely from a Western-based model of mental illness risks pathologizing symptoms that may be culturally bound (Chandra et al., 2006).

Language differences can create a barrier to service delivery. Counselors benefit from using intervention strategies that require less verbal expression such as play-based interventions (Hebert & Ballard, 2007; Wehrman, 2005, 2007). Culturally contextual play-based activities are useful in working with children and adults because all people can engage in play. It is also important to be mindful of practices specific to the culture such as the typical work week, religious holidays, or rituals. When working with Arab or Middle Eastern cultures, it is common to hear the Islamic call to prayer played over loudspeakers or on the local radio station throughout the day. Counselors may benefit from reviewing region specific information developed by the World Health Organization before they deploy.

The National Board for Certified Counselors-International (NBCC-I) has developed a comprehensive program to help improve access to culturally and regionally appropriate mental healthcare through the utilization of mental health facilitators. Counselors should collaborate with locally trained facilitators to determine if such services are being provided in the region.

Utilize Resources and Influential Community Members

Compile a list of local resources, key community figures, and important information (addresses, phone numbers, hours of operation, and points of contact). Counselors providing disaster response services will be asked about local resources, such as where to obtain food, shelter, or medical care.

Have a Plan for Individual and Group Self Care

Because crisis and disaster response is very emotionally draining and physically tiring, a plan for self care is as important as helping others. Knowing personal limits and having a plan for debriefing and self care are vital to providing effective services. Counselors should examine their own regular coping techniques used to decompress in day-to-day life and determine if they are transferrable to the new setting. Reading a book in the evening is easily transferred; however, working out at the gym or playing golf may not be possible. When travelling with a team, have a plan for group self care—whether it is a buddy system or nightly debriefings to allow members to process the experience. Discuss what worked well each day and what could be changed or adjusted for the next day.

Counselors work as part of a larger team that provides a variety of services (water purification, medical triage, construction, and food distribution) with conditions and circumstances often changing on an hourly basis. A high degree of flexibility and adaptability is required. Inability to accommodate these adjustments can lead to counselor impairment. Services typically are not provided in isolation, thus counselors also may function in a role such as debriefing other first responders or relief workers and promoting self care.

Come with Compassion and Appreciate the Experience

Attributes and characteristics of counselors who are successful in providing crisis or disaster response services include genuine compassion for others, a flexible nature, and an understanding that all situations are unique, unpredictable, and can change at a moment's notice. Developing these skills and having access to opportunities to provide these services takes many years.

Joseph D. Wehrman, PhD, LPC, is assistant professor of Counselor Education and coordinator of the Community Counseling program in the Department of Counseling and Human Services at the University of Colorado at Colorado Springs. He is a former Medical Service Officer and veteran of Operation Iraqi Freedom and has provided humanitarian aid after the 2004 Indian Ocean tsunami and Hurricane Katrina.

REFERENCES

Boase-Beier, J. (2004). Saying what someone else meant: Style, relevance, and translation. *International Journal of Applied Linguistics, 14*(2), 276–287.

Chandra, V., Pandav, R., & Bhugra, D. (2006). Mental health and psychosocial support after the tsunami: Observations across affected nations. *International Review of Psychiatry, 18*(3), 205–211.

Goodman, R. D., & West-Olatunji, C. A. (2008). Transgenerational trauma and resilience: Improving mental health counseling for survivors of hurricane Katrina. *Journal of Mental Health Counseling, 30*(2), 121–136.

Hebert, B. B., & Ballard, M. B. (2007). Children and trauma: A post-Katrina and Rita response. *Professional School Counseling, 11*(2), 140–144.

Rogers, J. R. (2007). Disaster response and the mental health counselor. *Journal of Mental Health Counseling, 29*(1), 1–3.

Santiago-Rivera, A. L., Arredondo, P., & Gallardo-Cooper, M. (2002). *Counseling Latinos and la familia: A practical guide.* Thousand Oaks, CA: Sage.

Wehrman, J. D. (200, August). Mining report: Adjustment following war, natural disaster, and crisis. *Association for Play Therapy.* Retrieved from http://www.a4pt.org/download.cfm?ID=20551

Wehrman, J. D. (2005, May). A Sri Lanka experience: Providing relief for wave related fears. *Counseling Today,* 10–12.

INTERNET RESOURCES

The Centers for Disease Control – www.bt.cdc.gov
The International Federation of Red Cross and Red Crescent Societies – www.ifrc.org
The National Center for PTSD – www.ncptsd.va.gov
The National Child Traumatic Stress Network – www.nctsnet.org

Section Two

Lessons Learned from Hurricane Katrina and Other Disasters

COUNSELING SURVIVORS OF HURRICANE KATRINA 7

Barbara Herlihy and Zarus E. Watson

On August 29, 2005, Hurricane Katrina struck the Gulf Coast, setting into motion a series of successive traumas for its survivors. When the levees that had protected New Orleans failed, 80% of the city and its environs was flooded, causing fatalities, property destruction, and infrastructure collapse. Tens of thousands of citizens were trapped in the Superdome and Convention Center where they were abandoned, not to be rescued for days. More than one million other residents who had evacuated watched with horror the televised images of the dead and dying, submerged neighborhoods, widespread looting, and civil unrest. The multisystemic and pervasive nature of the destruction made it impossible for residents to return for several weeks to several years, creating a diaspora of 1.5 million displaced individuals who had lost their homes and their jobs and who were separated from family, friends, and community support networks. Even today, New Orleanians continue their struggle to cope and recover.

Every Katrina survivor has a story, and each story is unique. The stories of three survivors are shared in this chapter.

Ernesto, 72-year-old African American Jazz Musician

Ernesto, a resident of the Upper Ninth Ward, evacuated New Orleans with his wife the day before Katrina made landfall. They arrived at the home of a cousin, one of many extended family members who lived in or near Atlanta. As Ernesto sat glued to the television, he knew that his home of 50 years had been flooded and all of his prized possessions destroyed. Due to his experience with Hurricane Betsy 40 years earlier, he realized that it would be a long time before he could go home. Not wanting to impose on any one set of rela-

tives for too long, he and his wife moved several times over the next few months before settling with a nephew. More than one year passed before anyone returned to his neighborhood to begin the basic work of cleaning up debris and gutting houses. Ernesto and his wife longed to come home, but they were concerned about their safety because their neighborhood was sparsely inhabited and thus was a target for continued looting. They became trapped in a waiting game, with no resident of the area willing to return until others had returned. Ernesto's savings continued to dwindle as other members of the family needed financial assistance in their own struggles to survive and rebuild. He applied for a grant from the Road Home program, but his application remained mired in bureaucratic red tape.

As of this writing, nearly 4 years after Katrina, Ernesto is finally about to come home. His home has been gutted and is being rebuilt. However, he continues to deal with complications such as contractor fraud, sparse neighborhood services, and relatives who still ask him for help. Ernesto alternates between periods of hope, especially when he visits New Orleans and sees old friends, and periods of hopelessness and depression when he is alone with his thoughts, and realizes that even when he returns, life will not be the same.

Joann, 63-year-old White Corporate Executive

Initially, Joann planned to ride out Katrina, assuming she would be safe in her century-old home that had withstood numerous hurricanes before. However, she left when the mandatory evacuation order was issued, intending to shelter with her sister in Houston. Caught in the evacuation gridlock, 12 hours later she found herself only 65 miles from New Orleans. With the hurricane fast approaching, she found shelter in the home of family members of one of her colleagues from work. After a 3-day stay with these strangers who welcomed her into their home, already overcrowded with their own family members who had evacuated, she made it to her sister's home in Houston. Six weeks later, she returned to New Orleans and found her home damaged but inhabitable. With funds provided by her homeowner's and flood insurance, she began repairing her home. After several uncomfortable weeks without electricity or other basic services, her life in New Orleans began a slow and gradual return to normal.

Today, Joann's life is much like it was before Katrina. She is quick to point out that she is one of the fortunate few in post-Katrina New Orleans who still have their home and jobs. She finds it hard to believe that "someone like me, with a six-figure income," once accepted free meals from the Red Cross wagon as it drove through her neighborhood. She continues to experience survivor guilt and admits that she feels worn down by the daily reminders—when she drives through blighted neighborhoods or interacts with people at the office who are still living in FEMA trailers—that her beloved city is a long way from full recovery. When the economic crisis hit in 2008, she started to have panic attacks and other symptoms of anxiety. Her company has begun to lay off employees, and she fears she may lose her job. With her retirement savings decimated by the stock market plunge, she cannot afford to retire and worries that she will be unable to find another job at her age.

Rodney, 41-year-old African American Unemployed Veteran

Rodney, a U.S. Army veteran, became addicted to alcohol and drugs after he returned from his service in Desert Storm. He lost his job and his family, ended up on the streets, and eventually was admitted into a residential substance abuse treatment facility near downtown New Orleans. As Katrina bore down on New Orleans, the residents of the facility needed to evacuate, and Rodney arranged to be picked up by his brother. His brother never showed up, and Rodney ended up back on the streets and then at the Convention Center where he sheltered for several days. When no food or assistance arrived, he set out on his own, and he survived by looting and "staying drunk" for the next several weeks, until he was found unconscious by a National Guard patrol. Because no detox facilities were available in or near New Orleans, he was taken by ambulance to a hospital in northern Louisiana. When he completed detox, he returned to New Orleans by bus. Over the next 3 years, he alternated between resi-

dency at the treatment facility and living on the streets.

Today, Rodney is back at the residential treatment facility for the fourth and final time allowed under its policies. His cognitive functioning has declined as a result of his long-term abuse of drugs and alcohol, and it is becoming increasingly doubtful that he will be able to return to gainful employment and independent living. The Veteran's Administration hospital in New Orleans was destroyed by Katrina and never rebuilt, and there are no other social service agencies in the city that can accommodate Rodney when and if he completes his treatment program. He may end up homeless and surviving on the streets once again.

THE COUNSELING NEEDS OF SURVIVORS

In the *immediate aftermath* of Katrina (the first few weeks), almost all survivors were in need of some sort of crisis intervention services. Those (like Rodney) who were trapped on rooftops or in the Superdome or Convention Center needed immediate assistance in meeting their basic needs for shelter, food and water, and safety. Although those who evacuated were more fortunate, many had been separated from family and friends and were desperate to find out whether loved ones were safe. They were continually retraumatized by the horrific scenes from home that played endlessly on television and they were confronted rapidly with their unpreparedness to cope with a prolonged evacuation. They had left home with supplies (e.g., clothing, cash, medications) for a 2- or 3-day absence, and these supplies were soon depleted. Crisis workers were needed throughout the diaspora to provide intensive case management services linking evacuees to services that could assist them with meeting concrete and practical needs.

In the *short-term aftermath* (several weeks to 6 months post-Katrina), many evacuees (like Ernesto and his wife) were living nomadic lives, with frequent and multiple relocations, and could not establish predictable routines or new support systems. Others (like Joann) had returned to New Orleans but often were finding "home" to be unfamiliar territory, with even simple tasks like purchasing food almost impossible to accomplish. Acute stress disorder symptoms became common among survivors; these symptoms were complicated by their grief over all they had lost and uncertainty about the future (Madrid & Grant, 2008).

Numerous relief organizations sent crisis workers to New Orleans and other locations with large concentrations of evacuees (e.g., Baton Rouge, Houston, and Atlanta), but they were able to provide only short-term, crisis-oriented services. A survey conducted by the Centers for Disease Control in October of 2005 found that half of respondents had a possible need for mental health services, and one-third clearly needed intervention, but only 1.6% reported that they were receiving help (Weisler, Barbee, & Townsend, 2006). In New Orleans, the Charity and VA hospitals, which had provided most of the acute psychiatric care to the poor and uninsured, had been destroyed. Community based mental health services that had been inadequate even before Katrina (Madrid & Grant, 2008) were almost nonexistent. Very few of the city's own mental health workers had returned. Six months after Katrina, only 11% of the psychiatrists had returned, and most of the other mental health professionals remained displaced because their homes or workplaces had been destroyed. Those few mental health practitioners who had remained or returned were themselves overwhelmed and traumatized (Madrid & Grant, 2008).

In the *long-term aftermath* (1–4 years post-Katrina), recovery is ongoing but slow. The long-term effects are becoming evident, including high incidence of complex PTSD; an increase in suicidal ideation, suicides, and murder-suicides; and a three-fold increase in heart attacks (Hurricane Katrina Community Advisory Group, 2008). Exhaustion, depression, and hopelessness are increasing, especially as the economic crisis causes setbacks for survivors just when they have started to make gains. There is a deep cynicism about the ability, or even the willingness, of government at the local, state, or federal level to assist its citizens when disaster strikes.

Initially, Katrina seemed to be an "equal opportunity event" that blurred the lines between rich and poor, Black and White, and young and old. Over time, however, we are observing a growing gap between those survivors who had resources before the disaster and those who did not. Many survivors whose pre-Katrina resources included good mental and physical health and adequate financial means have essentially returned to their pre-Katrina level of functioning, although they remain a bit more fragile. Many of them still experience over-reactivity to events such as storms and find that seemingly minor disappointments or frustrations can trigger episodes of anger, anxiety, or depression.

The survivors who remain at the highest risk for mental health problems are those who are more vulnerable due to pre-Katrina traumatization, lack of resources, or age. Prior to Katrina, a significant portion of the population of New Orleans was struggling to survive in a social system plagued by intergenerational poverty, racism, adult illiteracy, unsafe neighborhoods, high rates of violent crime, failing schools, and inadequate mental health treatment services. Ninety-three percent of Katrina evacuees in Houston were African American, and nearly 60% had pre-Katrina annual incomes under $20,000 (Brodie, Weltzien, Altman, Blendon, & Bensen, 2006). Most of those who remain displaced have lost their homes and jobs and have nothing tangible to which they can return. The low-income housing developments in which many of them resided were razed after Katrina and nothing has been built in their place. Many of these displaced individuals are third- and fourth-generation natives of New Orleans who feel a tremendous pride of place. For them, the possibility that they might never come home is devastating.

Children also are highly vulnerable to long-term ill effects of the massive disruptions in their lives. Although many remained with their families, nearly 5,200 were reported missing in the wake of the hurricane, and one-third were separated from their primary caregivers at some point during the aftermath (Drury, Scheeringa, & Zeanah, 2008). As families moved from one temporary location to another, some children missed an entire year of school or attended a series of schools for brief periods of time. They could not establish predictable routines, form new friendships, or experience the stability that was needed to mitigate their fears and confusion (Madrid & Grant, 2008).

Perhaps most vulnerable of all are squatters sleeping in abandoned homes in New Orleans. They are the chronically mentally ill, elderly, and developmentally disabled whose family networks and places of residence were destroyed, leaving them on their own for possibly the first time in their lives. The long-term mental health counseling needs of these at-risk populations have not been systematically addressed (Drury et al., 2008). Hurricane Katrina survivors will continue to need mental health services for many years to come.

LESSONS LEARNED AND RECOMMENDATIONS FOR COUNSELORS

In the aftermath of a multisystemic disaster like Katrina, recovery is slow and may have no relationship to the amount of time that has passed since the initial trauma. Counselors should avoid assuming that they know what survivors need—instead, ask! As an example, a number of church leaders in New Orleans established counseling services for their congregants and community members during the first year or two after Katrina, and they reacted with bewilderment when very few people came. Survivors are unlikely to seek counseling services when they are still struggling to get their practical needs met and put their lives back in order.

Counseling interventions are more effective when they are community based. If counselors carefully assess and continually reassess the needs of a community, their interventions are more likely to be culturally appropriate, well timed, and specifically targeted to meet community needs. In particular, we recommend that counselors working in disaster areas help to establish and facilitate neighborhood-based groups that would meet on a regular basis. Such groups, free from any stigma that might be associated with seeking counseling, can help survivors re-establish connections and reduce isolation, create mutual support networks, and share information about how to obtain resources to aid in recovery.

In addition to working with communities, it is important for counselors to work with families, particularly in the long-term aftermath of Katrina. Among natives of New Orleans, the definition of "family" may include a large number of people, both related and not related by blood, who form an extended kinship system. These families are being splintered by multiple, prolonged stressors such as living together in cramped quarters such as FEMA trailers or inequities in the amount of government assistance received by different family members (such as insurance awards, Road Home monies, and FEMA grants). Counselors can play a vital role in helping to restore the family cohesion that is a source of strength and support for many survivors.

Counselors should advocate for themselves to ensure that they have a place at the table in the system-wide recovery planning process. Multisystemic disasters require multisystemic interventions, and mental health services must be integrated into the larger recovery system. Counselors need to collaborate and develop partnerships with medical health providers, housing and relief agencies, educators, the criminal justice system, and religious leaders to create the kinds of multifaceted, holistic interventions needed most by survivors of large-scale disasters.

People are remarkably resilient. Goodman and West-Olatunji (2008) have suggested that resilience theory may be a useful lens through which to view those populations of Katrina survivors who can be understood only within the context of transgenerational trauma. Their histories include elements of not just despair

and destruction but also renewal and recovery. For instance, Ernesto's experiences with Hurricane Betsy may have served as a protective factor as he faced another slow process of rebuilding. Other survivors discovered untapped sources of resilience within themselves. Joann, who had led a comfortable middle-class life for 60 years, embraced her new existence as an "urban pioneer" when she returned home. Even survivors such as Rodney whose personal resources seemed the most depleted by previous traumas were able to call upon their survival skills. Rodney's experiences had made him sufficiently "street wise" to survive the first few weeks in an environment of utter devastation.

Each Story is Unique

Over the long term, the counseling process needs to move beyond a trauma focus, toward helping survivors find meaning in their experiences and opportunity in their losses. Pipher (2009) stated that "regardless of the crisis, the cure is always growth" (p. 173); posttraumatic stress can lead to posttraumatic growth. Growth occurs in connection, which is a common theme in the recovery stories of our three survivors. Each of them is grateful for having been helped by someone, somewhere along the way, and has felt a need to "give back" in some way. Ernesto feels good about providing continued help to his children, grandchildren, nieces, and nephews and has no regrets that helping others has slowed his own progress in returning home. Joann volunteers on Sundays for Habitat for Humanity, helping to build houses for those who are still displaced. Rodney is working through the steps of his recovery and, as an "old hand" at the treatment facility, he mentors newcomers.

We, too, are survivors of Hurricane Katrina. This narrative is colored by our own experiences and how we have interpreted them. It is not the same story that other survivors would tell, nor is it the same story we would tell 5 years from now. Counselors who work with survivors of multisystemic disasters such as Hurricane Katrina should anticipate that their clients' needs will be complex and varied and will change over time. Each story will be unique.

Barbara Herlihy, PhD, LPC, is university research professor and coordinator of the Counselor Education Program.

Zarus E. Watson, PhD, LPC, is associate professor of Counselor Education.

Both are at the University of New Orleans.

References

Brodie, M., Weltzien, E., Altman, D., Blendon, R. J., & Benson, J. M. (2006). Experiences of Hurricane Katrina evacuees in Houston shelters: Implications for future planning. *American Journal of Public Health, 96*(8), 1402–1408.

Drury, S. S., Scheeringa, M. S., & Zeanah, C. H. (2008). The traumatic impact of Hurricane Katrina on children in New Orleans. *Child and Adolescent Psychiatric Clinics of North America, 17*(3), 685–702.

Goodman, R. D., & West-Olatunji, C. A. (2008). Transgenerational trauma and resilience: Improving mental health counseling for survivors of Hurricane Katrina. *Journal of Mental Health Counseling, 30*(2), 121–136.

Hurricane Katrina Community Advisory Group. (2008). *Hurricane Katrina victims' mental health worsens*. Retrieved from www.hurricanekatrina.med.harvard.edu

Madrid, P. A., & Grant, R. (2008). Meeting mental health needs following a natural disaster: Lessons from Hurricane Katrina. *Professional Psychology: Research and Practice, 39*(1) 86–92.

Pipher, M. (2009). *Seeking peace*. New York: Penguin Books.

Weisler, R., Barbee, J., & Townsend, M. (2006). Mental health and recovery in the Gulf Coast after Hurricanes Katrina and Rita. *Journal of the American Medical Association, 296*(5), 585–588.

CRITICAL INCIDENT STRESS MANAGEMENT FOLLOWING HURRICANE KATRINA

8

Charles Gagnon

Immediately following Hurricane Katrina on August 29, 2005, the Critical Incident Stress Management (CISM) team in Ouachita Parish, Louisiana, responded to a call to action (Louisiana CISM, 2009). The team, composed of two firefighters, a chaplain, a law enforcement officer, and a licensed professional counselor, originated 4 years earlier. The team members, all trained in the model of CISM by Mitchell and Everly (1993) (known as the Mitchell model), were called to respond to the incident command center (a command facility detached from "ground zero" but accessed easily) in Baton Rouge. However, the team chose to remain in northeast Louisiana in order to conduct CISM debriefings for first responders returning after a 2-week rotation in the Ninth Ward of New Orleans. The debriefings took place in Ouachita Parish, at one central location; a few were conducted in rural facilities to accommodate those responders living farther away.

CISM PROCESS

In compliance with the Mitchell model, team debriefings lasted approximately 1.5 hours and were conducted according to the following format:

Introduction. CISM team members introduce themselves using their first names. Then participants do the same with a brief description of their role in the incident.

Facts. The group being debriefed is asked to "paint a picture" of the incident, understanding that the CISM team knows nothing of their experience.

Thoughts. Participants share their thoughts/feelings about the incident before, during, and after the event.

Reactions. Participants describe their reactions to the incident.

Symptoms. Participants describe unusual symptoms or behaviors they experienced during the incident and since that time.

Teaching. Participants learn that what they are experiencing is a normal reaction to an abnormal event. The CISM team teaches those debriefed how to recognize symptoms they may experience and ways to destress. They also learn how to use the team and each other for ongoing support.

Re-Entry. Participants are reassured that the information shared is confidential and that the debriefing is not a critique; rather, it is an opportunity to process their participation in a catastrophic event.

Once the CISM debriefing is completed, the team interacts with those participants who remain in order to be available for individual processing. After the participants have left, the team processes the debriefing and makes plans to follow up with participants, particularly those experiencing an unusually high level of stress. If individual participants do not contact any of the team members, the follow-up takes place within 2 days after the debriefing.

The number of participants in a group averaged between 12 and 20. The largest group, with 30 participants, was from the Office of Public Health—whose members were responsible for treating evacuees located in all outlying shelters in northeast Louisiana.

First Debriefing

The team conducted the first of 10 debriefings on Sunday, September 4, 2005, two weeks after Katrina made landfall. All participants in the debriefings took part in rescue and recovery operations following the subsequent levy breach, particularly in the Ninth Ward in New Orleans. Although the individuals included law enforcement, paramedics, and firefighters, the one common factor was that the participants of each debriefing were at the same location and event during the incident. One debriefing was composed of firefighters; another was a combination of all three professions. All rescue and recovery participants described incidents in which they felt as though they were "in a war zone." Events included scenes of houses moved off foundations and destroyed by the flooding, people stranded on the tops of houses, and "dead bodies everywhere." When asked to clarify their experiences, participants described situations in which they felt helpless in boats, standing at the ready for hours at a time and being forced to stay out of the affected area without direction from incident commanders. Several participants stated that they took it upon themselves—against orders—to venture into the hurricane-ravaged area looking for survivors.

One rescuer described taking gunfire from survivors sitting on the peak of a rooftop after the survivors were left behind because the boats were full. Others heard children screaming but were unable to locate or access the source of the voices. Responders described seeing babies and small children floating face down in the flooded streets as they passed by, wanting to retrieve the bodies but needing to focus on rescuing survivors. This was a common description in most debriefings.

Following the Mitchell model, all supervisors, police and fire chiefs, and state police supervisors participated in separate briefings that allowed them to share more openly and to interact with just their peers rather than with those they supervised. It is important to understand that during the traumatic event, the supervisors were working side by side with those personnel whom they normally supervise; however, once they returned to their duty stations, their role reverted to administrative disciplinarians. Thus, these briefings allowed the first responders to participate freely, not intimidated by the presence of a supervisor. In one of two debriefings that week, a fire chief described performing CPR on a child who died in his arms. The chief became tearful and said that he would never allow himself to cry in front of his firefighters.

The CISM team also conducted debriefings with Hurricane Katrina responders who were not participating in the New Orleans rescue operations, including Region 8 Incident Command Center staff, public health nurses, and evacuation shelter staff. Individuals in these groups reported feeling overwhelmed by the large number of evacuees who suffered from both medical and psychiatric/psychological conditions. These responders also expressed anxiety as a result of the number of times they had to prepare for a large influx of patients and evacuees being sent via medevac to the area, then to stand down due to a change in plans, only to be required to repeat the process several times a day.

Debriefing CISD Team Leaders

At the end of each day of team debriefings, the team leader reported the findings to personnel at the Louisiana Critical Incident Stress Management (LCISM) headquarters in Shreveport, Louisiana. Team leaders stated that reporting to the LCISM professional staff was another way of decompressing from the day's events. The CISM team members had some flexibility in their work schedules but did not deviate from their regular work duties during this period.

The CISM team responded to all requests for debriefings, remaining vigilant to their own symptoms of vicarious trauma. Given the team members' various professions, they not only conducted the debriefings but also interacted with 5,000 victims/survivors of the hurricane who evacuated to Ouachita Parish. With the influx of evacuees came a sudden rise in crime and rapid depletion of resources available to local residents. This led to an increase in the stress level of already-fragile first responders, creating a hypervigilant state that made them more prone to overreact to routine calls.

Individual Processing

After the initial wave of debriefings, the number decreased from 10 per week to an average of one debriefing every 2 weeks. Although rescuers in the initial groups did not participate in subsequent debriefings, those who continued to experience nightmares, isolation, and loss of appetite requested individual processing sessions. Any available CISD team member responded to these one-to-one requests and conducted individual sessions in the following manner. First, a debriefing participant contacts the team member. The participant shares memories of the event and subsequent personal dilemmas. The team member is careful not to conduct psychotherapy; however, if the participant is unable to let go of the event, a counseling professional (not a CISM team member) becomes involved for in-depth psychotherapy. This allows the team member who is a mental health professional to maintain his or her role integrity as a CISM team member.

CISM TEAM MEMBER STRESS

The CISM team members conducted their own post debriefing interviews after each incident, providing an opportunity to process the information discussed in each specific group as well as a chance to debrief the debriefer. Having participated in multiple debriefings over a short period, the team members began to show signs of stress from listening to these horrific stories on a daily basis. After the first week, team members started to express concerns about their own psychological well-being. Symptoms expressed and observed included fatigue and a decrease in typical facial expression and verbal interaction during the debriefings. Because the team members had been working closely together for several years, they were able to recognize symptoms and decompress with the team and each other. This process proved to be very beneficial and allowed the team to facilitate other CISM debriefings whenever necessary.

CISM staff reported experiencing heightened levels of stress because of the unusual number of debriefings conducted in a short period. The CISM debriefing team remained intact during this time, participating together in all sessions. Once the number of debriefings declined, the team members maintained contact with each other through phone calls and occasional contact with no other activity planned. Interaction with each other after the debriefings and for several weeks after the hurricane proved to be a reliable source of support for a well-connected CISM team. During post-debriefing visits to participants, team members noted that they reported a decrease in typical post-critical event reactions and a gradual return to routine behavior. Given the number of first responders benefiting from the debriefings and the positive feedback regarding their progress after the trauma, the CISM team remains ready to move into action again with the hope that they will never need to do so.

Charles Gagnon, LPC, is a Mental Health Center Manager-A for the Region 8 Office of Mental Health, State of Louisiana, in Winnsboro and Columbia. He is also a counselor in private practice in West Monroe, Louisiana and a CISM team member with Louisiana Critical Incident Stress Management Inc. He is also a doctoral student at Argosy University.

REFERENCES

Louisiana Critical Incident Stress Management (CISM) Inc. (2005). *Critical incident stress team management.* Retrieved from.Lcisminc.com/Services.htm

Mitchell, J. T., & Everly, G. S. (1993). *Critical incident stress debriefing: An operations manual for the prevention of traumatic stress among emergency services and disaster workers.* (3rd ed.). Ellicott City, MD: Chevron.

Katrina: Ongoing Trauma, Ongoing Recovery

9

Michael Gootee

Looking back, we should have known that Hurricane Katrina was going to be an ongoing story of ongoing trauma and ongoing recovery, without a definitive end. At first, Katrina was a strong storm, but not the worst one. Overnight it blew up into a Category 5 hurricane—making landfall with a fury. New Orleans had a short sigh of relief—the hurricane came in weaker than expected. There was a brief moment of recovery; then, news came of levees breaking. As the waters continued to rise, people were stranded on their rooftops, floating in the water clinging to pieces of debris, or worse, trapped in their attics.

Next were images of recovery: police and other first responders, fellow citizens, and neighbors from local communities coming in boats to pluck people from the waters and bring them to safety, while Coast Guard helicopters lifted stranded persons from rooftops. Lawlessness and looting brought on more terror and trauma. Gangs broke into hospitals and shelters while criminals randomly terrorized others and shot at rescuers in boats and helicopters. The story continued, as did the powerful surge of the Gulf waters roaring in and washing out. The pattern was: in and out, ongoing trauma, ongoing recovery.

During the early days and weeks of ongoing recovery, the National Guard and military troops arrived to restore law and order and to deliver food and water. Busses and airplanes moved the sick and transported residents to shelters throughout generous towns and cities. Individuals, churches, and community groups provided shelter, clothing, food, comfort, and compassion. After many days, helicopters dropped huge sandbags to plug holes in the levees.

The city lay underwater for 3 weeks until it could be pumped out. The ongoing trauma included: days of stifling heat and nights of frightening darkness; look-ing for the dead or missing, or missing family and friends; mass dispersion across the country; loss of relational supports as well as utilities, food, and water. Ambiguous reassurance came from the presence of armed military throughout the city. We were grateful that they were there, unnerved that they needed to be there, and hoping they would be there at the right moment.

Some residents had suffered the death of a loved one; others relived the traumatic memories of narrow escape from death. Many lost their homes and jobs, along with the supports that we usually count on to help us through times like these. They lost the very fabric of their relational lives: neighbors and family members were dispersed many miles away; entire neighborhoods where families had lived their entire lives were destroyed; and the recovery and future of the city of New Orleans itself was in question. A powerful moment for me was when I went back to my home and neighborhood, which had been flooded by more than 8 feet of water for 3 weeks. I had a joyful reunion with a Vietnamese neighbor of many years, and, after sharing some of our stories, we discussed our future, including the possibility that neither family would return to rebuild our old homes. In parting, he turned to me and said in his gentle voice, "Well, goodbye. You have been a good neighbor." In that moment, the sadness and reality of how our lives had changed forever struck me.

A huge obstacle to recovery has been the enormous, and, at times, paralyzing uncertainty. It is hard to pick up the pieces of my life and reconstruct it when it continues to unravel, and when I do not know how much more it will unravel: no job, no home, and no neighborhood. Do I have a city to return to? Will it be livable? What kind of life will be possible? How long before basic utilities and services such as groceries and gas stations are restored? Will there be medical care and schools? Will my insurance pay fairly and in a timely fashion? Will I be stuck paying for a blighted house I cannot live in and can I afford to rent? Will my neighborhood come back? What if I rebuild only to have this all happen again? How do I make decisions about my future with all these unanswered questions?

ONGOING TRAUMA, ONGOING RECOVERY

Those who were able to sort out the confusion enough to make some initial, if tentative, decisions created a foothold to take the next step of ongoing recovery. Those who were paralyzed and unable to decide fell into limbo regarding their recovery. After a few days, my wife and I made the decision to stay in Lake Charles, Louisiana, where we had evacuated to the loving support of her sister and brother-in-law. After 2 days of re-traumatization watching TV news, we had had enough. We had to take action for our recovery to begin.

I contacted colleagues for a job at Family and Youth Counseling Agency (an organization that has played a major role in the ongoing recovery in Lake Charles and all of southwest Louisiana) and I started the next day, counseling fellow evacuees who were staying at a Red Cross shelter. This was a very helpful step for my recovery because we were now letting go of the city we loved, where I had lived most of my life, and where we had raised our daughter and son. I also let go of the private practice in New Orleans that I had built over 14 years. My wife began volunteering at the local HIV clinic until she received a permanent transfer months later. While we were there, a month after Katrina, Hurricane Rita hit, devastating Lake Charles and southwest Louisiana.

The next year, my wife was transferred to Lafayette where we lived for 2 years. I continued to get calls from former clients in New Orleans who wanted counseling, so I reopened my private practice in New Orleans 3 days per week, driving 2 hours each way for 2 more years. Gradually we took necessary steps and finally, after 4 years, we are back in the New Orleans area. We built a home in Covington, 45 miles away from our old home

in New Orleans, and although we are extremely grateful and love the peace and beauty of nature with our new country lifestyle, we miss being closer to our family and friends.

I continue to work with clients who are experiencing ongoing trauma and ongoing recovery, reliving traumatic memories from the hurricane, and moving through the waves of grief over not returning to their home and neighborhood in addition to the cascade of other losses. Some fight with insurance companies and government programs to rebuild their homes while still living in FEMA trailers or partly rebuilt houses. They have rebuilt their homes, living with a lack of services and safety while the neighborhoods continue to be blighted by flooded homes that have been neither repaired nor torn down. Others have been fortunate to live in parts of the city that have had a better recovery. If you continue to live in the New Orleans area, even if your neighborhood did not take the brunt of the hit, there is still a sense of sadness, scarring, and trauma that is not far below the surface; it still reverberates through you.

GRATITUDE

Fortunately, the ongoing recovery continues and people are rebuilding their lives, their homes, and their neighborhoods. The overwhelming generosity of individuals and faith and civic communities has been heartwarming and inspiring. Residents have been supported, uplifted, and comforted by their neighbors next door as well as individuals in communities throughout the state and the country.

There will be no end point, no closure, to the Katrina story in the foreseeable future, and perhaps never. The obstacles, pain, and triggers of traumatic memories and losses will be ongoing. But even more so, the strength, resilience, compassion, comforting, and healing of a community from within—and with help from the greater community—also will be ongoing. For all of that loving support, we are deeply grateful.

Michael Gootee, LPC, LMFT, is a counselor in private practice in New Orleans, LA.

The Kat-Rita Trauma: Reflections of a Traumatized Professional

10

Walton H. Ehrhardt

As a native of New Orleans, having returned to the area in 1969, I believed I knew much about hurricanes. I still recall my first hurricane experience 61 years ago at age 7, watching the movements of the empty rocking chair in the living room and laughing as I noted the serious expressions on the faces of my parents who realized the house was doing the "rocking."

Hurricane Camille (August 1969) served as a wake-up call. As an overconfident husband and father, I did not evacuate our Biloxi, Mississippi home at the storm's approach; rather, I chose to ride it out. That decision exposed us to an unforgettably frightening experience. My wife and I concluded that we would evacuate in any future storm of Category 3 or higher. We reasoned that we could return safely a few days later, experience a "resurrection to new life," clean up, and move on with normal living.

Katrina-Rita: Evacuation to Exile

On August 26, 2005, my New Orleans-based family (three married children with spouses and kids) numbered 11 with one more on the way. We gathered on my 65th birthday to enjoy a family dinner, and the restaurant patrons were all abuzz with Katrina talk. I was finalizing plans for our probable evacuation to my oldest son's home in Atlanta when the TV news interrupted with the governor's evacuation order and weather radar picturing the monstrous beast churning toward us.

We departed early to avoid the anticipated traffic, and arrived in Atlanta 8 hours later. The forecast was explicit: Katrina was a Cat 5 killer storm, pushing a dangerously destructive tidal surge. By Monday morning, it was over and New Orleans had dodged another one! We celebrated our blessings and made plans to return to New Orleans on Tuesday. As in pre-

vious evacuations, we knew what to expect and what had to be done when we got home: pick up tree limbs and other debris, repair any glass breakage, call the insurance company, and return to normal.

The Shock of Reality

The first levee break occurred at 4:30 a.m. on August 29 as Katrina was making landfall. Within 20 hours, 14 additional levee breaks flooded 80% of the city with salty waters, to the rooftops in some neighborhoods. Filthy sewer and chemically infested waters deluged 220,000 homes and remained for 3 weeks, only to return for another 10 days when Hurricane Rita pushed its surge into Lake Pontchartrain.

Communities southeast of the city in St. Bernard Parish were devastated, with 95% of the homes destroyed. West of New Orleans, Jefferson Parish flooded because the pumps had not been turned on for 2 days. The Mississippi coastal communities from Pass Christian to Biloxi were obliterated by a 30-plus foot tidal surge. Metro New Orleans was flooded for almost 6 weeks.

This was the genesis of what I call Kat-Rita. The hurricanes of August 29 and September 24, 2005 left indelible marks on the lives of residents of Alabama, Mississippi, Louisiana, and the Texas Gulf Coast. Our lives have been radically altered as a result.

Our Trauma Begins

According to van der Kolk, "Trauma is the result of exposure to an inescapably stressful event that overwhelms a person's coping mechanisms" (as cited in Ulman & Brothers, 1993, p. 16). Trauma greatly affects our ability to cope. Initially we were all plagued by numbness, emotional deadness, derealization, depersonalization, and denial; then depression set in. Crying, fear, rage at our helplessness, shame over feeling so nakedly needy, confused and overwhelmed, frustrated with broken communication systems, bureaucratic mismanagement—these were our early experiences.

For the Ehrhardts, the houses of two families were flooded and one was damaged by winds. We had packed for a quick trip; clearly, the exile would extend beyond our preparations. Our concerns were: jobs, schools for the kids, prenatal care for my daughter-in-law, how to manage our stay in Atlanta, and for how long?

Two contrasting experiences illustrate the bookends of our emotionality; on one side, housing and support were key pressures; there were 17 of us living in the Alpharetta house with eight pets, and we dreaded wearing out our welcome. The school-age children were enrolled in the Fulton County system, and to the relief of my wife and me, we learned that my bishop in the Lutheran Church would be providing income for both of us. The other bookend of our experience was one overflowing with gratitude. When we left Alpharetta 5 weeks later, we felt blessed by the hospitality of family, their neighbors, and friends who organized themselves into a hospitality community. They purchased two sets of clothing for each grandchild, donated food, prepared meals, held block parties to welcome us, and gave my three exiled children a gift of $500 per family.

Missing Pieces

My family was experiencing losses of significant coping function. From a Bowenian family therapy perspective, increased triangulation was occurring in this stressed, extended three-generation family system and much of it involved me (Bowen, 1978). I was over-functioning, and others were becoming overly dependent on me. The continuing effects of the Kat-Rita trauma directly influenced our capacity to perceive, recall, anticipate, and act in ways suited to the situation. I recognized that I was experiencing a breakdown, a collapse of these essential functions of reflection, regard, and judgment.

Adult Onset Trauma

Boulanger (2007) described adult onset trauma as experiencing the loss of safety and security, and feeling terrorized and persecuted by a reality that continually wounds. The hurricanes pressed all these aspects of terrorizing anxiety into consciousness: annihilation anxiety, separation anxiety, and persecutory anxiety.

We experienced a loss of agency, a crippling sense of helplessness that results in a constant sense of betrayal by reality. Thus, our core self is affected and we doubt the senses of agency, physical cohesion, continuity, and affectivity—all of these embody a baseline for ongoing self-experience. When significant others do not comprehend the nature of this wounded subjectivity, we experience further wounding (Boulanger, 2007).

Living and Working Inside the Trauma

Our home is in Mandeville, north of Lake Pontchartrain at an elevation of 26 feet above sea level; it did not flood but was damaged by wind. Our daughter and her family lived with us for 8 months while their house was being restored. They were among the more fortunate—their house sustained less then 2 feet of water. However, our son's house had 4 feet of flooding. After renting for 7 months, our son and his family were forced to return to live on the second level of their flooded house while they sought an "as is" buyer. This family of five had moved five times over a 20-month period.

During this early post–Kat-Rita epoch of confusion, depression, anger, and grief, I functioned as counselor, leader, group- and community-organizer in my professional roles, and as husband, father, and grandfather in my family roles. As clergy care coordinator for Lutheran Social Services of the South-Disaster Response, I was counselor to 50 Lutheran churches in the New Orleans metro area and in Baton Rouge (where the population swelled overnight by nearly 200,000 residents, all displaced by Kat-Rita). Essentially, I worked to rebuild community and communality by bringing people together to process losses, grieve, and begin healing, and I developed a series of presentations to be used in large and small group settings (Ehrhardt, 2006; 2006/2007). Little did I know the difficulty that this work would bring. I am chagrined to admit that I was working between 55 and 80 hours per week, which took its toll and led to compassion fatigue.

Loss, Suffering, and Death

More than 1,800 people from the metro New Orleans area drowned, and an estimated 300 remain missing (Louisiana Recovery Authority, 2009). The number of elderly who have died since Katrina has tripled, as has the rate of suicide (Tulane University School of Social Work, 2009).

The Displaced and Wounded

Officials estimated some 1.2 million people evacuated metro New Orleans. Approximately 120,000 did not have the means to leave; they were the poor of New Orleans crowded into the lower Ninth Ward, the lowest area of the city where the federal housing projects are located. Very little remains of the Ninth Ward. As of this writing, residents of many communities of New Orleans remain displaced, or they are residing in the remains of their damaged property, or in 8 x 20 FEMA travel trailers. Most of the 1.2 million evacuees were unable to return to their homes for weeks, and when they did, more than 80% learned their homes were uninhabitable. They have become the population of the *displaced-suffering-their-losses*, and their recovery after returning is painfully slow. Businesses, especially the small mom-and-pop ones, were obliterated. More than 800 schools were damaged or destroyed; neighborhoods, churches, synagogues, and communities were disrupted and many were gone. Government on all levels was dysfunctional and remains chaotic as of this writing. Mental health resources were decimated as therapists experienced tremendous losses in their client base. Medical infrastructure incurred drastic losses as 6,000 physicians prior to the catastrophe were now reduced to 2,000, and 16 hospitals before the event are now reduced to 6. We expect the effects of Kat-Rita to continue for the next 25 years.

Incidence of violence, substance abuse, and family chaos have escalated threefold. In January 2009, I experienced my first client suicide, and I am treating members of three different families who have lost sons to suicide. The number of fatal auto accidents has tripled. The number of homicides increased so much that the National Guard was activated with State Police to provide protection; only recently were they sent home—3½ years later. The son of one of my students at University of New Orleans was shot, robbed, and left to die; his parents removed him from life-support 4 days after he was identified. New Orleans now has the dubious distinction of being the murder capital of the country (McCarthy, 2009). Never in the history of my practice have I had to work with such violence in such compacted time and space.

THE BALM OF GRIEVING RELATIONSHIPS

How do we heal while living in this realm of threat and insufficient security? Most people are stuck in the current economic recession, and their post–Kat-Rita entrapment is further exacerbated. The emotional pain of traumatic loss is never quantitatively measurable, but it is qualitatively lessened by the process of grieving. Psychological and physiological benefits are reaped by enduring the emotional processes involved in grieving one's losses. In grieving, we transform what was once an externally priceless experience into internalized memory that contributes to our resilience.

Spirituality is a necessary, rather than adjunct, dimension of recovery and healing from trauma. Connecting to community and communality has been most beneficial to me. In my practice, I now make it a point to inquire about a person's spiritual resources. Griffith and Griffith (2003) defined spirituality as "a commitment to choose, as the primary context for understanding and acting, one's relatedness to all that is" (p. 15). The Kat-Rita trauma has affected our relationship to all that is. Griffith and Griffith explained:

> With this commitment, one attempts to stay focused on relationships between oneself and other people, the physical environment, one's heritage and tradition, one's body, one's ancestors, saints, Higher Power, or God. It places relationships at the center of awareness, whether they are interpersonal relationships with the world or other people, or intrapersonal relationships with God or other nonmaterial beings. (pp.15–16)

New communities are coming into being around a focused mission: helping one another and listening to our life stories. Connected with this are all the familiar communities, people, and places that have made the living experience of New Orleans such an *élan vital*. The new normal has not yet arrived for us; rather, it is still forming.

Resilience and Faith

In traumatic loss, our faith, intimacy, and resilience are inseparable (Walsh, 1982). Faith is more about spirituality than about religious experience, a spiritual reality of relationship with others. We have been blessed with people who came from outside to help us recover. When you have spent endless weeks and months engaged in tossing ruined possessions, tearing out walls, shoveling mud and filth, the body aching to the bone—the feeling of ecstasy is indescribable when a voice says: "Looks like you could use some help here. Where can I begin?" Both faith-based organizations and secular humanistic groups have driven the voluntary responses to the Kat-Rita wounded. More than 55,000 volunteers have come through the Lutheran Disaster Response and in July 2009, 35,000 Lutheran Youth spent 5 days helping us rebuild our lives. This faith is more a sense of trust in the goodness of other beings.

It has been my personal experience that hope is fostered through participation in a spiritual community, and healing involves building and maintaining significant relationships. Physical working out, music, laughter, drama, and the arts are all essential in building and maintaining resiliency. The communities of faith have provided the greatest positive influence in post–Kat-Rita life in terms of building resiliency and intimacy with self and others.

And Life Goes On

As we enter the fourth hurricane season since Kat-Rita, our family continues its healing. My practice is rebuilding slowly with noticeable effect of the economic downturn. I continue to assist my new bishop in a part-time staff position as director of specialized pastoral care, offering psychotherapy to individuals without insurance.

How do my wife and I renew? I take 3-day weekends as time off, and every other month we get out of town on a mini-renewal. The family carries the emotional scars of anxiety over any signal of seriously stormy weather. All of us are aware that "reality" will perhaps wound us again. Hurricane season brings the awareness that we are still vulnerable; 2012 is too long a time to wait for basic levee protection, but it is also part of life.

Reverend Walton H. Ehrhardt, EdD, LPC, LMFT, is director of specialized pastoral ministry, TX/LA Synod of the Evangelical Lutheran Church.

REFERENCES

Bollas, C. (1987). *The shadow of the object.* New York: Columbia University Press.

Boulanger, G. (2007). *Wounded by reality: Understanding and treating adult onset trauma.* New York: Routledge.

Bowen, M. (1978). *Family therapy in clinical practice.* New York: Jason Aronson.

Ehrhardt, W. (2006). Reflections on my Katrina experience. In R. McCullough-Bade & J. McCullough-Bade (Eds.), *Voices of faith in the midst of a storm* (pp. 1–12). Baton Rouge, LA: Future With Hope Press.

Ehrhardt, W. (2006/2007). *Our world is a mess! Spirituality for the long journey: Renewal of faith and hope.* Presentation to Members of Peace Lutheran Church Slidell, LA; Hosanna Lutheran Church, Mandeville, LA; Grace Lutheran Church, New Orleans, LA.

Ehrhardt, W. (2007). *Missing pieces: Loss of intimacy post-trauma.* Paper presented at the International Psychotherapy Institute Conference, Washington, DC.

Griffith, J. L., & Griffith, M. E. (2003). *Encountering the sacred in psychotherapy: How to talk with people about their spiritual lives.* New York: Guilford Press.

Louisiana Recovery Authority. (2009). *Annual report.* Baton Rouge, LA: Author.

McCarthy, B. (June 1, 2009). Despite drop in crime, N.O. still leads. *The Times Picayune.*

Tulane University School of Social Work. (2009). *Best practices seminars.* March 19–20. New Orleans, LA.

Ulman, R., & Brothers, D. (1993). *The shattered self: A psychoanalytic study of trauma.* London: The Analytic Press.

Walsh, F. (1982). *Normal family processes.* New York: Guilford Press.

Section Three
Support for Returning Veterans and Their Families

Returning Veterans: The Effects of Traumatization

11

Michael Rank, Michael Dubi, and Kristen Chandler

Since the beginning of the wars in Iraq and Afghanistan, considerable research has been conducted on the effects of trauma on veterans. However, significantly less research has been done on the effects that those veterans have on their family members, friends, and significant others upon returning home from overseas. Mental distress symptoms have been found in the children of veterans, as well as their spouses, therapists, and close friends (Dekel, Goldblatt, Keidar, Solomon, & Polliack, 2005). It is quite possible that the number of people in the U.S. affected by the Middle East wars will be in the millions.

Secondary Traumatization

Secondary traumatization can be a serious consequence for those associated with returning veterans; it occurs when people come into close contact with a trauma victim and vicariously experience the victim's emotional upset. Over time, the people closest to these trauma victims can become indirectly associated with the trauma itself and the resulting mental distress (Figley, 1983). Wives of returning veterans have complained of symptoms similar to those of their veteran husbands who have PTSD. Many wives also have experienced such symptoms as depression, anxiety, guilt, and distressing dreams. They feel as if the PTSD is running their lives and that having their husbands back is like having another child in the home (Dekel et al., 2005).

Secondary traumatization is not only a very possible side effect for families of returning veterans, it also can affect mental health professionals who listen to every detail of trauma day after day—and usually from many different clients. According to Figley (1995), secondary traumatization is "the natural and consequent behaviors and emotions resulting from knowing about a traumatizing event experienced by a significant other. The stress results from helping or wanting to help a traumatized or suffering person" and not being able to do so (Figley, 1995, p. 7). Kanter (2007) reminded us that mental health professionals must learn over time that they cannot help all clients, cannot resolve all problems, and can only do the best they can at any given moment. The impact of secondary traumatization on mental health professionals is similar to the effects mental disorders in returning veterans have on their families: "sleeplessness, nightmares, stomachaches, headaches, fatigue, memory loss, irritability, and sadness" (Naturale, 2007). These feelings are associated with compassion fatigue, secondary traumatization, and vicariously living out combat trauma.

Children and the Effects of Secondary Traumatization

Children are the youngest victims of the current wars in the Middle East. They are innocent, unable to speak for themselves, and easily affected in many ways. Children in military families deal with many stressors, even before their parents return from a war zone. Problems arise when issues such as frequent relocation and separation from family members are added to the process of reunification (Drummet, Coleman, & Cable, 2003). Older male children tend to take over the father position in the family informally in the absence of the real father and, upon reunification, that child may resent having to go back to child status. He may not only resent the father for taking his place back as the head of household but also may have difficulty in going back to the prior position.

Children thrive on consistency. Uncertainty can cause anxiety, stress, and depression in a young child. Military children also experience ambiguous loss in the new war-torn, post-September 11 era that to them seems uncertain, vague, unclear, or indeterminate (Boss, 1999). Children know that when their parent is deployed into a dangerous situation, there is always a chance that he or she may never come back. This creates a constant state of uncertainty and can lead to severe anxiety and other mental disorders. Children talk about having to take care of their parent at the same time as they are progressing further into an emotionally distant state of depression, stress, and anxiety. In addition, ambiguous loss can lead to resentment of guardians (Huebner, Mancini, Wilcox, Grass, & Grass, 2007). Children's grades often suffer because of the uncertainty of deployment and reunification. One mother reported that her son's grades dropped dramatically because "he worries more about daddy dying than just going away and coming back" (Lyle, 2006). Spouses often relate that, even though their partner has returned and are physically there, they are not psychologically present. Thus, they remain in the same position as single parents, just as when their spouse was absent (Dekel et al., 2005).

Roger's Story

Roger enlisted at 18, right after high school. He was deployed to a base outside of Kirkuk, Iraq where one of his responsibilities involved base security. He recalls being frightened and on edge for the first tour but nothing of any great significance happened to him. During the second tour, while walking to lunch, a mortar round exploded nearby, killing a friend. He remembers body parts flying in front of his face, being splattered with blood and debris, and being thrown to the ground.

A few days later, dreams and flashbacks began to occur and he could not control them; he began drinking alcohol heavily. He was frightened all the time. Subsequently, he was honorably discharged and returned home to live with his mother and sister.

Roger was drunk every day, would not bathe for days at a time or look for a job, and had regular violent outbursts. He threatened his mother twice with a pistol. His mother took him to the Veteran's Administration (VA) outpatient facility nearby. Roger believed that they were going to admit him to a psychiatric hospital. He panicked, ran from the facility, bought and consumed a pint of vodka, and then attempted to kill himself by running in front of a moving car. Rogers' pelvis was broken in several places. He broke both femurs and sustained other assorted injuries; his right leg was amputated just below the knee.

He returned home from the hospital and continued to drink and abuse his family. Roger threatened suicide.

His mother and sister took turns watching Roger, 24/7. He attacked and beat his sister and was arrested for domestic violence after which he agreed to seek treatment, but not with the VA. At the same time, his mother and sister began receiving psychotherapy because of their own traumatic stress issues.

The Future

Roger—as well as hundreds of veterans—returned home with multiple debilitating emotional, physical, and neurological problems. These problems have a deep impact not only on returning military but also on spouses, partners, children, and extended family. The war and the resulting mental disorders that can be attributed to it will affect soldiers, families, and mental health professionals for many years to come (Bride & Figley, 2007).

The clients who come to mental health professionals from the current wars in Iraq and Afghanistan are usually young, and they have seen atrocities that even the most hardened professional cannot comprehend. In order to prevent compassion fatigue, there must be some balance in the caseload of "successful clients" for counselors who work with veterans. Although this is usually so, mental health professionals may need to seek psychotherapeutic help themselves and should always consult their supervisors in times of need and uncertainty.

The debilitating effects on veterans returning from Iraq and Afghanistan are considerable. Mental health disorders can co-occur with physical problems; it seems that targeted early detection may be the best way to prevent this ripple effect on veterans and the people in their lives (Seal, Bertenthal, Miner, Sen, & Marmar, 2007). However, much more research needs to be conducted in order to understand the impact of the wars on veterans and their families. Mental disorders, somatic complaints, physical ailments, academic problems, and other issues are all direct risks for the families and loved ones of returning veterans. According to Galovskia and Lyonsa (2004), interventions for spouses and family members largely have been based on "improving relationships and reducing veteran's symptoms, rather than targeting improvements in the psychological well-being of the spouse and children" (p. 277).

Follow Up

Roger, his mother, and sister have been in treatment for more than 2 years and are doing well. He was convinced to attend individual psychotherapy with an EMDR therapist, but took several weeks before he would talk about his experience and nightmares. Once EMDR sessions began, he was able to work on his traumatic experience, and the nightmares stopped after the fourth session. Roger has been fitted with a prosthetic leg and is learning to use it. He has plans to run a marathon some day. He is in college and has a job and a girlfriend. He lives on his own in the town next to his mother and sister.

Roger's story is a call to action for counselors and all mental health professionals to be prepared to understand the impact of traumatic events on returning military and to be competent in the assessment and treatment of trauma.

Michael Rank, PhD, is associate professor in the School of Social Work, and director, Traumatic Stress Studies, at the University of South Florida, Tampa, FL.

Michael Dubi, EdD, LMHC, is associate professor in the School of Psychology and Behavioral Sciences at Argosy University, Sarasota, FL, and is certified in Acute Tramatic Stress Manangement and Compassion Fatigue.

Kristen Chandler is a doctoral student in the School of Public Health, University of South Florida, Tampa, FL.

REFERENCES

Boss, P. (1999). *Ambiguous loss: Learning to live with unresolved grief.* Cambridge, MA: Harvard University Press.

Bride, B., & Figley, C. (2007). The fatigue of compassionate social workers: An introduction to the special issue on compassion fatigue. *Journal of Clinical Social Work, 35*(7), 151-153.

Dekel, R., Goldblatt, H., Keidar, M., Solomon, Z., & Polliack, M. (2005). Being a wife of a veteran with posttraumatic stress disorder. *Family Relations, 54*(1), 24–36.

Drummet, A. R., Coleman, M., & Cable, S. (2003). Military families under stress: Implications for family life education. *Family Relations, 52,* 279–287. Retrieved from ProQuest database.

Figley, C. (1983). Catastrophes: An overview of family reactions. In C. R. Figley & H. I. McCubbin (Eds.), *Stress and the family: Vol. II: Coping with catastrophe* (pp. 3-20). New York: Brunner/Mazel.

Figley, C. (Ed.). (1995). *Compassion fatigue: Coping with secondary traumatic stress disorder.* New York: Bruner/Mazel.

Galovskia, T., & Lyonsa, J. (2004). Psychological sequelae of combat violence: A review of the impact of PTSD on the veteran's family and possible interventions. *Journal of Aggression and Violent Behavior, 9,* 477–501.

Huebner, A., Mancini, J., Wilcox, R., Grass, G., & Grass, S. (2007). Parental deployment and youth in military families: Exploring and ambiguous loss. *Family Relations, 56* (4), 112–122.

Kanter, J. (2007). Compassion fatigue and secondary traumatization: A second look. *Journal of Clinical Social Work, 35*(9), 289-293.

Lyle, D. (2006). Using military deployments and job assignments to estimate the effect of parental absences and household relocations on children's academic achievement. *Journal of Labor Economics, 24*(2), 319–350.

Naturale, A. (2007). Secondary traumatic stress in social workers responding to disasters: Reports from the field. *Journal of Clinical Social Work, 35*(6), 173–181.

Seal, K., Bertenthal, D., Miner, C., Sen, S., & Marmar, C. (2007). Bringing the war back home: Mental health disorders among 103,788 US veterans from Iraq and Afghanistan seen at Department of Veterans Affairs Facilities. *Archives of Internal Medicine, 167*(5), 476–482.

DEPLOYMENT COUNSELING: SUPPORTING MILITARY PERSONNEL AND THEIR FAMILIES

12

David L. Fenell and Joseph D. Wehrman

As part of an all-volunteer force, many military personnel have been committed to battle in multiple theaters of operation and on multiple combat tours—a reality that often creates stressful and challenging conditions for warriors and their families. Following September 11, 2001, the military forces of the United States shifted from a post-Cold War operational stance of training cycles and preparation for the possibility of war to a wartime emphasis. After 8 years of continuous combat several hundred thousand troops have been deployed to Afghanistan, Iraq, and other Middle Eastern countries for 6 to 18 months serving nearly 3 million combat tours (Tan, 2009a).

STAGES OF DEPLOYMENT

The five-stage deployment cycle model focuses on the impact of deployments from the first Gulf War and Bosnian conflicts (Pincus, House, Christenson, & Adler, 2001). This adapted model incorporates experiences of the Global War on Terrorism. The model is divided into three developmental stages with each having distinct and identifiable stressors experienced by the service member and family: preparation for separation, separation, and reunion. Counselors can provide services to military families targeting each stage of the cycle of deployment (Fenell & Fenell, 2008; Fenell & Weinhold, 2003; Mabray, Bell, & Bray, 2009; Sloane & Friedman, 2008).

The first stage of the cycle, *preparation for separation*, begins when the family receives the news of the upcoming deployment. This news usually comes as no surprise because, in an effort to allow some predictability for families, the military schedules deployments as far in advance as possible. Counselors can help children and adults to explore and express their fears and

encourage parents to respond to thoughts and feelings that otherwise might remain unspoken. The family may benefit from meeting with a counselor knowledgeable about military issues who will help prepare a response plan to the challenges ahead (Fenell & Fenell, 2008). The counselor needs to find a balance between the utilizing strength-based approaches, while recognizing and normalizing the fears and uncertainties that emerge during the preparation for deployment.

Separation, the second stage of the cycle, is the actual deployment. While the service member is in the combat zone, primary care-giving responsibilities fall on the parent or members of the child's extended family at home. This may be an overwhelming emotionally and physically draining experience often resulting in anxiety and depression for those at home attempting to "do it all." Communication is unpredictable, occurring daily or every few weeks by telephone, videoconferencing, e-mail, or chat. Establishing an effective long-distance communication pattern is important, as too much communication can distracts the service member by taking focus off the combat mission, and too little communication can create anxiety for both the deployed and family members at home (Fenell & Fenell, 2008).

Counseling normalizes feelings, develops methods of coping with anxiety and stress, and prioritizes responsibilities separating the most critical responsibilities from those that can be temporarily set aside. Counseling also supports children who develop symptoms of anxiety, have difficulties in school, or begin acting out. Joint sessions with the parent and child as well as individual sessions provide the adult with appropriate parenting strategies and the children with a means for understanding and responding more effectively (Fenell & Fenell, 2008; Fenell & Weinhold, 2003;

Hall, 2008; Jowers, 2007; Mabray et al., 2009; National Military Family Association, 2009; Sloane & Friedman, 2008).

The third stage of the cycle, *reunion*, occurs as the family anticipates and prepares to be reunited. This is a time of excitement and anticipation, but it is also a time of concern for some families. The service member often returns from combat expecting the family to be the same as it was before the deployment; however, this is rarely the case. Children have grown and developed, the spouse is more independent and competent, and the service member has changed during deployment and combat. Service members deployed for 6 to 18 months in a new, hostile environment may have developed new habits and interests that could surprise family members. Thus, the reunion can be a complex and difficult process as the family begins reintegrating the changed service member into the changed and reconstituted family structure (Fenell & Fenell, 2008; Fenell & Weinhold, 2003; Hall, 2008; Mabray et al., 2009; Pincus et al., 2001; Sloane & Friedman, 2008). Counseling can assist the couple and family in assessing their current family situation and help incorporate the changes in each family member.

The reunion presents additional challenges if the service member returns with severe emotional or physical challenges such an amputated limb or posttraumatic stress disorder (PTSD) (Roche, 2007). Medical and mental health treatment systems become an integral part of the reunion process and a new part of the family system during the recovery process. If the family is not included in the treatment process, reunion and stabilization are unlikely. Family counseling is also important when each parent has different ideas about continuing on active duty with an impending deployment or leaving the service altogether (Hall, 2008). If it is not resolved effectively, conflict about future deployments can break up relationships.

The stabilization component within the reunion phase of the deployment cycle is designed to assist families to adapt to changes made by members to get "back to normal" and establish homeostasis (Minuchin, 1974). Unfortunately, because it is almost certain that the soldier will be deployed again within 18 months, stabilization is hindered with the turmoil from thoughts and feelings about the next deployment cycle.

In reality, the reunion and preparation for separation stages of the deployment cycle are not distinct—these two phases overlap with frequent, multiple deployments. For most military families, stabilization does not occur during the reunion phase because the family attempts to enjoy one another while preparing for the next deployment. Some critics have called the reunion cycle the "reunion spiral" (Jowers, 2006) because frequent combat tours are accompanied by a downward spiral of morale for the military families, presenting severe challenges to their emotional well-being. A counselor familiar with military deployment issues can be of great assistance to these families.

NOT A JOB FOR ALL COUNSELORS

Many counselors have limited or no exposure to military life and culture. Without a direct frame of reference, counselors could unknowingly adopt stereotypical views about military organizations and personnel. Attitudes held about war and international conflict might have an impact on the counselor's effectiveness in working with military families (Fenell, 2008; Fenell & Fenell, 2008; Hall, 2008). Military families are commonly perceived as highly patriotic, religious, rule conscious, systematic, organized (their work requires this), holding conservative political beliefs, and following lawful orders from superiors without question. Service members may inflict deadly force during combat operations, which could conflict with the values and beliefs held by some counselors. Enlisted military personnel from all walks of life quickly identify a helper who does not respect or value their chosen profession of arms (Fenell, 2008; Fenell & Fenell, 2004, 2008; Price, 2008; Sue, Arredondo, & McDavis, 1992).

The cornerstone of multicultural counseling is the ability to empathize and enter into the world of the client. Counselors must hear the client accurately, understand the client's worldview, value the client, and communicate empathic understanding and valuing to the military client (Fenell & Weinhold, 2003; Rogers, 1951). Those who serve in the military enter a diverse culture with its unique lifestyle, similar to other diverse groups needing counseling support. If counselors are culturally encapsulated, they may rely on their internalized value systems to determine what is good for clients, ignore cultural differences, and define reality for clients according to rigidly held personal beliefs (Pederson, 1990; Wrenn, 1962).

Sue et al. (1992) identified several cross-cultural competencies that have been modified to guide the counselor's treatment of military personnel and their families:

1. An awareness of personal values and biases regarding military service and war

2. An ability to appreciate and work comfortably with military personnel and their families

3. An ability to share the military worldview without critically judging that view

4. An awareness and appreciation of the barriers that may prevent military personnel from seeking counseling services

5. A general knowledge about the history, traditions, and values of military culture

6. An ability to adjust the counseling approach to accommodate the needs of the military client

With the complexity and richness of within-group variance that exists in every cultural group, counselors should be aware that the military is a diverse culture unto itself, composed of culturally, ethnically, and religiously diverse individuals. Often the differences within a cultural group are as significant as those *between* cultural groups. For example, although many military personnel hold conservative values, not all do. It would be a therapeutic mistake if the counselor does not obtain data in the counseling session to support this assumption (Fenell, 2008). When asked about their ethnicity, Army and Marine Corps often respond, "We are all green," or members of the Navy, Air Force, and Coast Guard say, "We are all blue." Although these service members have voluntarily elected to be part of a culture of warriors, they do not relinquish their individual ethnic, cultural, and gender identities.

COUNSELORS' ROLE IN MULTIPLE DEPLOYMENTS

As couples spend more time apart some find that the advantages of being married are outweighed by disadvantages such as loneliness, fear, and frustration. Recent post-deployment follow-up surveys revealed that upon redeployment one-third of young combat veterans experience sexual difficulties related to trauma experienced in combat with most reporting that the dysfunction was severe ("Trauma, Sex and Health," 2008). While separated by deployment, spouses often identify their own wants and needs and may determine that they desire a career or do not wish to remain married. Anecdotally, it has been reported that infidelity is increasing because separated couples may meet their sexual needs with another partner (Vandevoorde, 2006). Other problems that result from multiple deployments include

PTSD (Roche, 2007), depression and withdrawal from family and friends, and increased alcohol consumption, all of which can severely undermine relationships. Although there is concern within the Department of Defense (DOD) that continued frequent deployments will result in a spike in military divorce rates, a Rand study (Karney & Crown, 2007) suggested the divorce rate is slightly over 3%, not much different from that of non-military couples. According to Sheila Casey, the wife of Army Chief of Staff General George Casey, Jr., many Army spouses who would seek divorces do not because they are overwhelmed by the responsibilities of multiple deployments and do not have time to take action. She said, "What military families need more than anything else is less deployment time" (as cited in Maze, 2009). General Casey has publicly stated that he hopes to give army troops more "dwell" time at home after the Iraq drawdown in 2010 (Reed, 2009).

Military Suicides

Multiple deployments coupled with psychological symptoms, heavy alcohol consumption, and failed relationships have been linked to an increase in the suicide rate for military veterans. With the current suicide rate in the military the highest in recent history (Tan, 2009b), the DOD is trying to reduce the frequency of deployments to solidify family relationships, reduce mental health issues, and reduce suicide attempts (Drummet, Coleman, & Cable, 2003). Because frequent and multiple deployments take a tremendous toll on the military and their families, mental health services need to be available to both.

Given the geopolitical complexities of the 21st century, military deployments are likely to continue. As of January 2009, more than 700,000 service members have experienced *multiple* deployments, and more than 1,178,000 have been deployed once since September 11, 2001 (Tan, 2009a). Many service members and their families will face years of separation in service to our nation. The stress created by multiple combat deployments for our nation's soldiers and their families has increased the need for counseling services by well-trained and culturally competent counselors.

As of this writing, the Veterans Administration has yet to promulgate rules for the creation of positions employing qualified counselors and family therapists within its mental health care system. Professional counselors often are required to receive a physician's supervision and referral to provide mental healthcare to the soldiers and their families through the military's

TRICARE health insurance system but social workers and family therapists are not. This complicates the help-seeking process for military clients and some may not seek needed care. Intensive advocacy efforts are needed to ensure that counselors have an equal standing in the mental health care community in order to provide critical services to returning veterans and their families.

Note: The thoughts presented in this chapter are those of the authors and do not necessarily reflect policies of the DOD.

David L. Fenell, PhD, is professor of Counselor Education and chair of the Department of Counseling & Human Services at the University of Colorado at Colorado Springs. He is also a Colonel (retired) in the U.S. Army Reserve Medical Service Corps and served as a behavioral sciences officer with U.S. Army Special Operations Command, Ft. Bragg, NC. Dr. Fenell was deployed to Afghanistan in 2002–2003 and to Iraq in 2007.

Joseph D. Wehrman, PhD, LPC, is assistant professor of Counselor Education and coordinator of the Community Counseling program in the Department of Counseling and Human Services at the University of Colorado, Colorado Springs. He is a former medical service officer and veteran of Operation Iraqi Freedom.

REFERENCES

Drummet, A. R., Coleman, M., & Cable, S. (2003). Military families under stress: Implications for family life education. *Family Relations, 52*(3), 279–287.

Fenell, D. L. (2008, June). A distinct culture: Applying multicultural counseling competencies to work with military personnel. *Counseling Today,* 8–9.

Fenell, D. L., & Fenell, R. A. (2004). Counseling services for military personnel and their families. *Counseling and Human Development, 35*(9), 1–20.

Fenell, D. L., & Fenell, R. A. (2008). *The effects of frequent combat tours on military personnel and their families: How counselors can help.* Retrieved from http://counselingoutfitters.com/vistas/vistas08/Fenell.htm

Fenell, D. L., & Weinhold, B. K. (2003). *Counseling families: An introduction to marriage and family therapy* (3rd ed.). Denver, CO: Love Publishing.

Hall, L. K. (2008). *Counseling military families: What mental health professionals need to know.* New York: Routledge.

Jowers, K. (2006, April 10). Survey: Families carry worry from one deployment to the next. *Army Times,* 10–11.

Jowers, K. (2007, November 5). Helping children of deployed soldiers. *Army Times,* 23.

Karney, B., & Crown, J. (2007). *Families under stress.* Rand Corporation. Retrieved from http://www.rand.org/pubs/monographs/2007/RAND_MG599.pdf

Mabray, D., Bell, M., & Bray, D. (2009). Redeployment and reintegration: Military family issues. *Family Therapy Magazine, 8*(2), 30–36.

Maze, R. (2009, June 15). Stretched and stressed: Families need help now, *Army Times,* 12.

Minuchin, S. (1974). *Families and family therapy.* New York: Routledge Press.

National Military Family Association. (2009). Challenges for military children. *Family Therapy Magazine, 8*(2), 45–46.

Pederson, P. (1990). The multicultural perspective as the fourth force in counseling. *Journal of Mental Health Counseling, 12,* 93–95.

Pincus, S., House, R., Christenson, J., & Adler, L. (2001). The emotional cycle of deployment: A military family perspective. *U.S. Army Medical Department Journal, 8,* 38–44.

Price, M. (2008). Culture matters. *Monitor on Psychology, 7*(37), 2–53.

Reed, B. (2009, May 8). Casey: Army wants to give more time at home. *Colorado Springs Gazette,* A8.

Roche, J. D. (2007). *The veteran's PTSD handbook.* Dulles, VA: Potomac Books.

Rogers, C. (1951). *Client-centered therapy.* Boston: Houghton-Mifflin.

Sloane, L. B., & Friedman, M. J. (2008). *After the war zone: A practical guide for returning troops and their families.* Philadelphia: Da Capo Press.

Sue, D. W., Arredondo, P., & McDavis, D. (1992). Multicultural counseling standards: A call to the profession. *Journal of Counseling & Development, 70,* 477–486.

Tan, M. (2009a, May 4). OEF, OIF deployments total nearly 3 million. *Army Times,* 24–26.

Tan, M. (2009b, February 16). Suicides surpass combat deaths in January. *Army Times,* 14–15.

Trauma, Sex and Health. (2008, November 10). *Army Times,* 6.

Vandevoorde, S. (2006). *Separated by duty, united in love.* New York: Citadel Press.

Wrenn, C. G. (1962). The culturally encapsulated counselor. *Harvard Educational Review, 32,* 444–449.

Additional Resources: Websites

Purdue University's Military Family Resource Institute

http://www.cfs.purdue.edu/mfri Provides links to a variety of information that is useful for helping combat veterans and their families.

Military OneSource

http://www.militaryonesource.com Provides referral to a therapist who will provide six free counseling sessions for combat veterans and their families. They will also provide assistance with other matters such as advice on childcare and finances.

Military Child Education Coalition

www.militarychild.orgProvides information to assist military children in transition.

Family Resources for Surviving Deployment

http://www.survivingdeployment.com/links.html

PTSD Guide for Families: Returning from the War Zone

http://www.mentalhealth.va.gov/MENTALHEALTH/ptsd/

Battlemind

http://battlemind.org Provides information about the mindset of the warrior in combat and the changes that need to be made in that mindset to return home.

Sesame Street Workshop for children of deployed warriors

http://archive.sesameworkshop.org/tlc/

Video for children dealing with multiple deployments

http://a836.g.akamai.net/7/836/12038/v001/doditc.download.akamai.com/12038/MHF/sesame/Homecomings_for_Grown_Ups.asx

TREATING VETERANS AND THEIR FAMILIES: WHAT CIVILIAN COUNSELORS NEED TO KNOW

13

David L. Albright and Gayle Rosellini

More than 400,000 National Guard and Reserve troops serve alongside regular troops in military operations around the world. The U.S. Army Medical Department (2008) estimated that 78.4% of recent war zone veterans have been exposed to incoming artillery, rocket, or mortar fire; 72.1% have known someone seriously injured or killed; 61.1% have seen destroyed homes and villages; and 60.2% have seen dead bodies or human remains.

Some Guard and Reserve units are on their second, third, and even fourth deployment while their families remain in their hometown, often hundreds of miles away from medical and psychological counseling at military bases. These families face all of the usual problems of civilian families; however, they face the real possibility that their loved one could be captured, killed, injured, or psychologically wounded in action.

Deployed troops experience significant mental health problems upon returning home (Britt, 2007; Hoge et al., 2004). More than 30% of all service members meet strict criteria for mental disorder, but fewer than half (23%–40%) of these will seek care through the military system (Department of Defense, 2007). When veterans reside far away from Veterans Administration (VA) hospitals, civilian counselors become the first line of defense when life problems can no longer be ignored. These problems are manifested as acute stress, anger, anxiety, depression, chemical dependency, post-traumatic stress disorder, and an increase in suicide thoughts and behaviors. Problems often erupt in ways that bring police scrutiny and court referrals for domestic violence, anger management, alcohol and drug treatment, or child welfare interventions. Other more subtle forms of deployment stress exist for active duty families as with the wife of a Guardsman on his second deployment to Iraq.

Shauna

I didn't share my husband's gung-ho attitude. He'd come home from his first tour changed, with a quicker temper and less patience. We argued over money, sex, and the way he expected the kids to follow orders without question. I constantly felt guilty for my angry feelings because I knew he's been through a lot, but he wouldn't open up to me. He said the only problem was me. I didn't know if our family could survive another tour. His unit left with a parade, TV cameras rolling, and front page stories. Everyone was acting like this was the greatest thing in the world, but we weren't even talking to each other. I couldn't sleep, I couldn't eat, I couldn't think. After 2 weeks, I worked up the courage to call my doctor for an appointment. I knew I needed counseling to get through this, but I didn't know where to turn. I needed a referral. The nearest military facility was a 6-hour drive, and I needed a counselor in my home town. As the nurse checked me in, she beamed all over me and said, "You must be so proud of your husband." I froze. I didn't know what to say and I never told the doctor I needed help. I was so ashamed of myself for feeling the way I did.

POST DEPLOYMENT STRESS

Many individuals mistakenly believe that families of Guard and Reserve troops called to active duty can easily get counseling services through the military. However, long waiting lists, limited clinic hours, breakdowns in the referral process, and facilities in hard-to-reach areas have become the norm. Stigma and negative attitudes within the military about seeking mental health counseling also create obstacles (Hoge et al., 2004). Guard and Reserve families suddenly deal with changes in social opportunities, the loss of income and benefits the deployed spouse provided through civilian employment, as well as the fearful separation of their loved one being deployed to a combat zone.

These families may be particularly stressed and isolated within their larger community as their friends and neighbors go on with life as usual. Veterans and their spouses who have trouble adjusting to civilian jobs are often referred to employee assistance programs, either voluntarily or as a condition of keeping employment. Anti-poverty and job training programs find unemployed and underemployed veterans and their families among their client base. Addressing the impact of deployment stress on veterans and families becomes part of the mix of providing comprehensive services. When help is sought, it most likely will be from a civilian counselor at a local mental health clinic, school, church, employee assistance program, chemical dependency treatment program, Boys and Girls Club, battered person's program or, perhaps, even a counselor picked at random from the phone book.

Children and Families as the Identified Clients

Compared with the military veteran, spouses are more likely to get mental health assistance (Milliken, Auchter-lonie, & Hoge, 2007). Thus, family members often become the identified clients, and it is important to invest counseling efforts toward them. In 2007, 700,000 children in the U.S. had at least one parent deployed overseas for military duty (American Psychological Association). When children suffer, counselors in the community will be called upon to intervene, evaluate, and provide support, treatment, and referrals.

When children are in trouble, clinicians trained in child therapy represent the ideal community resource. In the real world, parental denial, long waiting lists, and financial obstacles may delay or prevent a parent from seeking help for a troubled child. Counselors can make proper referrals if they remain alert to the signs and symptoms commonly seen in children troubled by a parent's deployment. Children's responses to deployment are individualized and depend upon the developmental age, but there are certain key behaviors that serve as warning signs when families undergo emotional trauma.

Parents' Influence on Children's Reactions
Infants and children under a year old tend to be sensitive to changes in their surroundings, schedules, and the availability and emotional state of their caregivers. If schedules and the level of nurturing are severely disrupted, the child may refuse to eat, lose weight, and become apathetic. These changes may be noticed first by a grandparent, aunt, pediatrician, or nurse-practitioner.

Toddlers between the ages of 1 and 3 tend to take their cues from their primary caregiver. If the caregiver copes well, the child is likely to cope well. If the caregiver develops emotional problems or becomes emotionally or physically unavailable, the toddler may develop sleep problems, throw temper tantrums, or become sullen and tearful.

Preschoolers between the ages of 3 and 6 may use their imaginations to develop personalized, self-blaming explanations for the deployed parent's departure. "Mommy left because I was bad." "Daddy came home angry because I was bad." They have a clearer awareness of a parent's absence than do younger children and may respond with regression to thumb sucking, wetting or soiling, sleep disturbance, clinginess, and separation anxiety. Other problems may include irritability, depression, somatic complaints, bullying, or emotional withdrawal.

If toddlers and preschoolers exhibit troublesome changes in their behavior, it may first be observed and reported by daycare providers and nursery school workers. Young children can best be supported and reassured by parental attention, emotional and physical warmth, and maintaining family routines. This may be difficult if the non-deployed parent or other primary caregiver feels overwhelmed by the stresses of deployment. Often the best way to help young children is to intervene with the parent who is not coping well by offering support and referral to counseling services.

Children between the ages of 6 and 12 may have a clearer awareness of the risks and realities of military deployment. It is normal for a child who is old enough to have experienced the death of a pet, watch television news, or listen to adult conversations to worry about death and dying. If the child is exposed to too much adult information or if the non-deployed parent is unavailable or is experiencing emotional difficulty, the child may act out aggressively or with irritability, whining, separation anxiety, school refusal, or obsessive-compulsive behaviors. This may happen around issues of safety, security, and fear of death of both the deployed parent and the primary caregiver.

Teenagers may challenge the authority of the non-deployed parent's household rules, either through open rebelliousness, falling away from normal school and sports activities, covert rule breaking, or risky behaviors. They may feel all the distressing emotions that an adult might feel—sadness, anger, loneliness, anxiety, restlessness—while lacking the maturity and experience to know how to cope with such feelings.

It is sometimes easier to medicate anxious, aggressive, irritable, misbehaving children and teenagers than to intervene in the behaviors and emotions of the non-deployed caregiver. Exploring the impact of deployment stress on the family dynamic can be a better *first step*, especially with young children who are reacting to their home environments and taking their cues from the primary caregiver—be it a mother, father, grandparent, or other relative.

Catherine and Jack

Jack had been a happy and cooperative child but at age 10 his behavior became progressively more difficult. He did not pay attention in class, he ridiculed smaller children, and his grades fell. He brought cigarettes to soccer practice and urged his pals to sneak a cigarette with him. Each offense seemed minor especially because there were days when Jack acted like his old sunny self. But over time he became a disruptive force in the classroom and on the playing field. When his teacher or coaches tried to discipline him, he'd angrily shout, "You're not the boss of me!" When a stray soccer ball hit his coach in the nose, bringing a trickle of blood, Jack tearfully wrapped his arms around the coach and pleaded, "please don't die." Other boys laughed at his "baby" behavior. Humiliated by his tears, Jack slapped and punched the other boys, then ran off the field and did not come back.

Catherine Johnson's lifeline was an activities counselor at the Boys and Girls Club where her 12-year-old son Jack had spent many happy hours as young child. Noah, a master's-level counseling intern, called Mrs. Johnson and asked her to meet with him. Catherine recalls, "I knew what was coming. I knew he was going to tell me I was a rotten mother, that I'd ruined my son. I lit up, waiting for the ax to fall, but it didn't. He was nice to me. I expected anything but kindness." Slowly, Noah elicited a story from Catherine of nearly paralyzing symptoms of despair, fear, guilt, and resentment:

"It all came out. It was everything I wanted to tell the doctor months before when I first tried to get help, when I froze. I froze because I was supposed to be proud that my husband might get killed, proud that I'm left to take care of the kids with about half the money we had before, I'm alone and I don't know what's going to happen to us. I work hard to accept things the way they are.

Emotionally, I can accept it, but my body—I get choked. I get physical symptoms. I stay in my room. Jack brings me food, tries to get me to eat, but I can't, I gag, it's like I'm choking on my emotions. He's 12 years old, and he's trying to take care of his mom. It's all wrong. We need help."

Noah offered to act as Jack's advocate within the Club and to help Catherine find a qualified therapist experienced in working with adults and families in the throes of traumatic life changes. Jack's behavior began to improve, then took a short-term turn for the worse when his father returned safely home. Catherine continued with therapy, successfully learning to accept life's difficulties without choking up. "We're heading toward marriage counseling and a referral to the VA. I'm going to keep taking care of myself and the children. We're going to make it."

Noah has since attended training to learn more about the way military deployment can put children and families at risk. If more had been known about the impact of military deployment on children, Jack's problem could have been recognized earlier. It might have been tempting for Noah to try to solve Jack's and Catherine's problems himself. He chose instead to follow the American Counseling Association Code of Ethics (2005) by practicing within the scope of his professional competence, education, and supervision. Like Noah, counselors can stay within the parameters of their expertise while learning to recognize the signs and symptoms of deployment stress on children and non-deployed parents.

WHAT CIVILIAN COUNSELORS CAN DO

Non-military counselors may feel ill-equipped to deal with the most serious mental health repercussions of deployment and combat. But counselors can make a referral. A comprehensive evaluation before referral is ideal; however, agencies conduct an intake before services are provided. Questions concerning military deployment, combat injuries, combat stress problems, and access to military or veterans' psychological and medical services can and should become a basic component of intake interviews for all types of counseling services.

Counselors can ask any client experiencing a traumatic life transition simple questions that do not sound clinical or coldly professional. Their simplicity may help break through the first layer of denial and stigma. One or two yes's means the service members or families are admitting, perhaps for the first time, that they are troubled and suffering. This opens the door for offering a referral to a higher level of care.

- Do you feel pushed and shoved to the breaking point at times?
- Do you ever feel like you can't think straight?
- Do you ever feel as if you might start screaming or crying and not be able to stop?
- Do you fly off the handle over little things?
- Do you feel overwhelmed much of the time?
- Is your stomach tied in knots or do you feel pressure and choking sensation in your throat or chest?
- Do nameless fears and a sense of doom plague you?
- Are things so bad that you want to hide or jump in your care and keep driving?
- Have you lost hope? Do you feel your efforts to make things better are futile, so you've given up trying?
- Do your thoughts scare you? Do you sometimes feel like you might hurt someone?
- Do you ever think you'd be better off dead?

Providing help in finding the most appropriate care provider within the civilian community or the military system is a high priority for counselors in all practice settings. In this way, civilian counselors can become a vital force in the process of bringing our service members and their families back to wholeness and health.

Counselors and agencies can develop comprehensive lists of services and therapists available in the community for a variety of needs and income levels. Veterans in need of diagnosis and treatment for psychological, medical, and chemical dependency problems related to their military service are eligible for treatment at regional VA hospitals and satellite clinics. Although most vets know this, they may not know how to access those services. Civilian counselors can serve a vital function by learning how to negotiate the bureaucracy and walking their client through the process of obtaining services. This is especially important when clients demonstrate symptoms of depression or low frustration tolerance.

It is our job to be there for veterans. If their problems go beyond the scope of our training and experience, we must find resources for them, their families, and their children. We can negotiate the bureaucracy, help fill out the forms, and arrange appointments. It does not sound heroic, but it is the kind of quiet battle counselors fight every day because, in the long run, we know it saves lives.

David L. Albright is a doctoral student studying combat stress in the College of Social Work at Florida State University in Tallahasee, FL.

Gayle Rosellini is volunteer community activist and a retired social worker who worked extensively with combat veterans and their families.

REFERENCES

American Counseling Association. (2005). *ACA code of ethics.* Alexandria, VA: Author.

American Psychological Association Presidential Task Force on Military Deployment Services for Youth, Families, and Service Members. (2007). *The psychological needs of U.S. military service members and their families: A preliminary report.* Washington, DC: Author.

Britt, T. W. (2007). The stigma of mental health problems in the military. *Journal of Military Medicine, 172,* 157–161.

Department of Defense Task Force on Mental Health. (2007). *An achievable vision: Report of the Department of Defense Task Force on Mental Health.* Falls Church, VA: Defense Health Board. Retrieved from http://www.health.mil/dhb/mhtf/MHTF-Report-Final.pdf

Department of Veterans Affairs. (2004). *Iraq War clinician guide* (2nd ed.). Retrieved from http://www.ptsd.va.gov/professional/manuals/iraq-war-clinician-guide.asp

Hoge, C. W., Castro, C. A., Messer, S. C., McGurk, D., Cotting, D., & Koffman, R. L. (2004). Combat duty in Iraq and Afghanistan, mental health problems, and barriers to care. *New England Journal of Medicine, 35,* 1–10.

Hutchison, J., & Banks-Williams, L. (2006). Clinical issues and treatment considerations for new veterans: Soldiers of the wars in Iraq and Afghanistan. *Primary Psychiatry, 13,* 66–71.

Milliken, C. S., Auchterlonie, J. L., & Hoge, C. W. (2007). Longitudinal assessment of mental health problems among active and reserve component soldiers returning home from the Iraq war. *The Journal of the American Medical Association, 298,* 2141–2148.

U.S. Army Medical Department. (2008). *Mental Health Advisory Team V Report.* Retrieved from http://www.medicine.army.mil/reports/mhat/mhat_v/mhat-v.cfm

RESOURCES FOR CIVILIAN COUNSELORS

Armstrong, K., Best, S., & Domenici, P. (2005). *Courage after fire: Coping strategies for troops returning from Iraq and Afghanistan and their families*. Berkeley, CA: Ulysses Press.

Capella University. *Joining forces America: Community support for returning service members*. Retrieved from http://joiningforcesamerica.org/

Ellis, A. (2006). *How to stubbornly refuse to make yourself miserable about anything: Yes anything!* Yucca Valley, CA: Citadel.

Friedman, M. J., & Sloane, L. B. (2008). *After the war zone - A practical guide for returning troops and their families*. New York: Perseus Book Group.

Grossman, D. (1996). *On killing: The psychological cost of learning to kill in war and society*. New York: Back Bay Books.

Paulson, D. S., & Krippner, S. (2007). *Haunted by combat: Understanding PTSD in war veterans including women, reservists, and those coming back from Iraq*. Wesport, CT: Praeger Security International.

Substance Abuse & Mental Health Service Administration (SAMHSA). SAMHSA veteran resources. Retrieved from http://www.samhsa.gov/vets/index.aspx

U.S. Army Family and Morale, Welfare, and Recreation Command Child and Youth Services. Resources for military children affected by deployment. Retrieved from http://www.armymwr.com/cysimages/Deployment%20 A%20Compendium%20of%20Resources.pdf

Whealin, J. M., DeCarvalho, L. T., & Vega, E. M. (2008). *Clinician's guide to treating stress after war: Education and coping interventions for veterans*. Hoboken, NJ: Wiley.

Post Deployment Counseling: Assisting National Guard and Reserve Families with Reintegration

14

Joseph D. Wehrman and David L. Fenell

Not since WWII has the armed forces utilized National Guard and Reserve (NG/R) to the extent and duration seen today. The call up of these soldiers has had a ripple effect through the entire nation as teachers, police officers, firefighters, and businessmen and women leave their civilian jobs to support their calls to duty. With advanced technology and more efficient demobilization, NG/R soldiers are back in their civilian communities significantly faster than in the past—sometimes without time to work through and process deployment experiences with other service members.

Between 2001 and 2007, nearly 500,000 NG/R soldiers have been deployed to Iraq and Afghanistan; 46% has served one or more deployments (Employer Support of the Guard and Reserve, 2008; Waterhouse & O'Bryant, 2008). Women are moving closer to the front lines of combat, and authors are beginning to discuss women's experiences as well as those of men who stay at home (Gambardella, 2008; Rychnovsyk, 2007). Slightly more than half the soldiers serving in the NG/R are married, with more than 90% of spouses at home during separation being women (National Health Marriage Resource Center, 2007).

Often the complexity of serving in the NG/R is overlooked, as these soldiers have many competing obligations and responsibilities. The nation is engaged in two overseas wars, numerous support operations across the globe, border security, and response to state and national disasters. While supporting these missions, NG/R soldiers leave communities and separate from their families and civilian careers. They face a variety of emotions and adversity during familial separations that bring stress, uncertainty, and fear for families.

The exceptional circumstances of military separation paired with the dangers soldiers face differs from other types of familial separation (Vormbrock, 1993). This phenomenon is not new; however, with changes in society, technology, and expectations, differences exist. To assist military families, counselors first need to understand the deployment and post-deployment process and the unique challenges families face upon reunion. As early as 1945, Duvall wrote that she felt it was easier to explain the process than to be the counselor working with each family because each is unique.

POST-DEPLOYMENT REINTEGRATION

Although the timeframes vary for each family, post-deployment usually encompasses the day of reunion to 6 months after reunion. Counselors who do not have past military experience or a frame of reference may find the three-phase model—preparation for separation, separation, and reunion—useful as they work with military families (see Chapter 12). The family reunion is commonly filled with joy; however, post-deployment is also a challenging time of role renegotiation, exploring intimacy, civilian occupation reintegration, and finding a balance again as a family. Immediately upon reunion, the couple often experiences greater cohesiveness, like a honeymoon, followed by challenges in making readjustments (Drummet, Coleman, & Cable, 2003; Wood, Scarville, & Gravino, 1995). Initially, disagreements and turmoil tend to be pushed aside, making way for reconnection and reunion. When exploring the reintegration of NG/R soldiers into civilian life, counselors should consider the setting. NG/R soldiers reintegrate directly into their home communities while active duty soldiers return to a military post. An NG/R soldier may be the only service member in the community, feeling isolated or unique among civilian counterparts.

Post-Deployment Reintegration into Civilian Life

Rural communities experience significant impact as a result of deployment of NG/R units with notable disruptions in places of employment such as schools, the fire department, police department, or other vital community businesses or services. NG/R soldiers return to different levels of support and fanfare depending on the military presence and proximity to military installations. Some communities show support with local news covering redeployment ceremonies, ribbons on vehicles, signs around town, or discounts at local establishments.

NG/R soldiers face the historic challenge of balancing roles, norms, and expectations found in civilian life with those in military settings. Compounding this readjustment is the awareness that civilian occupations frequently do not function with the same hierarchy and organizational requirements that exist in the military. Going back to the place of employment and reintegrating into the former civilian occupation is often an awkward and isolating task. NG/R soldiers worry about loss of their civilian careers or future opportunities for advancement (Doyle & Peterson, 2005). Self-employed individuals or small business owners might face starting over from the ground up as a result of long absences.

IMPLICATIONS FOR COUNSELORS

As they return to their civilian occupations with limited interaction with military personnel, NG/R soldiers can fall through the cracks of mental health counseling services. Rural members struggle to find access to Veterans Administration services. Civilian employers may not fully understand or be able to identify warning signs when a soldier needs assistance; thus, counselors should conduct a thorough assessment to determine the mental health needs of the soldier and family.

Family members who are most successful in finding the balance between post-deployment and reunion communicate through the process letting each other know their expectations and needs. Without communication, they often make assumptions about one another's behavior, leading to difficulties in the relationship and family. The counselor's primary focus should be on facilitating the communication process, developing adaptive coping skills, and emphasizing resilience as a therapeutic primer (Sammons & Batten, 2008).

Joseph D. Wehrman, PhD, is assistant professor of Counselor Education and coordinator of the Community Counseling program in the Department of Counseling and Human Services at the University of Colorado, Colorado Springs. He is a former medical service officer and veteran of Operation Iraqi Freedom.

David L. Fenell, PhD, is professor of Counselor Education and chair of the Department of Counseling & Human Services at the University of Colorado at Colorado Springs. He is also a Colonel (retired) in the U.S. Army Reserve Medical Service Corps and served as a behavioral sciences officer with U.S. Army Special Operations Command, Ft. Bragg, NC. Dr. Fenell was deployed to Afghanistan in 2002–2003 and to Iraq in 2007.

REFERENCES

Doyle, M. E., & Peterson, K. A. (2005). Re-entry and reintegration: Returning home after combat. *Psychiatric Quarterly, 76*(4), 631–370.

Drummet, A. R., Coleman, M., & Cable, S. (2003). Military families under stress: Implications for family life education. *Family Relations, 52*(3), 279–287.

Duvall, E. M. (1945). Loneliness and the serviceman's wife. *Marriage and Family Living, 7*(4), 77–81.

Employer Support of the Guard and Reserve. (2008). *Annual report 2008.* Arlington, VA: Author.

Gambardella, L. C. (2008). Role-exit theory and marital discord following extended military deployment. *Perspectives in Psychiatric Care, 44*(3), 169–174.

National Healthy Marriage Resource Center. (2007). Military service and marriage: A review of research. Retrieved from http://www.healthymarriageinfo.org/docs/review_mmilitarylife.pdf

Rychnovsky, J. D. (2007). Postpartum fatigue in the active-duty military woman. *Journal of Obstetric, Gynecologic, & Neonatal Nursing, 36*(1), 38–46.

Sammons, M. T., & Batten, S. V. (2008). Psychological services for returning veterans and their families: Evolving conceptualizations of the sequelae of war-zone experiences. *Journal of Clinical Psychology, 64*(8), 921–927.

Vormbrock, J. K. (1993). Attachment theory as applied to wartime and job-related marital separation. *Psychological Bulletin, 114*(1), 122–144.

Waterhouse, M., & O'Bryant, J. (2008, January). *National Guard personnel and deployments: Fact sheet* (Report for Congress Order Code RS22451). Washington, DC: Congressional Research Service.

Wood, S., Scarville, J., & Gravino, K. S. (1995). Waiting wives: Separation and reunion among Army wives. *Armed Forces and Society, 21*(2), 217–237.

THE SCHOOL COUNSELOR'S ROLE IN SUPPORTING STUDENTS WITH DEPLOYED PARENTS

15

Ruth Ann Fenell, David L. Fenell, and Rhonda Williams

Deployment creates significant challenges for school-age children of military families. A student's age and developmental maturity play an important role in how well a student manages the challenges. To help families understand and respond effectively to a deployment, Fenell and Fenell (2003) developed a model describing three phases of the cycle of deployment: preparation for separation, separation, and reunion. (See Chapter 12.) School counselors familiar with the distinct challenges children and parents face within each phase of the deployment cycle can create and implement proactive and responsive strategies to support students throughout a parent's deployment (Military Child Education Coalition, 2003).

CYCLE OF DEPLOYMENT

Resilient Students

Not all students will have difficulty with the deployment; some students handle the separation better than others do. Positive factors associated with deployment include: (a) gaining maturity by assuming additional family responsibilities, (b) discovering new interests and skills, (c) developing autonomy and self-confidence, (d) developing resilience and the ability to handle adversity, and (e) strengthening family bonds. Resilient children who make developmental gains during their parents' deployment are significant resources; for example, they can serve as trained peer counselors to helping students who are not coping well with deployment (Virginia Joint Military Family Services Board, 2001).

Phase I: Preparation for Separation

During the first stage, the school counselor's role is proactive. Whether the school district serves a significant number of deploying military or a handful of families with a member of the National Guard or Reserve, it is important to publicize how families can access support during a deployment by publishing information on the school and district websites and in newsletters (Military Child Education Coalition, 2003). When deployment orders are received, the military command encourages parents to contact their children's school counselor with information about the timing and projected length of the deployment. Communication is key and e-mail is a robust communication tool for the deploying parent. Due to long training hours required by the service member before a deployment only the non-deploying parent typically meets with the school counselor (Fenell & Fenell, 2003; Pincus, Christenson, & Adler, 2001). Closer to the deployment date, the deploying parent may have more time available.

During the initial meeting, the school counselor can highlight how the school's website may help the deployed parent monitor their students' academic progress online and stay informed about the activities throughout the school year. A policy for students receiving cell phone calls from a deployed parent must be communicated to families, students, teachers, and administration. If the student of a deployed parent will graduate, webcasting the graduation ceremony could be arranged with the command and the school district.

Many school personnel may be unfamiliar with the challenges of deployment and the military culture; therefore, presentations and workshops will help teachers and staff understand the distinct challenges of each phase of the deployment cycle and typical student responses to each phase. Staff and faculty can be enlisted to help monitor students for signs of stress and anxiety. A confidential communication process may be needed to address the security issues unique to families with a deployed parent.

Children become anxious because they are unsure of what to expect when the parent deploys and may worry that the other parent will leave them as well. The most important factor influencing children's attitudes about deployment is the attitude assumed by the non-deployed parent. Children often sense the anxiety of their parents and are uncertain how to react. Their questions should be answered as fully as the child's developmental ability allows. The following are examples of typical questions:

With my parent deployed, how much extra work will I have?

What is this war about anyway?

What will happen to us if you (the non-deployed parent) die?

Regular check-ins with the student provide the school counselor an opportunity to monitor the student's progress. As family members begin to anticipate the separation of the parent from the family for the next 6 to 18 months, mental and physical distancing begins even before the actual deployment.

For the elementary student, bibliotherapy and calendar activities (Vandesteeg, 2001) are especially helpful in dealing with the concrete reality of the deployment and the abstract concept of leaving the family with the expectation of returning. During check-ins with the middle and secondary school student, the school counselor provides information about how this phase typically affects families. Regular counseling sessions and journaling are effective tools to help the student accept the inevitability of the parent's deployment and develop strategies for coping in a healthy and positive manner. Students who are able to discuss or write about the feelings and concerns are less prone to express them in dysfunctional ways.

Phase II: Separation

For most children, separation is the longest and most stressful phase. Children worry about the safety of their parent, while they try to adjust to life at home without the deployed parent. They may have difficulty sleeping, appearing tired and irritable at school. Students may feel numb, sad, and alone, as well as distracted, disoriented, and overwhelmed (Fenell & Fenell, 2003; Military Child Education Coalition, 2003). They also experience feelings of relief, especially when there are several false starts

and delays to the actual deployment date. Younger children can regress and issues such as bed-wetting reoccur. High school students who try to take on a parent role in the family can create conflicts with the non-deployed parent and their siblings (Minuchin, 1974).

Students who demonstrated vulnerability before the deployment escalate their behaviors during this phase (Chartrand, Frank, White, & Sharpe, 2008). Their grades decline. Children who have not done so previously may complain about teachers and situations in the classroom, engage in irresponsible or aggressive behaviors, and begin to skip school. With its predictable daily routine, the school may be one of the few stable environments available to students with a deployed parent.

Students of all ages are likely to struggle with feelings of sadness and concern for the non-deployed parent. Deployment groups provide students with a safe place to discuss concerns and express feelings during the emotionally challenging first days of the separation phase (Rush & Akos, 2007). Focusing on the students' personal safety and support system and the safety of loved ones helps reassure the student. Normalizing feelings of anger, frustration, and fear in a developmentally appropriate approach allows students to understand the grieving and separation process (Military Child Education Coalition, 2003). When a student needs additional support, the school counselor can invite the student to an individual meeting and include the parent with the student's permission. For middle and secondary students, regular check-ins and journaling are invaluable in supporting students through early days of the separation.

Deployment does not affect just one student at the elementary level; it may have an impact on an entire class. Classroom sessions offer support to students directly affected by the deployment and provide other students support strategies that they can use to help their classmate. Classroom projects include "adopting" a student's deployed parent and sending letters, cards, and gift packages around holidays. As a morale builder, classrooms send "Flat Stanley" to the deployed parent who then poses for pictures with "Flat Stanley," sending the photographs back to the class (Vandesteeg, 2001).

Collaboration among all grade levels creates a sense of community. For example, a "Military Night" for elementary students whose parents are deployed can be facilitated by their middle and high school siblings who babysit preschool siblings and lead activities. Older students with deployed parents also "adopt" elementary students as their pen pals or buddies sending them cards of encouragement (*Parent's Guide,* 2009). Middle and high school students with deployed parents can become involved in meaningful community service activities including sending letters and practical gifts, supporting blood drives for military personnel, and collecting used cell phones for deployed personnel.

When problems at school emerge and the non-deployed parent is contacted, it is important to communicate appreciation for the efforts the parent has made to resolve the student's problems. A team of school professionals can collaborate with the parent and student, to clarify academic and social expectations and develop a plan for help. Team unity and caring send a powerful message that the student is not alone. Military communities provide counseling support to family members struggling with the challenges of deployment. Counselors, social workers, and chaplains are available for deployment counseling (Fenell & Fenell, 2004), and families can take advantage of free confidential counseling outside of their military communities (see Additional Resources).

Phase III: Reunion

The reunion of the deployed parent and the family is a time of great anticipation for all family members (Fenell & Fenell, 2003; Pincus et al., 2001). Children become excited and anxious about the reunion, and these emotions distract them from their academics. This reaction is expected and it is helpful to acknowledge the student's excitement while encouraging quality efforts in the classroom (*Educator's Guide*, 2009).

Elementary school counselors can help prepare for the reunion by suggesting ways to chronicle changes in the student such as creating a time capsule (box or scrapbook) with bits of the student's personal history during the deployment. Outlines of hands and feet as well as monthly height measurements are concrete and positive ways to share changes that have taken place (Vandesteeg, 2001). Sharing an online photo album chronicling physical changes and experiences helps reestablish relationships. A schoolwork portfolio and a scrapbook of events, movies, vacations, and activities generate family conversations about how family members spent their time during the deployment (Military Child Education Coalition, 2003).

When the initial glow of the reunion wears off, parent-child problems can develop as the returning parent resumes family leadership roles. If relationships are strained between parent and child, family therapy helps to restructure roles and rules while recognizing the contributions of each family member (Fenell & Fenell, 2003;

Fenell & Weinhold, 2003).

Children of deployed military parents face unique challenges when a parent departs for duty in a dangerous location. School counselors play a key role in designing school-wide programs to support students through individual and group counseling, classroom activities, and team interventions. School counselors who are knowledgeable about military culture, the deployment cycle, and the developmental needs of their students will be most effective in supporting students through the phases of deployment.

Note: The information in this chapter does not necessarily reflect the policies of the US Department of Defense.

Ruth Ann Fenell, LPC, *is a school counselor at Cheyenne Mountain High School, near Fort Carson in Colorado Springs, Colorado.*

David L. Fenell, PhD, *has served combat tours in Afghanistan and Iraq. He is professor and chair of the Department of Counseling and Human Services at the University of Colorado at Colorado Springs.*

Rhonda Williams, PhD, LPC, *is assistant professor in the same department and is a former school counselor.*

REFERENCES

Chartrand, M. M., Frank, D. A., White, L. F., & Sharpe, T. R. (2008). Effect of parents' wartime deployment on the behavior of young children in military families. *Archives of Pediatrics and Adolescent Medicine, 162*(11), 1009–1014.

Educator's guide to the military child during deployment Retrieved from http://www.ed.gov/about/offices/list/os/homefront/homefront.pdf

Fenell, D. L., & Fenell, R. A. (2008). Separated again: Professional and personal reflections on mobilization, deployment and well being of military families. *Family Therapy Magazine, 2*(4), 18–23.

Fenell, D. L., & Fenell, R. A. (2004). Counseling services for military personnel and their families. *Counseling and Human Development, 25*(9), 1–20.

Fenell, D. L., & Fenell, R. A. (2008, March). *Combat stressors affecting military personnel and their families: How counselors can help.* Presentation to the American Counseling Association Annual Conference, Honolulu.

Fenell, D. L., & Weinhold, B. K. (2003). *Counseling families: An introduction to marriage and family therapy.* Denver: Love Publishing.

Military Child Education Coalition. (2003). *How to prepare our children and stay involved in their education during deployment…*[Brochure]. Harker Heights: Author.

Minuchin, S. (1974). *Families and family therapy.* Cambridge, MA: Harvard University Press.

Parent's guide to the military child during deployment and reunion. (2009). Retrieved from http://www.uswestaap.org/Parent_Guide_Deployment.pdf

Pincus, S., Christenson, J., & Adler, L. (2001). The emotional cycle of deployment. *U.S. Army Medical Department Journal*, Apr-Jun.

Rush, C. M., & Akos, P. (2007). Supporting children and adolescents with deployed caregivers: A structured group approach for school counselors. *The Journal for Specialists in Group Work, 32*(2), 113–125.

Vandesteeg, C. (2001). *When duty calls: A guide to equip active duty, guard, and reserve personnel and their loved ones for military separations.* Enumclaw, WA: Wine Press.

Virginia Joint Military Family Services Board. (2003). *Working with military children: A primer for school personnel.* Retrieved from http://www.nmfa.org/site/DocServer?docID=642

ADDITIONAL RESOURSES

Army: www.myarmyonesource.com/

Marine Corps: www.usmc-mccs.org

Air Force: www.afcrossroads.com

National Guard: www.guardfamily.org

National Guard Youth Site: www.guardfamilyyouth.org

Reserves: www.defenselink.mil/ra/

National Military Families Association: www.nmfa.org

Military Child Education Coalition: www.militarychild.org/pdf_files/deploymentr2.pdf

Military One Source: www.militaryonesource.com

Section Four
Virginia Tech and Other University Tragedies

Virginia Tech: A Campus and a Community Respond

16

Gerard Lawson, Nancy Bodenhorn, and Laura Welfare

The April 16, 2007 shootings on the Virginia Tech campus prompted a massive response of law enforcement, emergency medical, governmental, and mental health resources. Students and faculty who were injured were evacuated by police and treated by the Virginia Tech and Town of Blacksburg volunteer rescue squads. These organizations were called upon to respond to a horrific act of violence that involved their community and, in the case of the Virginia Tech Rescue Squad (a student-run volunteer organization), their classmates. Similarly, local law-enforcement agencies that are trained to deal with violent occurrences were confronted by an event with a scope and magnitude that was dwarfed by the very personal connection many of them had to the victims and the community. Mental health resources were mobilized immediately because officials realized the large-scale traumatic effect it could have. As soon as the campus was secured, mental health resources were activated for faculty, staff, and students, and there has been a concerted support effort throughout the response and recovery.

Valuable Lessons

Valuable lessons were learned about dealing with trauma of this scale; many of them have more to do with preparation than intervention. For example, colleges and universities can begin to prepare by identifying the qualified mental health professionals on their campus and organizing a specific mechanism for utilizing those professionals in the event of an emergency. Within academic settings in particular, it is important to pay attention not only to mobilizing mental health resources but also to streamlining the chain of command so that first responders and external sup-

port personnel have a clear and centralized command structure. Once the individuals and agencies involved have been activated, regular and frequent communication and coordination are required to be sure needs are adequately addressed, and to avoid duplicating services. Unmet needs or duplication of services can demoralize volunteers and add frustration to the range of emotions that victims' families are already experiencing.

During the response and recovery, counselors need to be flexible, continually reassessing the needs of those they serve. Needs shift rapidly during a crisis for both individuals and communities. Often the most valuable intervention is a minimal one such as "compassionate loitering," but trained counselors also need to be ready to step into a more formalized role if called upon. Finally, whether actively engaged in the crisis response or not, counselors need to be aware of their own needs. Counselor self care is often a low priority, and it can sink further down the list when there is a crisis—a time when self care is even more important. In a crisis, counselors need to be knowledgeable about disaster response; counselors who are not disaster mental health specialists also may be called upon for support. For this reason, the Council for Accreditation of Counseling and Related Educational Programs (CACREP, 2009) has added competencies for crisis, disaster, and trauma response, which are now part of the core and specialty curricula.

Impact Phase

The National Institute for Mental Health lists five essential elements for trauma intervention: promote a sense of safety, promote calming, promote a sense of self- and collective efficacy, promote connectedness, and promote hope (Hobfoll et al., 2007). The sense of safety often falls to law enforcement and community messaging, but the other responsibilities are, at least in part, the domain of counselors and mental health workers.

Virginia Tech's Cook Counseling Center and the local Community Services Board (CSB), the public mental health agency, were responsible for assisting witnesses and bystanders after their statements were given to police and they were cleared medically. Simultaneously, students were beginning to gather in the common areas around campus, looking for information and support. "Drop-in centers" were established in the Squires Student Center immediately after the campus was secured and it remained open for weeks, providing walk-in counseling support. One of the challenges was that there was no widely understood mechanism for mobilizing crisis-counseling resources for a large-scale event on campus. Offers of assistance came in from alumni from our program, counselors, and others. At the same time, the campus was monitored closely, several agencies became involved in coordinating services, and a true picture was emerging of the response needs. It was difficult to turn away well-meaning offers of support, but most counselors understood that protocol demanded this.

Within hours of the shootings, the CSB along with the American Red Cross and Virginia State Police began preliminary death notifications with the family members who started to arrive in Blacksburg. This is an incredibly difficult process that requires specialized training. Police officers and chaplains accompanied each mental health worker in order to provide factual information with compassion, dignity, and support. Unfortunately, because of the intensive interest, and with so many people involved—each having different pieces of information—the notification protocol was violated. Some families heard the news that they were dreading from strangers and from the media. Fortunately, these were isolated incidents and those families were well supported.

On the morning of April 17, the Mental Health Advisory Group met for the first time, convened by Dr. Chris Flynn, the director of the Cook Counseling Center. It was composed of representatives from the local community mental health agencies, the psychological services center, international student services, human resources, and the marriage and family therapy and counselor education programs. The immediate and short-term (first week) response issues were discussed, and critical decisions were made. A key decision was that the mental health community needed to adopt a stance that, despite the reports in the media, there was not going to be a meltdown; we wanted an overt, visible, caring presence with resources available to anyone for any reason. On the individual level, these interventions took the form of psychological first aid that is designed to "reduce the initial distress caused by traumatic events, and to foster short- and long-term adaptive functioning" (NCTSN, 2006, p.5). Psychological first aid also provides individuals with support and resources, and helps to identify and support those with an elevated risk so they can be connected with other services. Some of this support involved providing direction for the community on how to move forward.

After ensuring the support of the families and affected students, the next task was the convocation, the first public acknowledgment of the tragedy in our community, and, as it turned out, the beginning of the healing. Expressions of grief were expected; counselors were charged with identifying individuals experiencing extraordinary emotion who needed assistance or those who did not have established support systems. Most people were struggling with or unable to keep their composure or they were staring into space with dazed looks of shock and disbelief. There was grieving, crying, and comforting everywhere. On any other day, such a widespread display of emotion might be a concern, but it all seemed very appropriate on this day. A few people lingered in the stands after others left the stadium, indicating to the counselors that they just needed some time on their own. Counselors offered handouts on normal reactions to tragedy, self care tips after trauma, and resource lists. Volunteers were instructed to be present, visible, and engage and support people who seemed to be struggling. We referred to this stance as "compassionate loitering."

By this time, most of the families had been notified that their loved one was killed, based on preliminary identification (a driver's license). However, scientific identification requires fingerprints, DNA, or dental records. The rationale is that a slower but more definitive process prevents misidentification. Compounding this problem was the fact that the medical examiner in southwest Virginia was accustomed to three or four homicides per year. With 32 deaths in one day, the system was overwhelmed, and it took days to convey required information and to complete the autopsies so that families could begin funeral arrangements. This delay resulted in feelings of anger and frustration as well as a desperate hope that the preliminary identification was somehow wrong. Counselors from the university and local community helped gather information for the formal identification of the victims, assisted families in arranging for items to be reclaimed from apartments or dorm rooms, addressed questions or concerns, and provided general support.

The other challenge was systemic. Although the Cook Counseling Center is clearly identified as the entity responsible for the mental health of students at Virginia Tech, the broader campus system was less well defined. The American Red Cross, Salvation Army, and the local Community Disaster Response Coalition are accustomed to a centralized command structure for disaster response. Most universities have a very decentralized structure. With each new question or need, there was a process of deciding who was responsible for that area, which delayed meeting some of those needs. Ultimately, each family was assigned a liaison from the Dean of Students office who was charged with assisting the families in navigating the university system. They were often supported by the Red Cross or other disaster mental health volunteers, but the consistent point of contact was a representative of the university.

Rescue Phase

Throughout the first week, the drop-in centers remained open on campus and were staffed by counselors from the Cook Counseling Center and employee assistance counselors from Value Options (the EAP Provider for the Commonwealth of Virginia). Although some were designated as faculty/staff centers and others for students, there was an unspoken agreement that it was more important to serve someone who showed up rather than check identification. If a staff member without university insurance or a student showed up at the EAP drop-in center, they were seen, no questions asked.

By the end of the first week, the Mental Health Advisory Group gathered again to discuss resuming classes. Monday, April 23, would be the first day back into classes, and a variety of issues were anticipated. The general plan included having two counseling support members in each class that had been affected by the shootings. The actual classes in which the shootings took place were no longer going to meet. However, the university registrar's office tracked every class in which an injured or killed student would have attended on Monday or Tuesday, every class that an injured or killed faculty member would have taught, and every class the shooter would have attended. This process was an incredible administrative effort by the registrar's office. Every one of those class meetings had counseling support present. In addition, support was provided to any faculty member who requested it. Thus, more than 200 class meetings and a

large number of common areas would require a supportive presence. Because it was a weekend, we began the digital-age version of the telephone tree with e-mail and phone calls. Master's level counselors who could work an entire 6-hour shift and leave at the end of the shift were requested because housing was not available.

At 5:30 a.m. on Monday, April 23, the Advisory group assembled in the Lane Stadium press box because it was big enough for large groups of counselors and it had telephone and radio support. Cook Director Dr. Flynn tells the story of going across the street to his office at 6:00 a.m. to make more copies, wondering if enough volunteers would show up with less than 36 hours notice, on a weekend. When he returned, a line of counselors formed at the door of the stadium, waiting to check-in and serve. More than 300 volunteers left their practice, school, college, office, or classroom for the day, and came to help us get back to the business of teaching and learning.

The volunteers were assigned to specific classes or areas and provided with instructions. First, the culture of higher education was explained--the belief that the classroom is the professor's, and that visitors need to be invited into class. Volunteers were told to meet with each instructor before the class and offer to help in whatever way they would like, such as saying a few words at the beginning, making resources available, or waiting in the back of the class or out in the hallway. Most faculty wanted them to say a few words to their class about what was to be expected after a tragedy; some asked the volunteers to stay and lead a discussion for the entire time. Volunteers were asked to use language that communicated the message, "Whatever you want or need to help you move forward again, please let us know," in an effort to help everyone understand that there was no threshold of distress that had to be met before you could request assistance. Volunteers also were instructed to provide handouts with resources and information and that no one was to do any critical incident debriefing or try to engage in an impromptu process group. Every class had at least two counselors, and all counselors were asked to return to the stadium to be reassigned or to debrief before leaving for the day.

We recognized two important points from this process. First, in the resumption of classes, Monday was very different from Tuesday. We failed to recognize the natural evolution, even day to day, in the affective response on campus. For example, on Monday volunteers were assigned to the dining halls because it is a normal gathering place, but debriefing with the volunteers indicated that no one in the dining halls would speak to the counselors. As a result, on Tuesday those counselors were reassigned to other areas. However, by lunchtime the managers of the dining halls called to report that staff members were struggling because kids were coming through the lunch lines in tears. Whereas on Monday, students had been somewhat anxious and even fearful, on Tuesday they were experiencing remarkable grief and sadness. EAP counselors and our volunteers came back to the dining halls and common areas, which turned out to be a very meaningful place for support and intervention. All volunteers had purple armbands and credentials to identify them. About once per hour someone came back to the command center and reported through the debriefing that a student had stopped them and said, "Thank you for being here." They did not want to talk and did not have any specific needs, but the presence of the counselors helped them feel better. No volunteer was allowed to leave without a formal administrative debriefing where they shared information on any students or faculty that might need follow-up, and the volunteer was provided an opportunity to discuss his or her own reactions to the day.

Recovery Phase

The American Counseling Association (ACA) offered support to our program and campus from the first day of the tragedy as well as in the weeks after the tragedy and provided publications to help prepare volunteers. Dr. David Kaplan, ACA Chief Professional Officer, had asked if there was anything else ACA could do to help with our recovery, and we responded that because we were just a few weeks from the end of the term, we were concerned about our students being away from campus for the summer and wished there was a way to make counseling services available. Dr. Kaplan responded saying that was no problem, and that if we could tell ACA where they lived they would identify counselors in the area. He had interpreted the statement about "our students" to mean the 60 or so students in the counselor education program, when in fact we had meant "our" 28,000 students. To their credit, once we clarified that, ACA did not change its answer, and they began work on the summer pro bono counseling initiative. Dr. Kaplan came to Blacksburg and met with Dr. Flynn and the counselor education faculty to develop a mechanism for providing support to Virginia Tech students while they were away from campus over the summer. ACA issued a call to licensed counselor members asking if they would commit to providing up to five free sessions for a Virginia Tech student over the summer. Within 48 hours, more

than 1,300 counselors responded, volunteering their services. In the first week of the summer, an e-mail went out to all 28,000 students letting them know that they could receive free counseling in their home community over the summer.

Ultimately, 69 counselors in 13 states provided more than 200 hours of services pro bono, which conservatively was a gift of $20,000 to Virginia Tech students, but more importantly, this was a gift in human terms. Caring professionals supported 60 of our students when they were away from the friends, campus, and community that they love. The compassion that was so present on our campus went home with them, and they were able to continue to work through their grief and sadness. Just as important, all 28,000 students knew that they were not alone and that we were thinking of them even when they were away.

Ongoing Recovery

As of the publication date, we have passed the second Day of Remembrance on our campus, and we continue to spend time and resources on the ongoing recovery issues. The university established the Office of Recovery and Support to serve as the single point of contact for all services and needs for the victims who returned to school and the families of the deceased.

The campus is very different now. Surveys done the summer after the shooting found that most students had no more than two degrees of separation from a victim of the shootings. After this year's class had graduated, only about one quarter of the remaining student body was enrolled at the time of the tragedy, so most of the students do not have the firsthand point of reference for the tragedy. Many of those who remain, however, have ongoing mental health needs, and the number of students exposed to a trauma at our university continues to be higher than that of other universities by 2:1. The faculty and staff see much less turnover than the student body. Many of them continue to struggle while others want to move on, presenting a real challenge in how to meet the needs of very different constituencies.

Each of the victims was awarded the degree they were seeking posthumously. There is a permanent memorial on the campus drill field, which is the central point of the campus directly in front of Burruss Hall, the main academic building. For our campus and community, the focus has become one of celebrating the lives of those lost and honoring their memory through service, while trying to revitalize the learning community.

Key Lessons Learned

1. Be prepared by identifying the qualified mental health professionals on campus and organize a specific mechanism for utilizing those professionals in the event of an emergency.

2. Streamline the chain of command.

3. Once the individuals and agencies involved have been activated, ensure regular and frequent communication and coordination to be sure needs are adequately addressed and there is no duplication of effort.

4. Adopt a "compassionate loitering" stance.

5. Ensure counselors are taking care of themselves.

Photo: Kristine Halls Reid

Visitors to the Chapel on the Drillfield read these words: "Write your wishes, thoughts, and prayers on a ribbon and tie it on a string to blow in the wind. This place of remembrance, reflection, and respect sponsored by the Graduate Arts Council, Hillel at Virginia Tech, Living Buddhism, & the Unitarian Universalist Congregation."

Gerard Lawson, PhD, LPC, is associate professor.

Nancy Bodenhorn, PhD, is associate professor.

Laura Welfare, PhD, LPC, is assistant professor.

All authors are in the Counselor Education department at Virginia Polytechnic Institute and State University (Virginia Tech) in Blacksburg, Virginia.

References

Council for Accreditation of Counseling and Related Educational Programs (CACREP). (2009). *2009 standards*. Retrieved from http://www.cacrep.org/2009 standards.html

Hobfoll, S. E., Watson P., Bell, C. C., Bryant R. A., Brymer, M. J.., Friedman, M. J , ... Ursano R. J. (2007). Five essential elements of immediate and mid-term mass trauma intervention: Empirical evidence. *Psychiatry, 70*(4), 283–315.

National Child Traumatic Stress Network and National Center for PTSD. (2006). Psychological First Aid: Field Operations Guide, 2nd Edition. Available on: www.nctsn.org and www.ncptsd.va.gov.

Making Meaning With Memorials

17

Nancy Bodenhorn and Gerard Lawson

Making sense differs from *making meaning*. Making sense implies an understanding of the how and why, which may never be possible in the case of the random shootings at Virginia Tech on April 16, 2007. Making meaning implies developing coherence between how each of us sees and interacts with the world and how this new experience fits into that worldview or spiritual framework (Echterling, Presbury & McKee, 2005).

The process of making meaning through memorials occurred organically at Virginia Tech, reflective of the community and system surrounding us. No one started out with a plan; we were taking one hour at a time, then a day at a time, and eventually weeks and months at a time, providing enough outlets for most people to find some way to connect. Although there are innumerable stories of individual and family memorials, the focus of this chapter is the public, group process of memorializing and the avenues these memorials provided to make meaning of the tragedy.

Convocation and Candlelight Vigil: April 17, 2007

According to the Group Crisis Intervention model (Echterling et al., 2005), the first step toward recovery is to link with one another. The convocation was the first opportunity for Virginia Tech and the Blacksburg community to do this. For many of us, the convocation also started the process of moving further into the tasks of co-creating a collective survival story, helping the group manage emotions, and facilitating group coping.

When a university official directed us to "go where you can get the most hugs," it was because we all needed connection at that point. For some, it would come most directly on campus, for others at their homes with family. Being given permission to grieve and handle the immediate shock in our own time and in our own way was validating, and being told that we each had the wisdom to determine our own path for this process was empowering. Connection, validation, and empowerment were crucial in the process of being able to create the momentum for each of us to manage our recovery.

In her convocation address, Nikki Giovanni (2007) helped us start the process of making meaning. In very few words, Giovanni

- Described the collective sadness that everyone in the arena (and beyond) was experiencing ("We are not moving on, we are embracing our mourning.")

- Reminded us of our common bond in emotional reactions ("We are brave enough to bend to cry.")

- Informed us that we were not at fault or deserving of this tragedy.

- Led us into the determination to cope ("We are better than we think and not quite what we want to be. We are alive to the imaginations and the possibilities... We will prevail...We are Virginia Tech...").

Her address moved us from one plane of reaction to another. We moved together with her words right along the continuum of mourning to a sense of resolve that we would be better at the other end. We left the convocation as a different group of people than we were when we walked in.

One controversial moment occurred during the convocation when a student started the "Let's go Hokies" cheer at the end of Giovanni's address. We were originally shocked and concerned at the apparent inappropriateness, but soon were wound up in the spirit of the collective chant. After the convocation ended, when we were checking in on anyone in distress who remained in the arena, one student helped us to understand the chant from his perspective. He knew five of the students who had been killed, but reflected on their strong Hokie spirit and speculated that they would have loved the fact that the cheer was included. This changed our perspective—the cheer was for those 32 students and faculty who were no longer with us; the rest of the convocation was for those of us in the room. We also recognized that the avenues for making meaning from this crisis were going to be very different for each of us.

That evening, the Hokies United student group organized the first candlelight vigil. Thousands stood on the drill field (the center of our campus) honoring the slain victims, hearing details and identities of the injured, raw from the shock and mourning, needing to connect with the larger community, yet developing the hope and realization that together we were making progress. The next day we heard stories of candles being donated by other universities because the stores in our area had sold out. Knowing that the rest of the world was supporting us in our tragedy was an additional piece of the healing process that continued throughout the spring and summer.

Hokie Stone Memorial

Hokie stone comes from a local quarry and is the stone that covers the majority of the campus buildings. Hokies United brought in 33 stones and laid them in a semi-circle in the drill field directly in front of the administration building (next to Norris Hall where most of the shootings took place). Beside each of the 32 stones was the name of one of the shooting victims. This area became the central site of public mourning and gatherings where people left flowers, cards, mementos, and tears beside those they knew or had just been introduced to through the amazing stories of their lives. When the university administrators decided on the permanent memorial, dedicated in August 2007, they kept this design. In the middle of our campus, the memorial of 32 Hokie stones carved with the names of each victim serves as a way to "never forget," which is one of the vows that those on campus made.

Initially the 33rd stone created some controversy because it represented the shooter, whose name never appeared next to the stone. During the first week, the 33rd stone disappeared each night, and each morning it was replaced. Finally, the student who was replacing the stone wrote a letter to the editor of the university indicating that she was committed to replacing the stones because, like it or not, the shooter had been part of our community and that we do not choose our family. Our understanding is that the stone did not disappear after that letter was printed. When the temporary stones were there, the 33rd stone never had as many visitors or mementos as the others, but there were some cards or flowers each day. The permanent memorial consists of 32 stones, which was the understandable request of the families of the victims.

Spontaneous memorials such as the initial Hokie stones placed by the students are similar to the roadside memorial phenomenon; perhaps new rituals for mourning need to be developed in situations for which old practices do not seem adequate (Haney, Leimer, & Lowery, 1997). Certainly, this situation challenged us all in how to memorialize both the personal loss and the community anguish. Frequently, grief is experienced individually and privately (Clark & Franzmann, 2006), yet this situation called for public mourning.

We believe that the presence of the 33rd stone, the visibility of the identities of those involved, as well as the proximity to Norris Hall, required visitors to experience their anguish, shock, and anger simultaneously in a way that supported the process of making meaning. In traumatic situations, these emotions are overwhelming and seemingly incomprehensible. By confronting the variety of emotions in tandem, we realize that we need to incorporate all of them in a meaningful way.

Sign Boards

Within a few days of the tragedy, signboards were erected on the drill field. These were a series of two pieces of ply board, painted white, with hinges connecting them on one side so that they stood up like a pup tent. Visitors were encouraged to write messages that were a combination of communications and prayers to the victims, the families of the victims, the community, God, and the shooter. Mementos also were left at the site of the signboards, which were later moved inside the student center, out of the rain. The signboards allowed people to express themselves and provide public witness that they were a part of the recovery effort. Students, community members, and visitors read each other's messages (usually anonymous), experiencing a connection with the sentiments of the larger group.

The signboards were a witness to the resiliency process, a combination of grief and sorrow, commitments to better times and hopes for the future, and forgiveness. Similar to the site of the 33rd Hokie stone, the sign boards included an occasional message to the shooter, many indicating a bewilderment as to why, but also acknowledging that his pain must have been enormous to incite such action, and offerings of prayers for him as well. These messages were especially powerful as a reminder that in order to make meaning of the tragedy, we had to incorporate an understanding of the person responsible. Everyone comes to the idea of forgiveness in different ways and at different times, and for some, forgiveness is too much to ask in tragedies.

VT-Engage (October 16, 2007, 6-month anniversary)

University administrators realized that anniversaries were going to be important markers for the community to memorialize. The first of these anniversaries (at 6 months) focused on the community coming together to support each other. A community service fair was held on the drill field with representatives of nonprofit agencies providing information about their agencies and volunteer needs. The VT-Engage project was kicked off that day asking each student, faculty, staff, and alumni to donate at least 10 hours the next year to a volunteer agency in honor of the victims.

Many of the reactions to the tragedy centered on how each of us could make a difference; some editorials were phrased in terms of making ourselves worthy of the victims who were lost. The recognition of the potential that was lost created a sense of commitment to fulfill their promise to the world by volunteering with agencies that make a difference in the community (Echterling et al., 2005). This anniversary moved from mourning to a commitment of caring and action, formalizing the group survival story, which now was focused on promises, the future, and concern for others.

Day of Remembrance (April 16, 2008)

Classes were cancelled on the first anniversary, and will be for the next two years until the class of 2011 graduates. The day was bracketed with formal community-wide ceremonies, and the middle of the day was left open for small groups to meet or engage in activities of remembrance. The morning ceremony included reading the name of each victim with a short description provided by their families. The tone was very subdued out of respect for the victims, but the anguish exhibited a year ago was not present.

Unlike the year before when the weather had been cold and snowy, April 16, 2008 was warm, sunny, and breezy. After the somber tone of the morning memorial, students started returning to the drill field as one would expect college students to do on a beautiful spring day. Frisbees, kites, picnics, pets, footballs, musical instruments, and blankets scattered the area, as the students reclaimed the drill field as their own. Although some faculty and alumni expressed concern that locating the permanent memorial in the center of campus would cast a constant pall over the campus and the student body, on this day, the students seemed to disprove that concern.

The middle of the day was left open for smaller communities (faith communities, residential communities, or academic communities) that organized gatherings as they saw fit. This purposeful decision allowed individuals to choose their level of involvement and utilized the strengths of the community. Activities provided for expressive outlets; one area in the student center was organized as a painting center where children and families joined college students in painting rocks or decorating kites. There was and still is a respectful distance between game playing and the memorial, but the drill field, similar to our hearts, is large enough to handle both. Those of us in the Counselor Education program who had organized counselors to be available just in case, sat back and reveled in the resilience that had brought the community to this point. Students being students was truly a beautiful sight to see.

Photo: Kristine Halls Reid

Hokie Stones were quarried locally by university stonemasons and engraved with the names of students and professors killed in the shooting. This permanent memorial was inspired by the spontaneous semi-circular memorial created by students with smaller Hokie stones in the hours following the tragedy.

Hokies United organized the evening vigil with large candles by each Hokie stone memorial. As the victim's name was read, an individual student walked to the stone to light the individual candles from one that had been lit all day. The larger community had come together to support each other in our common grief and recovery. We felt comforted by the caring resolve of the communion; yet, we also recognized somehow that this would not last.

MAKING MEANING

We do not think about the tragedy on a daily basis as we did a year ago, but when we do it is not with tears and anger, it is with a resolution to create and renew a community of support. The campus memorials helped us by providing a public expression of communal grief and resilience in a space that has become sacred.

Photo: Kristine Halls Reid

The semi-circular Hokie Stone Memorial on the Drillfield in front of Burruss Hall, Virginia Tech's main administration building. A single stone in the center of the memorial honors all the fallen and injured victims of April 16, 2007.

Nancy Bodenhorn, PhD, and Gerard Lawson, PhD, LPC, and are associate professors in the Counselor Education department at Virginia Polytechnic Institute and State University (Virginia Tech) in Blacksburg, Virginia.

REFERENCES

Clark, J., & Franzmann, M. (2006). Authority from grief, presence and place in the making of roadside memorials. *Death Studies, 30,* 579–599.

Echterling, L. G., Presbury, J., & McKee, J. E. (2005*). Crisis intervention: Promoting resilience and resolution.* Upper Saddle River, NJ: Merrill/Prentice Hall.

Giovanni, N. (2007, April). *Nikki Giovanni convocation address.* Speech presented at Virginia Tech Convocation, Blacksburg, VA. Retrieved from http://www.vt.edu/remember/archive/giovanni_transcript.html

Haney, C. A., Leimer, C., & Lowery, J. (1997). Spontaneous memorialization: Violent death and emerging mourning ritual. *Omega, 35,* 159–171.

Pathways to Resilience at Virginia Tech

18

Lennis G. Echterling and Anne L. Stewart

Personal and community resilience has provided an exciting conceptual framework in the areas of health, stress, and coping (Norris, Stevens, Pfefferbaum, Wyche, & Pfefferbaum, 2008). Instead of concentrating only on identifying and treating the "psychological casualties" of catastrophes, counselors can broaden their mission to help all survivors develop their potential, discover new resources, and flourish under fire. We were not situated at the epicenter of the Virginia Tech shooting in the spring of 2007; therefore, we decided to promote resilience by complementing the essential frontline work of crisis counselors who were in the trenches at the school.

Resilience

After cataclysmic events, the general news media typically depict most survivors as overwhelmed victims and only a handful as inspiring heroes. However, in contrast to these simplistic and misleading portrayals, the vast majority of trauma survivors are neither helpless nor superhuman. Instead, they are regular people who are coping actively and facing their challenges with integrity. Of course, in the midst of the chaos and turmoil, survivors endure tremendous torment, anguish, grief, fear, and rage. In the wake of catastrophe, they may find themselves unable to perform their jobs, concentrate on their studies, or handle the day-to-day tasks of living. They may feel alienated, confused, and overwhelmed. At the same time, most survivors are immediately demonstrating resilience by their initiative, fortitude, compassion, and sense of hope (Echterling & Stewart, 2008b).

After four decades, researchers of resilience have completed studies in countries throughout the world, with people of all ages, and involving all types of ad-

versities. Their findings have demonstrated that resilience is much more common than was once believed (Ryff & Singer, 2003). In fact, resilience is the rule rather than the exception for those who have experienced traumatic events (McNally, Bryant, & Ehlers, 2003). According to Calhoun and Tedeschi (2006), when researchers have conducted follow-up studies months or years after the trauma, most survivors—between 75% and 90%—actually reported posttraumatic growth (PTG). Their accounts of PTG include feeling more confident, becoming more self-reliant, growing closer to others, feeling more compassion for humanity, appreciating life more deeply, and experiencing a more intense sense of spirituality. Ultimately, resilience is the process in which individuals become survivors who go on to thrive in their lives.

Studies of resilience consistently have identified four general factors that promote successful resolution of crises and traumas (Echterling, Presbury, & McKee, 2005). These four pathways to resilience—social support, making meaning, managing emotions, and successful coping—provided the conceptual framework for the public education materials and workshop content that we developed.

Social Support: Reaching Out

Resilient people are not islands unto themselves. Research on social support has shown that relationships offer survivors many vitally important resources, such as affection, advice, affirmation, and practical assistance. As Berscheid (2003) pointed out, our greatest sources of strength in troubled times are our connections with other human beings. In American society, with its emphasis on individualism, we typically do not appreciate just how embedded we are in a complex web of interdependence. However, as attachment theory and research have demonstrated, our lives are interwoven in an intricate tapestry of relationships that form, nurture, protect, enliven, and enrich us from birth to death. The Circle of Security is a model that highlights how attachment relationships provide a foundation of safety that enables a child to explore the world from this secure base (Marvin, Cooper, Hoffman, & Powell, 2002). From infant education through higher education, schools have an opportunity and responsibility to provide a physically and psychologically safe environment so that students and faculty are able to explore and learn together.

Making Meaning: Telling One's Story

In times of adversity, the narrative fabric of our lives is torn. Resilience involves re-weaving our shredded life story into a meaningful and integrated whole. Survivors who ultimately make meaning of their traumatic experience later report greater satisfaction, more positive emotions, and greater vitality (Emmons, 2003). Looking back on how they dealt with a trauma, many see themselves as having been on a mission and having served a higher purpose (Milo, 2002). Resilient individuals also are more likely to have shared their survivor stories. The narratives that they create do more than organize their life experiences. They affirm fundamental beliefs, guide important decisions, offer solace, serve as catalysts for growth, and deepen the sense of community. As one Virginia Tech educator stated, "We are not going to let one troubled individual define who we are. *We* are going to define Virginia Tech." As learning communities dedicated to exploring, discovering, and learning, educational institutions are ideal settings for promoting the process of making meaning.

Regulating Emotions: Taking Heart

Adversity is a time of intense emotions, but a common assumption is that individuals in crisis have only negative feelings, such as shock, rage, and grief. Studies have demonstrated that individuals actually experience not only painful reactions, but also feelings of resolve, such as courage, compassion, hope, peace, and joy (Larsen, Hemenover, Norris, & Cacioppo, 2003). Acknowledging and giving expression to the gamut of emotions—both negative and positive—can promote resilience. Even during the crisis experience itself, resilient survivors are able to take some pleasure in savoring the few desirable events that took place, appreciating discoveries that they made, and celebrating small victories (Stein, Folkman, Trabasso, & Richards, 1997). Laughter, even in the midst

of tears, is an example of how humor can be an expression of resolve that embraces the paradoxes and mysteries of adversity.

Creative Coping: Taking Action

Rituals and routines provide ways for individuals, families, and communities to affirm their collective identity, celebrate their roots, and offer structure (Echterling & Stewart, 2008a). Maintaining traditions while accommodating the new circumstances offers continuity and reinforces the "new normal" that is emerging. As they engage in the process of resilience, survivors begin to envision possibilities. Once articulated, goals serve as beacons that light the way. When they begin to see a future, survivors gain a sense of hope, become more motivated, and increase their momentum toward resolution.

PRACTICING RESILIENCE

When we heard the horrifying news at Virginia Tech, we found ourselves doing what the literature on crisis and resilience predicted—we reached out to one another for support, struggled to deal with our own strong feelings, strived to understand what had happened, and determined that one way we wanted to cope was by sharing the lessons learned from survivors of other tragedies. As a result, one of our interventions was to create resilience-based public education materials for use by schools, churches, agencies, and organizations throughout Virginia.

Public Education Materials

Earlier education materials on the psychology of catastrophes tended to focus on vulnerabilities, impairment, regression, and heightened risk for posttraumatic stress disorder (PTSD). Although we discussed these reactions, we deliberately highlighted resilience in three handouts titled, "What Educators Can Do," "What Parents Can Do," and "How You Can Help." (Available online at www.psyc.jmu.edu/gradpsyc/). As we adapted the information for Virginia Tech, we were careful in the language used; for example, we described common crisis responses as "reactions" rather than "symptoms," which suggests pathology.

More recent public education materials, such as those offered by the American Counseling Association and American Psychological Association, have emphasized resilience, but they have been necessarily generic in design in order to cover a wide range of possible disasters. Every catastrophic event is unique, and the public education material should address the singular challenges and distinct strengths of a particular community. For example, although the number of casualties at Virginia Tech was enormous, the infrastructure of the area was still intact, which is not the case in natural disasters. There was no need for widespread emergency shelter, food was still in abundance, the surrounding communities suffered no physical damages, and the communication system operated. This was a distinctive tragedy, and therefore, we recommended specific strategies that held promise for promoting the resilience of survivors.

We distributed the materials as electronic documents and encouraged recipients to use the information, which was not copyrighted, to create handouts, newsletters, and websites with their own logos and organization names. Every member of the Virginia Counselors Association, Virginia School Counselors Association, and Virginia Association for Play Therapy received the materials. Many then forwarded the documents to professional colleagues, leaders of faith groups, parents, teachers, and others.

We used the four dimensions of resilience as the conceptual foundation for writing the guidelines and recommendations.

Reach out. Social support is crucial after an act of extreme interpersonal violence because the public's sense of security has been violated. Therefore, in each brochure, we emphasized that every citizen could support Virginia Tech and promote safety in his or her local communities. In "What Educators Can Do," we suggested ways that teachers could encourage their students to learn from their experiences, even those that are catastrophic, by contributing to their community:

> Give them an opportunity to help. Many of our students, fortunately, have been spared from direct involvement in this incident. You may encourage these students to offer help to others in need in their local community. For example, they may want to donate toys to the domestic violence shelter or send a message of compassion to the victims.

Make meaning. Creating meaning from such senseless acts of carnage and brutality is especially challenging for children, who need developmentally appropriate information and the active involvement of caring adults. In "What Parents Can Do," our first recommendation is to bear witness to children's attempts to gain understanding:

> It may be painful, but the best thing you can do

for children is to listen to them talk about the catastrophe. Younger children may be drawing pictures of the event or acting it out in their play. Talking, drawing and play-acting are healthy and natural ways for children to work through their reactions.

Children are not the only ones struggling with meaning making. The graphic media accounts can disrupt this process for individuals of all ages. We offered the following in "How You Can Help":

> There is neither a simple nor logical explanation of the tragedy; however, you can bring meaning by being a part of the healing process. You can acknowledge the depth of pain and offer your own random acts of kindness to help others to heal and be comforted. The senseless actions of one troubled individual have wreaked havoc and confusion. Your actions can help reaffirm our collective sense of meaning, trust, and well-being in life.

Take heart. Survivors experience intense feelings of anguish, fear, and grief. Children, in particular, may be unable to regulate such overwhelming emotions. In "What Educators Can Do," we encourage teachers to normalize these feelings of distress:

> Remind them that these reactions are natural. Many young people, like adults, will believe that something is wrong with themselves for feeling the way they do. They will need reassurance that their feelings are normal reactions to an abnormal situation. Finding out that their fellow students are having some of the same reactions also can be a great relief.

Resilient survivors of all ages also give expression to emerging emotions of resolve and we encourage survivors to acknowledge their own feelings of compassion, hope, and courage. In "How You Can Help," we offered the following suggestions:

> Let yourself be inspired by the courage of those who risked their own lives to protect others. Allow yourself to be encouraged by the dedication of security officers and emergency medical teams who responded so unselfishly. Be touched by the many gestures of support that parents, teachers, and friends have offered. It's essential that you acknowledge the heartache and suffering, but don't lose heart about the future.

Taking action. Studies have documented that helping others can promote one's own resilience. Most people feel prepared to be a resource in such personal tragedies as the death of a loved one, but when a catastrophic event occurs, they may be at a loss to know how to help. We address this concern in "How You Can Help":

> However you connect, you can offer emotional support to those who have been affected by the recent horrific event. You may be worried that you don't know what to say, but don't let that stop you. There are no magic words or slogans, but you can make a difference by being there for others. They may forget your exact words, but they will remember your presence and compassion.

The feedback that we received from many people was that they appreciated the immediacy, specificity, relevance, and emphasis on resilience in the materials. Other learning communities have adapted these materials to use in more recent incidents of campus shootings.

Resilience Workshops

Our second intervention was a series of faculty development workshops, "Pathways to Resilience: From Surviving to Thriving," at the beginning of the 2007 fall semester sponsored by the Center for Excellence in Undergraduate Teaching (CEUT) of Virginia Tech to support faculty members in continuing the momentum of promoting resilience among their students and colleagues. Specifically, the objectives of this faculty development program were to:

- Appreciate the resilience of individuals who have been victimized by violence

- Recognize crisis as a turning point that involves both threats and opportunities

- Integrate techniques that enhance hope and resolve into instructional strategies

This 3-hour training session included brief lectures, demonstrations, experiential exercises, discussions, and practice. We began by acknowledging the tragedy and describing the resolve we observed. We shared our hope that this workshop would provide opportunities for participants to reach out to one another, make meaning of their experiences, share their feelings, and explore creative ways to cope. We explained that we would be offering activities for participants to engage in experiential learning that highlighted resilience—their survival sto-

ries—instead of directing them to relive any traumatic event.

We provided a brief introduction to resilience, the etymology of which is the Latin word *resilire*. In physics, to resile literally means to bounce back, rebound, or resume shape after compression. We also briefly reviewed the evolution of resilience theory, summarized the research findings, and offered an overview of the four pathways of resilience in which victims become survivors who can become thrivers.

Throughout each workshop, we emphasized the crucial role that educators play in promoting the resilience of students. For example, in introducing the factor of social support, we relied on attachment theory to point out how educators support two fundamental needs of students—a safe haven and opportunities to explore the world (Marvin et al., 2002). A learning community flourishes when its students feel connected to a secure base from which they can then embark on the collective enterprise of discovery. Using this conceptual framework of resilience and attachment, we invited participants to relate these concepts to their personal lives in the following exercise:

Experiencing resilience. Pick a time in your life in which you bounced back from a major disappointment, misfortune, or trauma. Reflect on that experience by answering the following questions:

1. How did you manage to be so resilient?

2. Who helped you see your resilience and strengths?

3. In what ways are you a different person as a result of that experience?

4. How did your relationships with others change as a consequence?

5. What important lessons about life did you learn?

When catastrophe strikes, educators can set aside lesson plans to focus on their roles as mentors, models, allies, and advisers. In this teachable moment, they are helping students to learn the truly basic lessons of life—how to deal with tragedy, contribute to healing, promote a sense of community, cope with the "new normal," and rebuild lives. Students feel compelled to make sense of their traumatic experience, discover its point or purpose, and integrate it within their worldview, values, and beliefs. Their professors can be invaluable resources as they embark upon these formidable tasks.

Contrary to the stereotypes of engineering and agricultural institutions, the participants were grateful for the opportunity to share their feelings at the workshop. At times, their narratives focused on their initial reactions of disbelief, shock, and overwhelming horror. At other times, they shared experiences in which they were touched by acts of kindness and compassion. The majority expressed a complex mixture of both positive and negative feelings. We invited participants to reflect on the range of emotions they have felt by responding to the task below:

A rainbow of resolve. Think about the times that you have gathered with relatives and friends to grieve over the death of a loved one. In addition to shedding tears together, you probably also laughed as you recalled joyful times, offered expressions of love to one another, and perhaps savored the small but wondrous consolations of life. In these moments, you were all engaged in one fundamental process of resilience—expressing both positive and negative emotions.

Finally, the workshop focused on creative strategies that faculty use when teaching in times of crisis. These specific techniques included being authentic with their own struggles, openly discussing the crisis during their classes, offering opportunities for memorial rituals, adapting the syllabus to accommodate the changed circumstances, integrating relevant issues into the course, promoting related scholarly projects, facilitating service projects, referring students to counseling resources, and celebrating their collective resilience.

The feedback regarding the workshop was powerful and overwhelmingly positive. The most frequent comment was regarding the benefits of gathering together to listen and share. One faculty member wrote, "Hearing others talk about experience/feelings was most beneficial—that sense of survival within our own community, that's where we are and that's what we need to hear/feel/know." Another said, "I needed—but didn't know I needed—this conversation! I was surprised at the emotions it dredged up, and I was grateful to be able to acknowledge them." During an interview after the shootings, one educator expressed eloquently the dedication of the Virginia Tech faculty by affirming, "I need to be here with these people. We're going to have students for four years who have gone through this and it's going to be a part of our history forever, and I love this place and this is where I belong and this is where I will stay."

Finally, at the convocation following the heartbreak at Virginia Tech, honored poet and professor of English, Dr. Nikki Giovanni gave an address in which she asserted their collective identity by stating, "We are Virginia Tech," and she gave voice to their resilience by proclaiming, "We will prevail" (Giovanni, 2007). She concluded by predicting posttraumatic growth, "We are alive to the imaginations and the possibilities. We will continue to invent the future through our blood and tears and through all our sadness."

As counselors, our mission is to bear witness to this resilience and promote the potential of all survivors to flourish under fire.

(If you would like to hear a recording of the speech and view powerful photographs of resolve by Casey Templeton, go to www.caseytempleton.com/start/index.htm and click on "We are Virginia Tech.")

Lennis G. Echterling, PhD, and Anne L. Stewart, PhD, are professors at James Madison University, Harrisonburg, VA.

REFERENCES

Berscheid, E. (2003). The human's greatest strength: Other humans. In L. G. Aspinwall & U. M. Staudinger (Eds.), *A psychology of human strengths: Fundamental questions and future directions for a positive psychology* (pp. 37–47). Washington, DC: American Psychological Association.

Calhoun, L. G., & Tedeschi, R. G. (Eds.). (2006). *Handbook of posttraumatic growth: Research and practice.* Mahwah, NJ: Lawrence Erlbaum.

DiPietro, M. (2003). The day after: Faculty behavior in post-September 11, 2001 classes. In C. M. Wehlburg & S. Chadwick-Blossey (Eds.), *To improve the academy: Resources for faculty, instructional, and organizational development* (pp. 21–39). Hoboken, NJ: Wiley.

Echterling, L. G., Presbury, J., & McKee, J. E. (2005). *Crisis intervention: Promoting resilience and resolution.* Upper Saddle River, NJ: Merrill/Prentice Hall.

Echterling, L. G., & Stewart, A. L. (2008a). Creative crisis intervention techniques with children and families. In C. Malchiodi (Ed.), *Creative interventions with traumatized children* (pp. 189–210). New York: Guilford.

Echterling, L. G., & Stewart, A. L. (2008b). Resilience. In S. F. Davis & W. Buskist (Eds.), *Twenty-first century psychology: A reference handbook* (Vol. 2, pp. 192–201). Thousand Oaks, CA: Sage.

Emmons, R. A. (2003). Personal goals, life meaning, and virtue: Wellsprings of a positive life. In C. L. M. Keyes & J. Haidt (Eds.), *Flourishing: Positive psychology and the life well-lived* (pp. 105–128). Washington, DC: American Psychological Association.

Giovanni, N. (2007, April). *Nikki Giovanni convocation address*. Speech presented at Virginia Tech Convocation, Blacksburg, VA. Retrieved from http://www.vt.edu/remember/archive/giovanni_transcript.html

Larsen, J. T., Hemenover, S. H., Norris, C. J., & Cacioppo, J. T. (2003). Turning adversity to advantage: On the virtues of the coactivation of positive and negative emotions. In L. G. Aspinwall & U. M. Staudinger (Eds.), *A psychology of human strengths: Fundamental questions and future directions for a positive psychology* (pp. 211-225). Washington, DC: American Psychological Association.

Marvin, R., Cooper, G., Hoffman, K., & Powell, B. (2002). The circle of security project: Attachment-based intervention with caregiver-pre-school child dyads. *Attachment and Human Development, 4*(1),107–124.

McNally, R. J., Bryant, R. A., & Ehlers, A. (2003). Does early psychological intervention promote recovery from posttraumatic stress? *Psychological Science in the Public Interest, 4,* 45–79.

Milo, E. M. (2002). The death of a child with a developmental disability. In R. A. Neimeyer (Ed.), *Meaning reconstruction and the experience of loss* (pp. 137–155). Washington, DC: American Psychological Association.

Norris, F., Stevens, S. P., Pfefferbaum, B., Wyche, K. F., & Pfefferbaum, R. L. (2008). Community resilience as a metaphor, theory, set of capacities, and strategy for disaster readiness. *American Journal of Community Psychology, 41,* 127–150.

Ryff, C. D., & Singer, B. (2003). Flourishing under fire: Resilience as a prototype of challenged thriving. In C. L. M. Keyes & J. Haidt (Eds.), *Flourishing: Positive psychology and the life well-lived* (pp. 15–36). Washington, DC: American Psychological Association.

Stein, N., Folkman, S., Trabasso, T., & Richards, T. A. (1997). Appraisal and goal processes as predictors of psychological well-being in bereaved caregivers. *Journal of Personality and Social Psychology, 72,* 872–884.

Lessons Learned from an Employee Assistance Counselor

19

Wanda Osburn

Sirens shrieked as law enforcement vehicles flashed by in a blur on Interstate 81. Our police officer son must be driving one, I thought; I called him to get reassurance. Once I was able to breathe, I continued down the road to Blacksburg.

When I arrived at my EAP office, I was told that there had been a shooting on the Virginia Tech campus and that I needed to go to a workplace in Blacksburg that asked for help. Supporting employees after a critical incident is one of the best functions of an employee assistance program (EAP) I told myself. Yet on this day, I needed more grounding than usual. Traffic was intense; it seemed as if I would never get there. Snow began curling around my car as I made it into the Blacksburg parking lot. Snow? It is April 16.

Responding

As I entered the city building, a member of management swept me away to an open area where employees were gathering. Fast talk accompanied our walk-run to the auditorium. I was urged to speak to them right away, as they needed "something." I began taking calming breaths.

I was introduced as some kind of an expert; *God help me*, I thought. I saw faces filled with panic, worry, and confusion, and then there was silence. All eyes were on me. I spoke slowly as I confirmed that there had been a shooting on campus, that we did not know the details, and that I was there to support them. I urged them to come and share individually with me. I extended compassion and care and felt my throat closing with emotion as I brought the session to an end. We were already bonded in this experience. Several frightened individuals approached me as I left the room, touching my arm to carry a stronger message. I

assured them I would be there for them and to come by as soon as they could. They agreed silently.

I settled into a chair at a small conference table inside the manager's office. She dashed about in and out of offices, popped back in, and closed the door. Her breathing was rapid and her face pink and tense. As she perched on her chair ready to leap, I began listening to her workplace story. I took out my pad and pen because I knew I would not remember anything and there may be important numbers, names, or go-to instructions.

Decisions were made quickly regarding safety precautions and emergency planning. All of this was underway and revisions were being made as new information was received. The supervisors who would need my assistance as they worked with their employees were named. I followed the manager to meet the management team. Their intense handshakes revealed how much they appreciated my presence. Expressions on their faces told me that I was already providing relief just by being there. They were all in high gear as they moved to maintain focus and complete their jobs. Wearing a large nametag, I walked from room to room, observing individuals, letting them know I was there. It was clear to me that this workplace was teeming with people doing their jobs at a time of crisis, and I needed to stay out of the way.

Upon returning to the office where I was stationed, I noticed a TV had been brought in. I sank into the chair and heard for the first time that more than 20 lives were lost, but this number was unconfirmed! I lost my breath as I thought I caught a glimpse of our son crouched behind a building. I reminded myself of his excellent training and ability; there is no way I would distract him now. I worked to focus my attention as the manager appeared again for another update.

I spent the next 2 days with the workgroup. We bonded in a way that only happens in a crisis. Our presence, our energy, and our compassion for each other filled the room. We were all mothers and fathers focused on the location and safety of our children. We were all vulnerable people living and working in a small town, and we were all shocked that something so warlike could be experienced in the midst of our simple lives; how could this be? There was fear as well as tremendous sadness, but we found the openings that compassion offered to this collective human experience.

In the following months, my journey as an EAP counselor took me to the campus many times, along with countless others, as we bore witness to the stories of April 16. I engaged individual employees in makeshift walk-in clinics when they needed to "touch base" and spent time with workgroups in various campus locations who needed "something." I provided campus building support and checked in with faculty, staff, and students as they worked to reacclimate. As I encountered people in their workplace, I gave them a little "Hokie Touchstone" that I bought to share. I kept the small, dark red and orange stones in my pocket—a symbol of unity. It always feels better to me to share something simple, especially at a time when words do not matter so much. Sometimes when I came to campus, I just provided a safe place, information, and my presence.

I returned to campus as a university employee a few months before the first anniversary of April 16 in order to create the beginnings of an employee-driven referral program. Workers at the university, regardless of insurance status, were invited to call on a mental health resource on campus. We did not know what the offerings would look like, but in these early stages, it was important to be present for those who had an immediate need, to help make connections to referral services, and to develop educational tools for the workplace.

The idea of providing a resource for personal emotional assistance on campus has grown to include a more comprehensive look at wellness, pointing to specific workplace needs. Workgroups are requesting help with stress management; managers are referring employees with emotional needs; individuals are working on anger management; and larger groups are requesting emotional educational tools. Individuals who may not have accessed a mental health resource in the past are coming in for assistance. When our workgroups are pressed with tight schedules, we have learned how to provide care. When other difficult life events take place, we are learning how to access support quickly and are more open to each other.

LESSONS LEARNED

I have reflected on all that I have learned while assisting in this workplace and on the unique needs that arise during the various recovery phases. Some of the lessons learned are described below.

Early Days

- *Personal reactions happen first.* We checked in with family, helped others in front of us, and did what was natural for us when we heard about the event. We followed our heart.

- *Presence was everything.* We connected freely, compassionately and without barriers. We needed the help of others.

- *Workplace leadership was essential.* We looked for guidance and decision-making. It helped to have a strong leader and responsive followers acting efficiently to put a plan into action.

Follow-up

- *We want to share our stories.* It helped to be able to say out loud what happened; this made it real. Acknowledging loss and having that validated was a powerful step in healing.

- *The workplace changed.* Many did not know what they needed. We learned that we needed to restore a feeling of safety as quickly as possible at work.

- *We focused on our jobs.* This gave us immediate purpose and helped at a time when we needed something to do. Our jobs acted as a distraction.

Middle Days

- *Transitions were quieting.* This was a time for unique personal work and reflection. We were trying to figure out what seemed right in the midst of the first anniversary.

- *Workplace grief.* Many identified with their own unique process of dealing with trauma. Workplace education provided a bridge to personal work.

- *Workplace guidelines.* We needed to address what actions workers might take to share responsibility when they identified behaviors of concern. This educational tool helped empower individuals.

Later Days

- *Individuals are asking for guidance.* Workers are coming forward to talk about personal issues, not necessarily addressing trauma. This has been an opportunity to put April 16 into the mix when it fits during these moments of personal reflection.

- *Anger and social issues are emerging.* Collectively and individually, workers are sensitized to all sorts of reactions. This leads to workplace program development opportunities with both workers and managers.

- *How do we know we are well?* By engaging in "what does *healthy* look like" education, we are learning that the workplace is responsive to the whole person. The education includes health tips and informal discussions.

Though far from complete, this list identifies some places we have been and some places we still need to visit. We remind each other that we have no experience traveling this pathway. We walk gently and briskly, one next to the other, knowing we are both fragile and strong, doing the best we know how. Although we have collaborated with many and still must walk our own pathway, I think we are all okay with that.

Wanda Osburn, LPC, is an EAP consultant with Carilion Medical Center in New River Valley, VA. She was an EAP case manager in Blacksburg on April 21, 2007 and later worked at Virginia Tech. She is a Virginia Tech graduate.

Hokie Healing: A Tale of Two Counselor Education Students

20

Monique Bates and Brandy Smith

In the mountainous regions of Southwestern Virginia, Virginia Tech stands as a symbol of success and pride. Hokie flags fly proudly from our houses and yards, Virginia Tech gear can be found at retail shops, and bumper stickers and emblems color our vehicles with the prestigious colors of maroon and orange. Students accepted to Virginia Tech are considered to have "made it." The letters "VT" inspire us to victory in both academic and athletic arenas. Recognition of Virginia Tech as a treasure is embedded in our regional culture.

On April 16, 2007, our icon would be forever changed. Knee-deep into our practicum as Counselor Education students at Virginia Tech, we regularly practiced, theorized, and wrote about what it took to support others as they attempted to overcome hardships and process grief. However, when the lives of 33 classmates were taken and many more injured in West Ambler and Norris Halls, the answers were not as clear. Though we knew we had to face the reality that tragedy had struck on our campus, none of us were able to comprehend how such heinous crimes could have been committed, much less process all of the thoughts and emotions that flooded our heads and hearts. However, we pressed toward healing, no matter how difficult and overwhelming a task. Despite efforts from the media to prove otherwise, the Virginia Tech community epitomized grace and dignity in the face of adversity.

After the shootings, we began to process our reactions. One classmate described this phenomenon as the cloud that blanketed the campus. The cloud served as a reminder that regardless of where we went, we would inevitably be connected to the events of April 16. In the weeks following the shootings, many traveled outside of the area donning our Virginia Tech shirts. Paraphernalia that previously had prompted questions such as "So, how's that Tech football team looking next year?" now prompted, "How are you all doing our there with that Virginia Tech stuff?"

Realizing students would need to process the shootings in different ways, the Virginia Tech community supported our freedom to redefine normalcy. There was no expected way to grieve. For some, the road to healing was a private one filled with intimate gatherings, introspection and processing. For others, connecting more with the Virginia Tech community helped to bring about healing and comfort.

Personalized Healing: The Account of Monique Bates

The shootings at Virginia Tech brought into question the stability of everything students trusted. The uncertain safety of our campus, community, and our own lives proved unsettling and required some to reevaluate the Hokie parts of our lives that we took for granted. Even more unnerving was that the person who had prompted this reevaluation of self and safety was one of *us*. The attacker, a Hokie, killed 32 of his own. Some found coming to terms could not be done while surrounded by hundreds flooding the campus to pay their condolences or even with large groups of fellow Hokies. Camera lenses, microphones, and police officers on every square inch of the campus limited the amount of space and freedom needed for some to resolve their feelings. Like so many, I had fallen into the mindset of "that would never happen here." However, once shocked back to the reality that tragedy *could* and *did* happen, I used scrapbooking and journaling multiple times per day as a means to process and restructure my definition of safety. Like many, I eventually derived at a definition of safety that accommodated the unexpected.

Regaining a sense of control was also central to healing and required much personal reflection. The shootings had unexpectedly snatched that control away. The tears, uncertainty, and sadness were part of the heart-wrenching process of recovery. Grief was all we knew for certain during these early stages of recovery. Surprisingly, knowing that I needed and had to grieve provided some comfort and hope that the cloud would not blanket the campus forever. In this way, our community's grief itself encouraged further healing.

Many students also needed to reconcile their incongruence of emotion. We all shared a personalized sense of Hokie Pride and a sincere love for our university. The shootings intermingled our immense love with sadness and sometimes anger at how someone could defile our campus. Most had not imagined that opposing views could exist together. This odd cluster of emotions left some not knowing which emotion was the most urgent to address. Through meditation, spiritual counseling, or accessing mental health supports, private processing allowed students to separate these emotions and personally identify the role that each played in their grief process. I found making a remembrance bracelet to be the most helpful when working through my feelings of incongruence. I wear my bracelet each day, and although it acts as a constant reminder of recovery, it also reminds me of how something of beauty can coexist with memories of hurt. For many Virginia Tech students, it may not be a bracelet but a t-shirt, pin, ribbon, or other token that brings to mind all of the personal trials and triumphs after the shootings and that continue to encourage healing.

Collective Healing: The Account of Brandy Smith

In the hours and days after the shootings, accessing avenues for togetherness was vital. During a national press conference, Chris Flynn, Director of the Virginia Tech Cook Counseling Center, advised students, faculty, and staff, "Go where you get the best hugs." His words were not only timely but also helped set the tone for keeping ourselves healthy by sticking with those we love as we attempted to wrap our minds around the unthinkable. Families and close friends provided comforting words, strong shoulders, untiring ears, and warm embraces. Many of us met with faculty, doctoral supervisors, and each other. At peer gatherings, we shared the same loss of words, but found it reassuring to know that this tragedy had not penetrated the sincere care and compassion we had for one another.

Many of us stood hand-in-hand at memorial services and candlelight vigils. We sat together as we watched leaders from our campus, state, and nation offer comforting remarks during Virginia Tech's convocation service. The poem "We are Virginia Tech" written and read by Nikki Giovanni (2007) united the Hokie Nation. Her words brought us to a place where hope once again seemed possible. During such a difficult time, Giovanni seemed to shine a light on embracing who we were. Our hearts were broken, but our bond as Hokies remained unscathed. She exemplified the importance of holding our thoughts and spirits high.

Giovanni concluded her address with the statement, "*We* will prevail. *We* are Virginia Tech." This powerful declaration made a lasting impact on me. I felt like I was a part of something bigger and stronger than myself. On campus, prayer and support from others were tangible. After hearing Giovanni's words and experiencing the outpouring of support, connecting to Virginia Tech seemed more important than ever. I chose to work as a volunteer with disaster mental health services the week classes resumed. I found solace being on campus in the company of others. I transported counselors to classes of victims and those injured. As counselors returned from visiting classrooms, most everyone made comments about the spirit of students taking care of each other. One person said to me, "My granddaughter will be applying for schools next year. Virginia Tech is not on her list, but she has to visit this campus—whatever these kids have here, she needs it." Such words reaffirmed the themes of resilience and determination in Giovanni's poem. Strengthening ties to the Virginia Tech community proved to be a continual source of strength and comfort.

Photo: Kristine Halls Reid

The forever helping hand, the American Red Cross, offering counseling and spiritual care at the Squires Student Center on the Virginia Tech campus.

Virginia Tech's motto "Ut Prosim" ("That I May Serve") stood out to all of us. Honoring the exemplary lives of those lost by serving others, such as volunteering for the VT Engage movement, helped us begin to heal our community's broken heart. Our Counselor Education program built homes for Habitat for Humanity and we worked as counselors at a youth grief camp. Counselor Education students also worked with the local community services board to provide "personal empowerment makeovers" to those receiving assistance through mental health programs.

Final Thoughts

In no way have the students of Virginia Tech fully healed from the events of April 16, but we do push toward healing each day, carrying and sharing our stories. Our personal and collective stories help to commemorate the lives of those lost by never allowing their passing to be forgotten. Nearly 2 years after tragedy, we are still asked, "Were you there that day?" or "Do you know anyone who was shot?" Having an intentional, concise, and prepared response appropriately answers such poignant inquiries. Sharing an unmitigated account of our experiences also plays a vital role in educating the world on the impact tragedy had on our campus. Though such accounts may be so painful that they may be shared on only a few intimate occasions in an entire lifetime, the raw account of our experiences related to the shootings allows students to slowly lighten their pain.

By sharing our stories, we demonstrate the strength, resiliency, and honor that characterize Virginia Tech and this assures all that "we will prevail." Furthermore, our stories remind us that while we must travel the road to recovery individually, we are still connected to thousands of other Hokies. As a body, we will stand beyond the shadow of the shootings even more tenaciously than before. We no longer question but embrace and grow from our experiences with tragedy. The lessons learned from the Virginia Tech shootings have shaped its students into better people, and for these authors, better counselors.

Monique Bates and *Brandy Smith* are school counselors in the Roanoke County school system. They are graduates of the Counseling program at Virginia Tech and were students in practicum on April 21, 2007.

REFERENCES

Giovanni, N. (2007, April). *Nikki Giovanni convocation address.* Speech presented at Virginia Tech Convocation, Blacksburg, VA http://www.vt.edu/remember/archive/giovanni_transcript.html.

A Campus Shooting: How Northern Illinois University Responded

21

Debra A. Pender and Jane E. Rheineck

We all knew a crisis like this *could* happen but we hoped it never would. Like any crisis, the February 14, 2008 shooting that killed six and wounded 18, offered a path of danger, a moment that defined who we were as a university community by the strength of our collective response: Together, Forward Together. *Communiversity* is a term developed to convey the connections between Northern Illinois University (NIU) and the greater DeKalb region (NIU, 2009). It resurfaced to honor what happened here and how the DeKalb community and greater DeKalb area came together to assist during both the incident and the aftermath.

Pre-Incident Planning

The university was prepared—campus safety had long been a priority at NIU. Using the all hazards model, a comprehensive crisis response plan was developed, based upon all known threats, defining the populations needing services, the types of services to be utilized, who should offer them, and when they would be offered (Flynn, 2003; Mitchell & Everly, 2006).

The NIU police department had strong relationships with local responders; they conducted many mutual aid drills and engaged in local emergency planning efforts. The dispatch center at NIU is linked with City of DeKalb 911 and DeKalb County 911 so that if the volume at any center is too high, the next center handles the overflow. The Counseling Student and Developmental Center (CSDC), the lead mental health unit, had good working relationships with both the local DeKalb County Mental Health Board (with a disaster behavioral health plan in place) and the Ben Gordon Center, a local community agency. Our counselor education program has strong connections to the Illinois Counseling Association, which was instrumental during the recruitment of counseling volunteers.

Crisis Communications

The 911 calls began within seconds of the shooting, which started about 3:05 pm. All three dispatch centers overflowed; at one point, 89 callers were on hold. The university was immediately locked down, and the message was conveyed through our campus Novell phone system, e-mails, and officer searches of every campus building. Effective crisis communication requires clarity, informs about risk status and facts about the event, reduces uncertainty, offers reassurance, and promotes self-efficacy (Reynolds & Seeger, 2005). The initial message from the Public Affairs office was clear and concise; as new information appeared, they did not remove old posts, but used the strikeout feature, providing the time of each post (clarity). This strategy greatly reduced the potential for confusion as messages changed (reduce uncertainty). When the university determined that the single shooter was deceased, and that emergency response had been immediate (understand known facts and emergency response efforts), a campus-wide message was sent: call your family and prepare to return to home (promoting self-efficacy).

Counseling Response in the Immediate Aftermath

Before the "all-clear" was given, the Provost's Office contacted campus service providers. The counseling program decided not to open the Counseling Lab but to take a team of faculty to the residence halls. Residence hall teams were composed of CSDC staff, counseling and psychology faculty and doctoral students, and counselors from the Ben Gordon Center in DeKalb. Teams also were established at the Holmes Student Center, including drop-in family centers. Triage for crisis response with immediate witnesses as well as law enforcement interviews occurred in the student center.

Very few students came down to the resident hall lobbies to talk, and the teams shifted to a floor-by-floor walk through with senior community advisors who assessed their residents. The teams checked to see if advisors had identified any persons of concern and determined how to discreetly connect the team with a student-in-need. Our message of respect for their abilities increased both the floor advisors' comfort with the teams and the number of requests for assistance with residents (building connections and fostering self- and other-efficacy (Hobfoll et al., 2007).

In each hall, teams conducted a crisis management briefing (CMB) with senior community advisors (Clark & Volkmann, 2005; Everly, 2000). The CMB intervention was selected because (a) the purpose was to convey details and updates, (b) it is unsafe to process event meaning when the group has diverse exposure levels, and (c) the immediate aftermath period is not an appropriate time for resolution work. The team's task was to offer group psychological first aid: reviewing and assessing needs, supporting natural cohesion and resiliency, assisting with problem solving, and empowering the pre-existing network of support within the format of the CMB (Everly, Phillips, Kane, & Feldman, 2006).

Most residence hall community advisors exhibited moderate to high levels of distress, and they struggled between their desire to go home and the university's need for them to stay in their positions (needs assessment). The team began discussing this dilemma from a crisis management viewpoint; officials need to keep key personnel in place during the early stages of an event. The team asked advisors what they do and conveyed why the university values them as key personnel (support natural cohesion and resiliency). This offered advisors an opportunity to discuss their crisis work with residents and to understand why their work was valued. This shift from affective experiencing into cognitive processing allowed advisors to reenergize for the task ahead; all but three were able to regroup internal resources. The three remaining advisors had very different needs than their peers who had deep connections to the class where the shooting had taken place. The faculty team engaged in problem solving about making contact with parents who had come to campus and siblings from other resident halls who came and spent the night. They ended with a commitment that the team would voice their concerns about having to stay when everyone else went home (problem solving and existing networks).

Large scale mental health responses should follow the national consensus guidelines for emergency mental health operations (National Institute of Mental Health [NIMH]), 2002. Campus mental health leaders followed these guidelines; the next morning they held a volunteer orientation meeting that addressed: (a) rules for campus intervention, (b) the mental health volunteer agreement, (c) licensure requirements, and (d) the role of clergy during the crisis response efforts. Micky Sharma, CSDC director and lead mental health provider for the crisis, relayed key themes from the first 24 hours of crisis assessment, asking for reports from those already serving. The team reported the need to rotate community advisors, give them time off, and develop a plan to send them home. By Friday afternoon, a rotation with 4 hours off had been established. By Sunday, the residence halls were staffed with volunteer experts in residential life from regional universities.

The university sponsored a candlelight vigil Friday evening in the bitter cold. Students signed large boards with their thoughts and expressions of grief. The university did not interfere with the spontaneous memorial area where five crosses were placed, sometimes six—one for the shooter. On-the-scene support followed national standards for assistance—without interference or imposition. Although counselors were available to assist those with acute reactions, most individuals came in small groups and assisted each other (NIMH, 2002).

WEEKEND OF PREPARATION, WEEK OF HEALING

Representatives from NIU Human Resources, CSDC, and three faculty liaisons met with external experts from Virginia Tech and the University of Arkansas. We developed a framework for ongoing response, roles and responsibilities of campus mental health professionals, faculty involvement in the return to campus support, and preparation of handouts on trauma and stress reactions.

Campus mental health services experienced a spike in walk-ins, and services remained at 50% above normal rates across all campus resources. The CSDC met the demand through spontaneous groups and one-and-done, single-session crisis counseling support. Our Counseling Lab expanded operating hours with doctoral students, volunteer alumni, and faculty. During the summer of 2008, the American Counseling Association, the Illinois Counseling Association, and DuPage County Mental Health office provided pro bono services for NIU students who requested assistance.

One point of service was established for all academic and post-event needs for bereaved parents and students who were affected by the shooting. One advocate assisted with any academic need, adjustment, or recovery support required. Eventually, this effort evolved into the Office of Advocacy and Support (http://www.niu.edu/osa/), which was similar to the model used after the Virginia Tech shooting and the Texas A & M bonfire tragedy. This office continues to provide recovery support for parents and students including academic assistance, crime victims assistance funding, academic accommodations, trauma therapy, and educational newsletters.

Many campus groups received informational briefings (modified CMB). The general order of these meetings was:

1. Use talking points developed by planning committee

2. Update on known/not known information about the shooting

3. Describe the process of returning to classes

4. Define crisis counseling and psychological first aid

5. Clarify the role of classroom support counselors

6. Allow question-and-answer time

Human Resources used a different model for their work with campus groups, combining elements of debriefing group work and group-specific plans for recovery. A lesson learned from the informational briefings was that facilitators should talk less and avoid war stories. Campus groups addressed the purpose of the group, mixing the level of exposure, and the timing of interventions (Everly, 2008).

Closing Cole Hall, the site of the tragedy, and moving the large lecture courses to other campus facilities was a complex task. Each time a class moved, 75 other classes were affected, requiring four attempts to figure out a space and place for all instructional needs. These new locations had to be communicated to faculty and students; the mental health team had to arrange for a volunteer counselor to be in every classroom when classes resumed. Student Affairs clarified academic guidelines for addressing trauma-based needs and changed graduation to a later date.

To manage volunteer classroom counselors, a system was necessary to register volunteers, establish credentials, sign volunteer agreements, deal with logistics, lodging, and food, and create an easy way to identify the classroom support counselors. Recruitment began with the DeKalb County Mental Health Board, but in the immediate aftermath, the Illinois Counseling Association registered 250–300 volunteers electronically, although 509 showed up. Volunteers met prior to the memorial service on Sunday. Credentials were verified and training was provided on how to conduct classroom support and obtain services for individuals needing crisis counseling, support, and assessment. According to CSDS Director Sharma, "It was like trying to organize a national conference in 6 days."

Evidence-informed crisis intervention practices (Hobfoll et al., 2007) establishes five essential elements for effective crisis intervention: (a) reestablish safety, (b) promote calming, (c) develop self-efficacy and trust in others, (d) build connections, and (e) offer hope. Our strategy included: (a) clear, concise, well-crafted messages immediately and throughout the crisis, (b) establishment of police and counselor presence immediately and throughout the crisis, (c) engagement and empowerment of the student support staff, faculty, parents, and the bereaved, (d) early encouragement to connect with family, and (e) careful selection of interventions for the week of healing.

Our loss was deep. Our responsibility was to honor the legacy of these young people. The collective promise is that their loss will be honored by our commitment to service, building community, and embracing diversity.

Debra A. Pender, PhD, LCPC, and Jane E. Rheineck, PhD, LCPC, are assistant professors in the Counseling, Adult and Higher Education Department at Northern Illinois University in DeKalb.

REERENCES

Clark, D. W., & Volkmann, P. (2005). Enhancing the crisis management briefing. *International Journal of Emergency Mental Health, 7,* 133–140.

Everly, G. S. (2000). Crisis management briefings (CMB): Large group crisis intervention in response to terrorism, disasters, and violence. *International Journal of Emergency Mental Health, 2,* 53–57.

Everly, G. S. (2008). *The changing face of crisis and disaster mental health intervention.* Ellicott City, MD: International Critical Incident Stress Foundation.

Everly, G. S., Phillips, S. B., Kane, D., & Feldman, D. (2006) Introduction to and overview of group psychological first aid. *Brief Treatment and Crisis Intervention, 6,* 130–131.

Flynn, B. (2003). *Mental health all hazards disaster planning guidance.* (DHHS Pub. No. SMA 3829). Rockville, MD: Substance Abuse and Mental Health Services Administration (SAMHSA), Center for Mental Health Services.

Hobfoll, S. E, Watson, P., Bell, C. C., Bryant, R. A., Brymer, M. J., Friedman, M. J., Friedman, M., Ursano, R. J. (2007). Five essential elements of immediate and mid-term mass trauma intervention: Empirical evidence. *Psychiatry: Interpersonal & Biological Processes, 70,* 283–315.

Mitchell, J. T., & Everly, G. S. (2006). *Critical incident stress management (CISM): Basic group crisis intervention* (4th ed., rev.). Ellicott City, MD: International Critical Inci-

dent Stress Foundation.

National Institute of Mental Health (NIMH). (2002). *Mental health and mass violence: Evidence-based early psychological interventions for victims/survivors of mass violence: A workshop to reach consensus on best practices*: NIH Publication No. 02-5138, Washington, DC: U.S. Government Printing Office, 2002.

Northern Illinois University. (2009). *Inventory of the audio-visual collection of the Northern Illinois University archives.* Retrieved from http://www.ulib.niu.edu/reghist/UA%20 11.pdf

Reynolds, B., & Seeger, M. W. (2005). Crisis and emergency risk communication as an integrative model, *Journal of Health Communications, 10,* 43–55.

Preparing College Faculty to Assist Students After a Traumatic Event

22

Carlos Zalaquett

Approximately 67% of young adult college students have experienced a potentially traumatic event caused by nature or humans (Schnider, Elhai, & Gray, 2007) or directly or indirectly experienced tragic events (hurricanes, shootings, fatal car accidents, or suicides) that can produce distress (Gill, Ladd, & Marszalek, 2007). More than 60% of college students affected by Hurricanes Charley and Frances reported moderate to extremely high levels of psychological distress. Distress and anxiety responses to traumatic events or disasters are observed worldwide. College students in New York, New Orleans, and other states and countries were troubled deeply by the destruction of the World Trade Center and the devastation caused by Hurricane Katrina. Students in places such as the Dominican Republic, Puerto Rico, and the United States exhibited significant degrees of distress after Hurricane Georges (Sattler et al., 2002).

Students show different levels of psychological distress based on proximity to the disaster, the resources they have lost, and the level of social support available to them. After September 11, international students experienced rejection and discrimination from their college community (Morgan, 2002). Others were subjected to bigotry and hatred and often consider leaving (Del Castillo, 2002). Most students will cope successfully with disasters, but some may find themselves overwhelmed, distressed, or suffering posttraumatic stress disorder (PTSD).

Students affected by traumatic events are especially likely to manifest impaired psychological and physical functioning, a diminished sense of well-being, an increased use of mental and physical healthcare services, and a decline in academic performance (Gill et al., 2007). According to Tolin and Foa (2002), female college students evaluate the world as more dangerous or negative and are more inclined than male students to assign self-blame. They also tend to exhibit more severe symptoms of anxiety, depression, and distress (Silverman & La Greca, 2002; Yule et al., 2000). African American and Latino/a students seem to be at increased risk for developing PTSD and are less likely to show a decrease in symptoms over time when compared to White students (Rabalais, Ruggiero, & Scotti, 2002). Horowitz, Weine, and Jekel (1995) suggested that adolescents with a history of oppression and living in urban poverty zones may suffer compounded community trauma and are more prone to develop PTSD.

College students suffering the negative psychological effects of a disaster may engage in avoidant coping to prevent or stop the uncomfortable emotions. Avoidant coping is a strong predictor of PTSD, and many international students or those attending college at a considerable distance from their families may rely on it to deal with a traumatic situation (Schnider et al., 2007). Students demonstrating impairment across the domains of personal, social, academic, and career development likely will benefit from intervention strategies that are coordinated with different college resources and community mental health services.

College Faculty

College faculty can be instrumental in identifying and referring students whose traumatization places them at risk for distress or PTSD (Lindsey, Fugere, & Chan, 2007). Faculty members usually find opportunities for students to express their distress in the classroom through discussions and assignments. After September 11, students found "in-class discussion" helpful. Class discussion helped students process and regain a sense of normalcy (Matthieu, Lewis, Ivanoff, & Conroy, 2007).

Some faculty suffer from "traumaphobia," the inability to care directly for those affected by traumatic events, but the majority would like to help their students. Most faculty want to help but do not feel adequately prepared. There is a need for colleges to focus on disaster planning and preparedness to guide faculty. Students feel conflicted if faculty ignore a major traumatic event and attempt to continue teaching as usual, conveying the message that faculty do not care about them (Matthieu et al., 2007).

Faculty as Supporters

Colleges utilize different information delivery systems to inform students about campus security, shelters, counseling outreach programs, financial aid, as well as opportunities to participate in local disaster recovery efforts. Faculty can distribute information and support prevention and relief efforts by relaying emergency plans, security measures, and culturally relevant resources such as ethnic support groups.

Faculty as Liaison

Faculty are in a unique position to identify and help students who are experiencing the impact of a tragic event; they often express a desire to help their students when tragedy occurs, but sometimes they feel underutilized (Matthieu et al., 2007). Many students may not understand the potential benefits of counseling or may not know the availability of services. Cultural factors also may lead to students' mistrust of such practices. Faculty are well positioned to clarify such misunderstandings, explain potential benefits of counseling and therapy, and provide specific directions to locate and access such service. In this way, faculty can assist their colleges to become more resilient institutions in the aftermath of a disaster by improving social support services (Gill et al., 2007).

Some students approach faculty with concerns, while others display their emotional distress through changes in their academic performance, class behavior, and physical appearance. Faculty can identify and react to warning signs such as ambiguous messages in student papers and projects, direct threats, rumors about guns at the college, victimization on campus, changes in emotions or interests, isolation, and lack of family contact and support. Student services would benefit by establishing a working alliance with faculty.

RECOGNIZING STUDENTS DISTRESSED

The following indicators may be useful in assessing whether a student is distressed:

Changes in Academic Performance

Examples of behavioral changes faculty might observe are: noticeable decline in academic performance, poor attendance, excessive tardiness, poor preparation, an uncharacteristic need for additional attention, repeated requests for extensions or special consideration (especially when this represents a change), unusual or changed pattern of interaction, avoiding participation, dominating discussions, becoming excessively anxious when called upon, and exhibiting disruptive behavior.

Changes in Mood, Appearance, or Behavior

Crying spells or outbursts of anger could indicate psychological distress. Some students simply would not reveal a problem to a professor, but changes or deterioration in their appearance or behavior can communicate their distress.

Changes in Personal Relationships

Isolation and avoiding people can be indicative of distress. Also, threats to classmates, aggressive acts, and harassing behaviors can be signs of distress requiring decisive intervention.

References to Suicide

A student who talks or writes about suicide should be taken seriously. Thoughts of suicide are dangerous and may indicate that the student feels overwhelmed or depressed. Faculty who become aware of a student thinking about suicide should refer the student to the campus counseling center, university safety or police, or a crisis team. To assume that talking or writing about suicide serves the purpose of getting attention is risky and can be an unfortunate mistake. Faculty should consult with the counseling center about how to intervene, particularly if the student is reluctant to take the referral.

References to Homicide

Homicidal threats, whether made in verbal or written form, are clear reasons for concern; action needs to be taken immediately to prevent them.

Leaving School

A student who is considering leaving school or transferring should be referred to the dean's office or counseling center.

USEFUL SUGGESTIONS FOR FACULTY

There is no one "correct way" to deal with every situation: however, the following suggestions may be useful for faculty. These guidelines were first developed after the destruction of the World Trade Center and were used during the 2004 and 2005 hurricane seasons.

Privacy

Speaking to the student in private minimizes embarrassment and defensiveness. Talk directly and honestly, letting the student know that you sense the distress. Express your concern in a nonjudgmental way, "I've noticed you seem upset by what happened last Friday, and I'm concerned," rather than "Why are you concerned about what happened last Friday?" Do not discuss concerns with other students.

Empathy

Put yourself in the student's shoes and make an effort to see the nature of the distress from the student's point of view. Acknowledge openly that you are aware of their distress, you understand what is happening, and you are willing to help explore ways of coping with it.

Inquire

Ask if the student is talking to anyone about the distress, such as family or friends. People tend to isolate themselves when in distress even though it is likely that they would benefit by having individuals to talk to about their feelings and concerns. Ask how the student feels about his or her reaction to the critical event.

Normalize

Let students know that a tragic event is not the norm but the exception. Most people do not suffer tragic accidents or resort to violent behavior. Help students understand that it is normal during stressful times to feel the need to talk with someone they can trust; let them know that there are different sources of help available.

Listen

Do not start by trying to fix, advise, correct, or disagree with students; listen to their thoughts and feelings. Communicate understanding by repeating back the essence of what the student has told you. Use expressions such as "It sounds like you're distressed by this tragic event and afraid that something like this may happen to you." A few minutes of intentional and attentive listening will help the student feel cared about and more confident.

Give Hope

Assure students that fear, sadness, grieving, or anger can and will get better. It is important to help students re-

alize that there are options and that things will not always seem so negative. Suggest approaching other people who can help—friends, family, or professionals on campus. If students express religious beliefs, suggest visiting with on- or off-campus clergy. Provide the student enough hope to enable consultation with appropriate persons or professionals because most faculty members are not trained to eliminate a student's distress.

Judgment

Avoid judging, evaluating, and criticizing because such behavior may push the student away from you and the help they need. Respond in a non-threatening, non-challenging way, respecting the student's beliefs, even if yours are different.

Roles and Expectations

Keep clear and consistent roles, boundaries, and expectations. It is important to uphold the professional nature of the faculty/student or staff/student role and relationship by maintaining academic expectations, exam schedules, and so forth.

Be Careful

Behavior that is strange or inappropriate should not be ignored. Comment directly on what you have observed and refer the student to appropriate sources. Contact appropriate professionals if the student's behavior seems dangerous.

Consult

Consult with campus professionals if you are unsure of how to intervene or if the student does not acknowledge the need for help. Consultation is urgent for students exhibiting: depressed mood, swollen or red eyes, marked changes in personal dress and hygiene, and falling asleep in class; difficulties communicating clearly (e.g., confusing conversation, inability to stay with the topic, random thoughts); obvious loss of contact with reality (e.g., cannot recognize where he or she is, or who you are, or seeing or hearing persons or objects that are not there); and thoughts of suicide or homicide.

Refer

Your goal is to provide support and to make referrals when support is not enough. Do not get involved beyond what seems comfortable, appropriate, or beyond your expertise. In making a referral, let the student know that: help is available, addressing distress is a good choice, and that seeking such help is a sign of strength and courage rather than a sign of weakness or failure. Prepare the student by sharing what you know about the referral person or service. Share your reasons for making a referral (e.g., lack of appropriate information, conflict of interest) and emphasize your concern.

Follow-Up

Meet with the student again to reinforce the decision to obtain appropriate help. By doing this, you also will demonstrate your commitment to assist in the therapeutic process. Check with the student later on to confirm that the referral appointment was kept and to hear how it went. Provide support.

First Anniversary

According to Sitterle and Gurwitch (1999), the first anniversary is a day of revisiting emotions of loss and helplessness and continuing the healing process. Anniversary dates of traumatic events can reactivate thoughts and feelings from the actual event, and students may experience peaks of anxiety and depression.

FINAL THOUGHTS

Preparing faculty to assist students who have experienced anxiety or distress following a traumatic event represents a higher order goal for counselors and other mental heath professionals. This provides a way to meet the mental health needs of victims and distressed students, promotes more adaptive coping with the traumatic event or disaster, and enhances their academic achievement.

Carlos P. Zalaquett, PhD, LMHC, is associate professor and coordinator of the Mental Health Counseling program in the Department of Psychological and Social Foundations of Education at the University of South Florida.

REFERENCES

Del Castillo, D. (2002, September 6). A Kuwaiti student forces herself to continue her studies in the U.S. *The Chronicle of Higher Education*, A14.

Gill, D. A., Ladd, A. E., & Marszalek, J. (2007, October 1). College students' experiences with Hurricane Katrina: A comparison between students from Mississippi State University and three New Orleans universities. *Journal of the Mississippi Academy of Sciences, 52*, 262–281.

Greenberg, S. F. (2007). Active shooters on college campuses. *Disaster Medicine and Public Health Preparedness, 1*, Suppl. 1, S57–S61.

Horowitz, K., Weine, S., & Jekel, J. (1995). PTSD symptoms in urban adolescent girls: Compounded community trauma. *Journal of the American Academy of Child & Adolescent Psychiatry, 34*, 1353–1361.

Lindsey, B. J., Fugere, M., & Chan, V. (2007). Psychological and emotional reactions of college students to September 11, 2001. *College Student Journal, 41*, 558–571.

Matthieu, M., Lewis, S. J., Ivanoff, A., & Conroy, K. (2007). School of social work disaster response following the World Trade Center disaster: MSW student and field instructor perspectives. *Brief Treatment and Crisis Intervention, 7*(2), 115–126.

Morgan, R. (2002, September 6). An international student adviser faces rumors, fear, and prejudice. *The Chronicle of Higher Education*, A11.

Rabalais, A. E., Ruggiero, K. J., & Scotti, J. R. (2002). Multicultural issues in the response of children to disasters. In A. M. La Greca, W. K. Silverman, E. M. Vernberg, & M. C. Roberts (Eds.), *Helping children cope with disasters and terrorism* (pp. 73–99). Washington, DC: American Psychological Association.

Sattler, D. N., Preston, A. J., Kaiser, C. F., Olivera, V. E., Valdez, J., & Schlueter, S. (2002). Hurricane Georges: A cross-national study examining preparedness, resource loss, and psychological distress in the U.S. Virgin Islands, Puerto Rico, Dominican Republic, and the United States. *Journal of Traumatic Stress, 15*, 339–350.

Schnider, K. R., Elhai, J. D., & Gray, M. J. (2007). Coping style use predicts posttraumatic stress and complicated grief symptom severity among college students reporting a traumatic loss. *Journal of Counseling Psychology, 54*, 344–350.

Silverman, W. K., & La Greca, A. M. (2002). Children experiencing disasters: Definitions, reactions, and predictors of outcomes. In A. M. LaGreca, W. K. Silverman, E. M. Vernberg, & M. C. Roberts (Eds.), *Helping children cope with disasters and terrorism* (pp. 11–34). Washington, DC: American Psychological Association.

Sitterle, K. A., & Gurwitch, R. H. (1999). The terrorist bombing in Oklahoma City. In E. S. Zinner & M. B. Williams (Eds.), *When a community weeps: Case studies in group survivorship* (pp. 163–166, 180–181). Philadelphia: Brunner/Mazel.

Tolin, D. F., & Foa, E. B. (2002). Gender and PTSD: A cognitive model. In R. Kimerling, P. Ouimette, & J. Wolfe (Eds.), *Gender and PTSD* (pp. 76-97). New York: Guilford Press.

Yule, W., Bolton, D., Udwin, O., Boyle, S., O'Ryan, D., & Nurrish, J. (2000). The long term psychological effects of a disaster experienced in adolescence: I—the incidence and course of PTSD. *Journal of Child Psychology and Psychiatry, 41*, 503–511.

Section Five

Responding to School Crises and Tragedies

The Best Laid Plans: Will They Work in a Real Crisis?

23

J. Barry Mascari and Jane Webber

On September 11, 2001, I worked for a school district that was 9 miles from the World Trade Center (WTC) and the towers were visible from some of our schools. At least two hijackers lived and worked near us, passing through our community every day. This was the largest scale crisis we ever faced and it tested the effectiveness of our crisis plans on a new level. Our crisis success and almost automatic response reinforced our belief that having a plan is essential. Over the course of my 20-year career as counselor and supervisor, I have directed the implementation of a number of crisis response plans that included student shootings after a battle of the bands, disclosure of sexual abuse by a school psychologist who spent 20 years in the district, a gangland-style murder of a student by two fellow students, the death of a popular high school vice principal, an apparent suicide by the senior class president 2 weeks before graduation, an accidental shooting death of a student by her husband, a middle school student killed by a car in front of the school, an elementary school student who accidentally hung himself while playing, and numerous deaths caused by auto accidents (Mascari, 2001a, 2005). Although each traumatic event was unique, none had the impact of the terrorist attacks.

Shortly before 2001, several school shootings had prompted the U.S. Department of Education and states to begin providing planning resources (Fairfax County Public Schools, 2009; Iowa Association of School Boards, 2009; U.S. Department of Education, 2007). After the terrorist attacks and the hurricanes of recent years, a plethora of resources have emerged (e.g., the America Prepared Campaign, 2004; Auger, Seymor, & Roberts, 2004; Center for Mental Health in Schools, 2007; Chibbaro & Jackson, 2006; Herbert & Ballard, 2007; Lerner, Volpe, & Lindell, 2003; Millner & Clark, 2009; National Child Traumatic Stress Network, 2008; Smith, 2006; Webber, Mascari, Dubi, & Gentry, 2006; Uhernik & Husson, 2009).

While planning a workshop on preparing for sudden loss in the schools, a colleague said, "Most people don't plan to fail, they fail to plan." Although we can never be certain that plans will unfold smoothly in a real crisis, being prepared always yields better results than being unprepared. Behavioral rehearsal helps create a sense of control and the ability to respond in healthier ways.

What Is a Crisis?

Using the September 11 attacks on the WTC and the Pentagon as an example of a crisis, the following demonstrates that they met all of the criteria for a crisis (Mascari, 2002, 2005) (See also James & Gilliland, 2001). In order to be a crisis, the event must:

1. Affect and distress many people (as opposed to an individual in crisis)

2. Be unexpected, having the element of surprise

3. Be a "disaster" of varying magnitudes involving more than one person (i.e., not an individual in crisis)

4. Involve some type of loss, including death, serious property loss, or the destruction of a community symbol

5. Disrupt normal routines at home

6. Result in people feeling "out of control" or fear and uncertainty about the future due to a loss of structure and predictability

7. Not go away overnight—people will not feel better about this event in the morning

When assessing the level of response, it is important to determine how many people will need assistance. Since the first edition of this book was published, crisis intervention practice has been reconceptualized as *psychological first aid* (Uhernik & Husson, 2009). The degree of crisis varies with each event; therefore, assessing the impact allows planners and responders to provide the appropriate level of response and not over-react or under-react. Sometimes an over-reaction increases the magnitude of the event by drawing additional people into the grieving process who would not normally be involved. This leads to the contagion effect where the crisis can spin out of control (see Chapter 25).

Assessing an incident's degree of trauma helps the response team provide the appropriate level of response. Oates (1992) developed a simple instrument that provides a quick way to assess a situation. Experienced crisis teams report that they learned to "feel" the level of an event's impact in a school or community.

PLANNING FOR A CRISIS

Three broad phases of crisis planning are useful (Mascari, 2001, 2005): (a) develop a plan before an incident, (b) develop intervention strategies to implement during the crisis, and (c) anticipate and plan for what will come after a crisis (often referred to as mop-up). Others stages or sub-stages in crisis planning have been identified (Greenstone & Leviton, 2002; Roberts, 1996).

The team responsible for implementing the plan should consider the entire process of managing the crisis as well as the aftermath; a planning chart helps structure three major phases. In any crisis, there is uncertainty about what will happen next and how long each phase will last. The chart could include three major phases:

Before (planning)

During (intervening in "the event")—includes two distinct parts: beginning (initiating the intervention plan) and middle (responding and adjusting interventions as the team meets)

End (closing activities and return to normalcy) and the *aftermath* (team debriefing and preparation for delayed responses, anniversaries, and pressure to memorialize the event)

The *before* phase of planning involves readiness to act and an assurance that the response will be swift and orderly.

To determine your program's level of readiness, ask these questions:

- Is there a written plan?

- Do all team members have a copy of the plan? Have they read their sections?

- Do all members know their responsibilities in advance?

- Does the plan cover all stages and various degrees of crises?

- Have all staff members who will be involved in each phase of the response been trained?

- Have you initiated the emergency call-up system? Do you have a chart to help organize members? (See Underwood & Dunne-Maxim, 1997). Who is in charge of what? For example, who handles the press?

- How fast can the team be mobilized following the initial call?

- What if you need more help? Whom can you call outside the team? Whom can you count on? (Being involved with community agencies and hospitals can pay dividends during a crisis.)

Preparing to Respond Effectively

The accepted keys to an effective crisis response are to provide *support, control,* and *structure.* The crisis response team leader should be a mental health professional whose expert advice is invaluable to the principal and superintendent. Although the administrators are "in charge," the team leader can prevent actions that could undermine the support, control, and structure that helps keep the event manageable.

The Red Cross Disaster Mental Health training reminds participants that most people in a disaster are normal people, experiencing normal responses to an abnormal situation. It is helpful to keep this in mind when providing interventions. By following the steps identified below, counselors will be better prepared to respond in a crisis:

1. Initiate your response early in the day (support). Meet with your faculty and teams *before* school starts. Using the emergency call-up procedure, schedule a meeting before the students arrive to ensure that everyone has the same information about the event. Have statements, handouts, details, or other information that you wish to share available at this time. This is also the time to prepare and send letters to parents and consider distributing a newsletter (see Figures 1 and 2).

2. Acknowledge your own fear (support). Crisis work is frightening and the uncertainty of it all makes even the most seasoned veteran apprehensive. Remember to focus and breathe.

3. Get back to normal as soon as possible (control, structure, support). Normalcy and routine help people feel more in control. Children especially respond to routine; it reduces their anxiety. On September 11, teachers were asked to keep televisions and radios off and to continue teaching. This action, more than anything else, prevented panic. Provide interventions for staff members who may have trouble carrying on as usual, or find substitute staff to help students keep calm. Children watch adults' reactions

as a guide for their own thoughts and feelings.

4. Speak with one voice (control). Be sure that the district designates one person who knows the big picture to speak with the press. Be prepared for the press to criticize the school and to interview students who may not be the best representatives of the school. The police can be particularly helpful in sealing off the campus from the press.

5. Remain flexible (support). Be prepared to adjust plans and responses. Meet with your response team once a day, or more frequently if needed, in order to keep your "finger on the pulse."

6. Know why you are making an intervention (structure). The team should always understand the goals of any intervention. Responses to students should be planned and coordinated based on evidenced-based practice or expert consensus—not conceived in the moment because it "felt" good.

Figure 1.

Sample letter - Student death

Dear Parent or Guardian:

The recent death of one of our students has both shocked and saddened the community. In our own way, each of us experiences a search in order to make sense of such an event.

Children's grief takes on many forms, and the school has made professional support staff available to assist them in addressing their concerns. We thought that you would like to know about this and be prepared to address unexpected questions or fears, which are children's normal responses to death.

The death of someone outside the family presents an opportunity to begin addressing, in an age appropriate way, the experience that everyone must face at some time during the life cycle. This is an opportune time to share your views on death, especially in the context of family, religious, or spiritual beliefs.

Although the issue of death and grief may have been addressed in the classroom in a general way, we cannot offer a view that would include all possible religious, cultural, and family perspectives.

A topic such as this can often strengthen or make closer the parent-child relationship. If you find it difficult to begin the discussion and need some help, please feel free to call me at the school office for further information.

You may also want to consult with your own spiritual guide for advice in instructing your child in the context of your belief system.

The school community's heartfelt expression of sympathy is extended to the family. Your support and cooperation during this difficult time is appreciated.

Sincerely,
School Principal

Figure 2.

Sample letter - September 11, 2001

Dear Parent or Guardian:

The recent events in New York and Washington have made all of us, but most importantly children, uneasy. I am writing you to offer some simple suggestions about ways that you may make this period easier for your family.

Expect the unexpected from your children. This may include problems with sleep, being excessively "clingy," or having angry outbursts; they are responding differently because their world has changed. You can help them by:

- Listening or responding to their behavior without punishing or criticizing them (remember that children respond differently and some may have a delayed response)

- Limiting the amount of television news they see you watching, or are actually watching themselves (information is important, but overload can be detrimental)

- Assuring them that they are safe and that their life has resumed normalcy (do all of the things that you would normally do)

- Making contact with friends, your clergy, or counseling services

Should you have any concerns and wish to speak with a counselor in the schools, contact the Principal or your student's assigned Counselor. Staff members are prepared to make referrals to local counseling centers to help families deal with possible loss.

My heartfelt expression of sympathy is extended to all who lost a family member. As always, I appreciate your cooperation during this difficult time.

Sincerely,
Superintendent of Schools

In planning age appropriate interventions, remember that children are not "little adults" (Herbert & Ballard, 2007; La Greca, 2005; Steigerwald, 2004). When a 4th grade student died, it was not appropriate to establish a walk-in triage for upset students as we had done after high school tragedies. Rather, the most efficacious intervention was sending a letter home that informed parents/guardians of the plan, then going into the classroom where students made cards and drawings for the family.

Older students often respond spontaneously. Although counselors plan to avoid memorializing an event or death, spontaneous gestures by older students peers may result in unanticipated memorials. In one case after a middle school student died, close friends wanted to decorate the chair and table in the lunchroom where the student normally sat. It is important to keep the tasks of grief in mind with school responses to death. Underwood and Dunne-Maxim (1997) expanded on Worden's work (2008) regarding the four tasks of grief:

1. To accept the reality of the loss
2. To work through the pain of the loss
3. To adjust to an environment in which the deceased is missing
4. To relocate the deceased emotionally and move on with life

Keep expectations for your plan reasonable. The objective is to maintain a safe, secure, and orderly environment. After a traumatic event, everyday routines may return, but individuals are personally changed in some way. They are not unhealthy—they are different. Some people become healthier after a crisis and report posttraumatic growth (see Chapter 18), for example, individuals who experienced an existential crisis (see Chapter 25).

Aftermath

No one is unaffected by traumatic events, not even counselors. When the response is over, your energy may be depleted and you will need some time to recover. Helping the helper, or practicing self care (Skovholt, 2001), is one of the most important elements in any plan and is often the most overlooked.

Early in our September 11 crisis response experience, two critical mistakes were made following the intervention period: failing to put closure on the response process and being blindsided by the aftermath and its effect on all parties involved, especially the response staff. Surveys of staff (Mascari, 2001b) who provided crisis response to the events cited above indicated that nearly all were affected emotionally (87%) and felt some type of debriefing was necessary (93%).

Vicarious traumatization—when helpers absorb the trauma from those they helped—is a serious effect. Most traumatologists recommend some intervention within 24 to 48 hours after the response because the events may have touched the "soft side of the turtle" (Skovholt, 2001). Skovholt also suggested activities for self care. The American Red Cross (2006) requires that all disaster response workers be offered a debriefing as a means of putting closure on the response experience and helping them to return to normal. The leader of the response team should bring another professional in to lead the ventilation or debriefing session in order to participate, rather than lead.

Will the Plan Work?

The nature of a crisis is that some actions will work as planned, others will not. The American Red Cross (2006) reminds disaster mental health response staff to be flexible. Success often depends on factors that are out of the counselors' control (e.g., an off-campus interview of a student provided incorrect information that needed to be countered). Once the crisis response is initiated, there is barely time to breathe. Deal with events you can control rather than focusing on those out of your control. Your goal is to help people through a difficult situation and, despite difficulties, they will be better as a result of your team's efforts.

J. Barry Mascari, EdD, LPC, LCADC, is chair of the Counselor Education Department at Kean University, Union, NJ and holds New Jersey Disaster Response Crisis Counselor certification (NJDRCC).

Jane Webber, PhD, LPC, is associate professor and coordinator of the Counseling Program at New Jersey City University. She is counselor in private practice and holds New Jersey Disaster Response Crisis Counselor certification.

References

America Prepared Campaign, Inc. (2004). *Preparedness in America's schools: A comprehensive look at terrorism preparedness in America's twenty largest school districts.* New York: Author.

American Red Cross. (2006). *American Red Cross disaster services 2006.* Washington, DC: Author.

Auger, R. W., Seymour, J. W., & Roberts, W. B., (2004). Responding to terror: The impact of September 11 on K-12 schools and schools' responses. *Professional School Counseling, 7*(4), 222–230.

Center for Mental Health in Schools. (2008). *Responding to crisis at a school.* Retrieved from http://smhp.psych.ucla.edu/pdfdocs/crisis/crisis.pdf

Center for Mental Health in Schools. (2007). *Screening/assessing students: Indicators and tools.* Retrieved from http://smhp.psych.ucla.edu/pdfdocs/assessment/assessment.pdf

Chibbaro, J. S., & Jackson, C. M. (2006). Helping students cope in an age of terrorism: Strategies for school counselors. *Professional School Counseling, 9*(4), 315–321.

Fairfax County Public Schools. (2009). *Crisis management workbook.* Retrieved from http://www.fcps.edu/fts/safety-security/publications/cmw.pdf

Greenstone, J. L., & Leviton, S. C. (2002). *Elements of crisis intervention: Crises and how to respond to them.* Pacific Grove, CA: Brooks/Cole.

Herbert, B. B., & Ballard, M. B. (2007). Children and trauma: A post-Katrina and Rita response. *Professional School Counseling, 11*(2), 140–144.

Iowa Association of School Boards. (2009). *Lessons learned: Natural disasters toolkit for schools.* Retrieved from http://www.ia-sb.org/Spotlight.aspx?id=7188

James, R., & Gilliland, B. (2001). Crisis intervention strategies (4th ed.). Belmont, CA: Brooks/Cole.

La Greca, A. (2005). *After the storm: A guide to helping children cope with the psychological effects of a hurricane.* Coral Gables, FL: 7-Dippity.

Lerner, M. D., Volpe, J. D., & Lindell, B. (2003). *A practical guide for crisis response in our schools.* Commack, NY: The American Academy of Experts in Traumatic Stress.

Mascari, J. B. (2005). The best laid plans: Will they work in a real crisis? In J. Webber, D. Bass, & R. Yep (Eds.), *Terrorism, trauma and tragedy: A counselor's guide to preparing and responding (2nd ed.)* (pp. 65–77). Alexandria, VA: American Counseling Association Foundation.

Mascari, J. B. (2001a). The best laid plans: Will they work in a real crisis? In D. Bass & R. Yep (Eds.), *Terrorism, trauma and tragedy: A counselor's guide to preparing and responding* (pp. 39–51). Alexandria, VA: American Counseling Association Foundation.

Mascari, J. B. (2001b). Unpublished data of Clifton Public School staff.

Millner, V. S., & Clark, J. N. (2009). Children's responses to disaster from moral and ethical reasoning perspectives. In G. R. Walz, J. Bleuer, & R. K. Yep (Eds.), *Compelling counseling interventions: VISTAS 2009* (pp. 43–53). Alexandria, VA: American Counseling Association.

National Academy of Sciences. (2003). *Definition of psychological first aid.* Washington, DC: Author.

National Child Traumatic Stress Network. (2008). *Child trauma toolkit for educators.* Los Angeles: Author.

Oates, M. (1992). *Death in the school community: A handbook for counselors, teachers, and administrators.* Alexandria, VA: American Counseling Association.

Roberts, A. R. (1996). Epidemiology and definitions of acute crisis. In A. R. Roberts (Ed.), *Crisis management & brief treatment* (pp. 3–15). Chicago: Nelson-Hall.

Skovholt, T. (2001). *The resilient practitioner.* Needham Heights, MA: Allyn & Bacon.

Smith, H. B. (2006). Providing mental health services to clients in crisis or disaster situations. In G. R. Walz, J. C. Bleuer, & R. K. Yep (Eds.), *VISTAS: Compelling perspectives on counseling 2006* (pp. 13–21). Alexandria, VA: American Counseling Association.

Steigerwald, F. (2004). Crisis intervention with individuals in schools. In B. T. Erford (Ed.), *Professional school counseling: A handbook.* Austin, TX: Pro-Ed.

Uhernik, J., & Husson, M. A. (2009). Psychological first aid: An evidence informed approach for acute disaster behavioral health response. In G. R. Walz, J. Bleuer, & R. K. Yep (Eds.), *Compelling counseling interventions: VISTAS 2009* (pp. 271–280). Alexandria, VA: American Counseling Association.

Underwood, M., & Dunne-Maxim, K. (1997). *Managing sudden traumatic loss in the schools.* Piscataway, NJ: University of Medicine & Dentistry of New Jersey.

U.S. Department of Education Office of Safe and Drug Free Schools. (2007). *Practical information on school crisis planning: A guide for schools and communities.* Retrieved from http://www.ed.gov/admins/lead/safety/emergencyplan/crisisplanning.pdf

Webber, J., Mascari, J. B., Dubi, M., & Gentry, J. E. (2006). Moving forward: Issues in trauma response and treatment. In G. Walz, J. Bleuer, & R. Yep (Eds.), *VISTAS: Compelling perspectives on counseling 2006.* Alexandria, VA: American Counseling Association.

Worden, W. (2008). *Grief counseling and grief therapy: A handbook for the mental health practitioner.* New York: Springer.

ADDITIONAL AND SEMINAL RESOURCES

Clayton, L.O. (1990). *Assessment and management of the suicidal adolescent.* Dallas, TX: Essential Medical Systems.

Deskin, G., & G. Steckler. (1997). *When nothing makes sense.* Minneapolis, MN: Fairview Press.

Dudley, J. (1995). *When grief visits school: Organizing a successful response.* Minneapolis, MN: Educational Media Corporation.

Dwyer, K., & Osher, D. (1998). *Early warning, Timely response: A guide to safe schools.* Washington, DC: U.S. Department of Education.

Lystad, M. (1988). *Mental health response to mass emergencies: Theory and practice.* New York: Brunner/Mazel.

Iraq War, Katrina, Virginia Tech: A Virginia High School Responds

24

Marie Bullock, Jessica Baith, and Caitlin Rose

Washington-Lee High School (W-L) in Arlington County, Virginia has not been immune to the shockwaves sent around the nation and the world by the Iraq War, Hurricane Katrina, and the Virginia Tech tragedies. In the public high school that educates students living on the Ft. Myer military base and others whose parents work at the Pentagon, all three events have been experienced "up close and personal" by our students, staff, and parents.

The Iraq War raised issues of personal vulnerability for students and parents. We welcomed Katrina refugees who were traumatized by this cataclysmic event that was watched by the whole nation. The Virginia Tech massacre came at a time when seniors were receiving acceptance letters from colleges, and the issue of whether it was safe to leave home confronted some of our students. As a counseling department, we needed to strategize about the best way to address students' concerns as each event occurred.

The Impact of the Iraq War

At the beginning of the Iraq War, we experienced the full range of emotions. Parents of some students were involved in the planning and implementation of the invasion of Iraq, while parents of other students were being deployed. The tension felt by the entire nation resonated through our hallways and classrooms. As students discussed the issues, emotions were running high. When the invasion was announced, we began to hear from parents who called to tell us that a dad or mom was being deployed, and from non-military families who told us that their student was concerned about conversations taking place at school.

Because we pride ourselves on being a community of respect, the W-L Counseling Department re-alized that it would be our job to bring students and staff to a place where they could listen to each other. Respect for differing points of view was paramount. To prepare ourselves, counselors took several steps to make sure we were in agreement about our plans. The Department staff needed to talk about individual thoughts and feelings; a roundtable discussion enabled us to share our own opinions about the impending invasion of Iraq and to be mindful of our personal reactions to the issues. Clear boundaries must be in place to focus on the human element rather than protocol issues. Although we did not all agree, the process allowed us to hear others and acknowledge all feelings of students and staff.

It was important for us to be proactive in creating "safe spaces" where students and staff could gather and discuss their feelings. We let everyone know that we cared about their points of view and respected their right to state them. We wanted to make sure all students, especially our international student population—of which many are Muslim—knew they were valued members of the school community. It was our priority that these students understood what was happening and could be a part of any discussion that occurred. In fact, their perspectives were often eye-openers for many of us. Our plan was as follows:

- Circulate a notice to teachers that counselors were available to come into any class to participate in discussions.

- Ask teachers to remain neutral and not to express political or personal points-of-view with students.

- Organize lunchtime discussion groups to create a respectful dialogue for all during both lunch periods for the first week of the invasion.

113

- Call the families of students who we knew had a parent in the military to ask if they had any concerns and how we could help. Numerous requests for individual sessions with students and for sessions with parents and students were honored.

- Notify students for several weeks via morning announcements that they were welcome to drop in the counseling office.

For several years, we continued to receive calls from parents as they were scheduled to deploy, and, as is the case in a volunteer army, many parents were deployed multiple times. Now, years later, although not as dramatic as the first weeks and months of the Iraq invasion, we still have students whose parents cycle through the process of deployment, return, and, often redeployment.

HURRICANE KATRINA: ONE SENIOR'S JOURNEY

In late August 2005, as Hurricane Katrina was about to hit the Gulf coast, W-L teachers were coming back to open the school year. As we watched the story unfold on TV, we did not really expect to have students from New Orleans come as far north as our school district. However, late Friday afternoon before school opened, a young woman ("J") came to the counseling office insisting on going to school, and she wanted to know what courses she could take to get her diploma. Our new student had spent the past 3 days and nights on an overpass with her father and a group of people she did not know. J was evacuated north with a family friend and had arrived in Arlington that morning, restarting her senior year in a new school and in a new state without her school records. The school she attended for 11 years had been destroyed in the hurricane and we were unable to speak with anyone about her placement. It was apparent that we were talking to a motivated student and we did not want to put obstacles in the way of what seemed so important to her, so we created a senior schedule. We wanted her to calm herself and we ensured J that she was going to be taken care of at W-L.

J's mother, a physician in New Orleans, had not been in contact with her family for over a week. Her father stayed behind in New Orleans to salvage as much as he could from their home. J could not reach her parents by phone and worried about them. Fortunately, she was in touch with her sister, a college junior, who confirmed that we were on the right track in selecting levels for the courses J needed to complete her senior year.

Our main goal was to provide a sense of normalcy and stability. Coming from a school of 300 students and a class of 45, J was very reluctant to go into the cafeteria with 800 students. At first, J ate lunch with her counselor, then one or two of her teachers were invited to join them, and finally a few students were added to the group; after 2 weeks she was ready to take on the cafeteria. The counselor and the social worker also discussed how to help J with clothes, transportation money, and school lunches. After 3 weeks, we were able to contact her mother; however, since she could not come to Virginia until November, the counselor set up a weekly phone appointment to keep her informed.

J tried hard to cover up the fact that anything unusual had happened in her life, and although she was ambitious about the courses she was taking, it became apparent that she was taking on work that she could not handle. She insisted on taking seven very difficult courses, joined a sports team, and tried to become part of several school activities. We recognized that much of the activity J was piling on was to help her ignore the current reality.

Neither school nor the living arrangements were going well for J. She reported difficulty sleeping and could not get to school on time. She lost assignments and books, was not able to keep up with the workload, and became very upset with herself if she received less than an A on a test or assignment. We had serious concern about J's stress level, and we consulted with the principal. We developed a plan that would allow her to:

- Drop her first period class, come to school late, and report directly to the counseling office in the middle of first period to meet with a counselor or to read

- Use a permanent pass to leave class and go to the counseling office as needed; teachers were all in favor of this

- Meet weekly with the counselor and social worker

In November, her teachers met with J and her mom. Our main goal was to make sure she met the requirements for a diploma, therefore, we allowed J to drop one more class and use the time to study in the library; her schedule could be further reduced if needed. The teachers were seeing more and more signs of stress, and they all agreed to follow the plan.

J became increasingly withdrawn from her peers and teachers. She was in touch with the members of her New Orleans senior class by e-mail, and, although this seemed a relief to her, she missed her previous life. J sought more contact with her counselor because she had great ambitions and high SAT scores; she wanted to apply to top colleges, but she no longer had a transcript. Her counselor explained the situation to each college and all were very willing to help allay some of her fears. Because J was a talented writer, her counselor suggested journaling about her experience and feelings. J shared her poems and essays with her counselor as well as her English teacher, and submitted her writing as part of her college application. Although all her school records were destroyed, her counselor in New Orleans was able to reconstruct J's transcript, and the headmaster certified her grades. J was still depressed, but she mobilized energy around the college search process and chatted online with her New Orleans friends about where they applied. We felt confident that J would be accepted and kept reassuring her of our belief.

As we worked with J, we discussed her symptoms of posttraumatic stress disorder, giving her permission to accept that she was working as hard as she could. She did not have to be perfect and needed to allow herself space and let others support her when she needed help. We were amazed by J's resilience and determination to go on with her life and could feel her resolve even when she was "down."

In mid-January, her parents appeared at the counseling office. J was nervous and reluctant to report to us that her former classmates' parents rented a building to bring the seniors together as a class in New Orleans. Some of the teachers were returning, the administration was in place, and J's classmates wanted her to return.

J was worried that because we had done so much for her, we would be disappointed that she was leaving. Although we were sad to see J leave, her classmates and counselors were very happy for her opportunity. She is now in college, and occasionally e-mails her W-L counselor, and she has stopped by to show us she is okay. J will always be a part of the spirit of our counseling office.

Impact of Virginia Tech Shooting

Each year, W-L sends about 8% of its senior class to Virginia Tech and many staff members, former students, and parents are alumni of the university. When we learned of the Virginia Tech shootings on the morning of April 16, 2007, our school community was stunned.

Word of the tragedy moved quickly around the school. Students were told that if they needed support, our counseling staff was available, and counselors reached out to students whose siblings were on campus and those who planned to attend Virginia Tech that fall. Our principal, a Virginia Tech graduate, sent a letter home explaining what the counseling office was doing during this time and how it would focus on the aftermath of the tragedy. The conversations about moving to college campuses continued; some worried about safety while others felt little impact, but everyone talked about it. The focus was on the sadness we all felt for the victims and their families and the pride in our own school community; after all, we were a school that came together in times of crisis to support each other.

A few days later several students wanted to hold a candlelight vigil for the victims. Some students attended but many did not. A sense of normalcy had started to return to our community and most of us returned to our routines. As counselors, we must reach students where they are emotionally in times of crisis and recognize that not everyone will be in the same place or need the same type of support.

Benefits of Having a Plan

The need for establishing a collaborative program in crisis situations is clear, particularly when outside events affect the counseling staff as well as the students. A strong counseling department allows for collaborating with colleagues, supporting each other, and knowing we can rely on colleagues to debrief and assist us in our work. We have protocols for handling traumatic events and are trained in counseling strategies to help support the school population, as well as individual students and persons who experience grief, distress, or personal crises. When large-scale events occur, we first meet to plan as a department, troubleshoot potential issues or concerns, develop an action plan, and proceed. The plan may include classroom presentations, group counseling, individual counseling, and referrals to outside resources. Encouraging a return to normalcy and routine after a set time helps students feel "normal" again. Allowing excessive unstructured time for grieving can be detrimental, whereas returning to the typical routines and structures helps students feel a sense of security.

In tough times, the most important role counselors can play is being the familiar face around the school. It is difficult for students to connect immediately with outsiders who may come in to assist; familiarity is very comforting in coping with traumatic events. When a good rapport with students and positive relationships already exist, it is easier for students to feel comfortable and trust counselors.

After a crisis, a collaborative counseling department becomes the backbone of the school, helping students build resiliency and learn how to bounce back. Counselors must be proactive throughout the year because this makes handling the tough times a little better. When we have relationships with students, we can truly make a difference.

Marie Bullock, PhD is director of Counseling Services.

Jessica Baith and *Caitlin Rose* are counselors.

All are in the Counseling Department at Washington-Lee High School in Arlington, VA.

Coping with Death: What School Counselors Can Do

25

Maureen M. Underwood

In recent years, schools have developed policies and procedures to address the plethora of administrative issues related to managing the impact of a traumatic loss event on the functioning of the school community (Underwood & Dunne-Maxim, 1997). Policies provide a general direction for a response guided by both best practice principles and an articulation of the school's critical but limited role in recovery. What they may not address are the practical implications for school staff when a death occurs. The following guidelines are from seminars provided by New Jersey-based Center for Families Going On After Loss.

Working With Grieving Students

Your school's policies and procedures are your starting point. For student or faculty deaths, these policies should provide a framework for integrating your role and responsibilities into the overall school response plan. Crisis teams may provide faculty with a written announcement of the death for reading to students and an outline of where and how to refer students needing support. A crisis team member might follow the class schedule of the deceased to address student questions and concerns. Emergency faculty meetings are scheduled for updates and briefings.

In situations such as the death of a parent, your role may be less clear. Usually in-class announcements about parental deaths are limited to the classroom of the bereaved student, especially in elementary or middle school. In high school, a simple, limited announcement may be made in a homeroom if it is appropriate. "I have some sad news. Alisha's mother died over the weekend. I know you will join me in sending her kind thoughts."

Whatever the circumstances of the death, it is very helpful to pay attention to the reactions of students. Although you expect students who had a relationship with the deceased to be affected by the news, remember that this event also has an impact on students whose connection to the death might not be apparent to you. Watch for students whose behavior or performance has changed since the event and alert the student's counselor or crisis team. If your school does not have a crisis or intervention team, you can talk to the parent or guardian about your observations.

Pay attention throughout the year to those students who were especially affected by the death. A decline in school performance, even months after the death, may signal delayed grief symptoms. Share your concerns with the counselors, teams, or parents and encourage their intervention.

If your school does not have policies and procedures relating to responding to deaths, talk with your school administrator about their utility. In the absence of a comprehensive district policy and school resources, you will rely more on community resources for support, so investigate what is available before you are in a crisis.

Reintegrating Students after a Death

Balance the uniqueness of each child and the individuality of grief reactions with the basic premise of respecting the privacy of the bereaved. Most children do not want their classmates to have much information about their loss. Bereaved students of all ages are often embarrassed by expressions of sympathy from peers, counselors, or faculty members, which they sometimes construe as "people feeling sorry for me." Especially as they approach middle school, students often feel that they have the right to share as much or as little information as they want. Many bereaved students report feeling different from their classmates at a time when fitting into their peer group is extremely important.

To acknowledge the death and respect the privacy of the bereaved student, invite middle school students to write individual sympathy notes to the bereaved student, especially if he or she will be absent for an extended period of time. The entire class can sign a sympathy card that is mailed to the home of the bereaved. Communicating personal expressions of grief in writing is often easier than verbalizing them and can reduce the anxiety that surrounds "not knowing the right thing to say." Asking students how they would like to be treated in a similar situation can sometimes facilitate sensitive and empathic responses.

In some cases, the bereaved returns to school the day after the death or before the funeral. The student may feel more comfortable with the routine, predictability, and support available in school. After acknowledging the loss, ask the student, "Is there any way I can help you over the next few days?"

Most bereaved students are absent for several days and require reintegration into the classroom. It is essential to treat the student's return to the classroom like absences related to other causes such as illnesses. Your consistency in response will not single out the bereaved for unwanted special attention.

Privately and simply acknowledge the death if you have not already done so. "I was sorry to hear about your mom's death." Validate the student's return to school. "I'm glad to see you back in school. We've missed you." You can suggest this same response to students who are unsure about what to say to the returning student.

Discuss missed class work and assignments and make arrangements for completion. Adjust immediate expectations; using a short-term strategy can reduce some of the academic pressure. "I know this has been extremely difficult for you and you are having trouble concentrating on school work. What do you think about a take-home assignment instead of having to turn in all your missed work?"

Encourage the student to use school resources. "If you need to talk to someone during the school day, you can always go to (name of school counselor or resource person)." Monitor the student's academic performance and social interactions from a discreet distance.

The long-term issues in reintegration require gentle and persistent attention to the academic performance and social behavior of the bereaved child. Decline in

performance may be expected in the aftermath of the death. Make realistic accommodations to compensate for the difficulty the bereaved may have in concentrating, studying, or completing assignments. However, these accommodations should only be used on a short-term basis. Students who have had their academic standards excused for longer periods of time sometimes report they think their teachers feel sorry for them by not requiring them to work competitively with the rest of their class.

Students who continue to have difficulty after 4 to 6 weeks may be experiencing emotional sequelae to the death such as depression and should be referred to the appropriate sources for assessment. The mental health professional who makes the assessment can guide teachers in their classroom expectations. It is critical that counselors and teachers become part of the team that is working to meet the needs of the grieving student.

Students Who Show No Reaction

We may be applying our adult understanding of appropriate grief reactions to children. Grief in children looks different from grief in adults; the way children react to most things in life is based on their emotional maturity and developmental level. Children generally approach death with emotional caution, which is similar to how they approach all life events that they find emotionally challenging. Because their immature ego structures do not have the capacity to tolerate intense emotions for extended periods of time, they experience feelings briefly and then back away from them.

When viewed from an adult perspective, children may seem to be denying what has happened, but they are simply trying to deal with the reality of the loss in small, more manageable doses. When they are ready, they will approach the death more directly again. Children work through painful feelings differently than adults. The play of children can serve many functions including helping children deal with and resolve painful emotions. Physical play or creative arts provide children with the outlets they need for emotional expression as well as to keep them connected to their peers from whom they receive support and validation. Frequent illness, somatic complaints, and visits to the school nurse are common reactions of grieving children. It can be helpful to point out to children how we sometimes use our bodies to express feelings that are difficult to put into words.

There are no "inappropriate" initial reactions to learning about a death; all reactions are emotionally functional. For example, silliness and joking are well known cover-ups for anxiousness and worry. Anger can often reflect our disappointment that the deceased did not take better care of himself or herself or the fact that this valued person is no longer an active part of our life. A simple statement like, "I want to understand a little more about why you feel this way," can sometimes cut through the cover-up feeling and get to that deeper level.

Another important difference about grief in childhood is that the meaning of a loss, especially the death of a parent or caregiver, will change as children grow and mature. At each developmental stage and passage, the reality of how that loss affects their lives will need to be reevaluated and re-grieved.

TOPICS THAT MAY UPSET GRIEVING STUDENTS

Some students are vulnerable to material that stirs memories and feelings about traumatic life events such as the death or disasters such as September 11 or Hurricane Katrina. Some subjects and topics in the curriculum that might create upsetting reminders are:

- Language Arts: stories about death, suicide, homicide
- History: traumatic historical events, upsetting current events
- Driver's Education: discussions about driver safety, car accidents, drinking and driving
- Health Education: death, suicide, alcoholism
- Science: natural disasters (floods, tornadoes, hurricanes, forest fires; forensic science)

In addition to specific curriculum content, also attend to language when material is presented. Although slang expressions are acceptable in personal conversation, they have the potential to be offensive to vulnerable students; for example, graphic descriptions used for violent deaths such as *blowing one's brains out*, being *wiped out*, or *knocked off*. Equally offensive are descriptive idioms for mental illness: being nuts, wacko, or looney. Chances are good that there will be students in your classes who have personal experience with one of life's calamities. Sensitivity to the way in which these topics are discussed can go a long way in decreasing the stigma that often surrounds them.

Review curriculum materials for topics that might touch on any type of loss or trauma so you can anticipate potentially challenging area and discuss with the student. If they indicate that they would be uncomfortable remaining in class, give them an alternative (e.g., work in the library).

The students you do not know about are more difficult. When you review class rosters for students who might have had recent exposure to traumatic loss, include students who have been affected by some type of loss within the last several years because their losses can be reactivated even after time has elapsed. Consider the use of a general disclaimer at the beginning of the school year. For example, "Sometimes things we talk about in the classroom can be upsetting. If we are covering a topic that is personally upsetting or distressing to you, let me know privately, and I will see how we can handle it." Ask the counselor or crisis response team for suggestions for responding to students who might get upset in the classroom.

CHILDREN'S VIEW OF TRAUMATIC EVENTS

Understanding the ways children conceptualize traumatic events is an essential first step. Children view traumatic events differently than adults do. Unless they are personally touched by the event, they might not react at all. Traumatic events that take place in different states or communities may seem worlds apart, and events in their hometown may feel distant unless someone whom the children know personally is involved. Because children tend to focus on the immediate present rather than on the past or future, they are able to put all events, even traumatic ones, behind them in a short period of time. However, when a child is personally impacted, reminders of the trauma keep the event a part of the child's current reality.

Young children may underreact to trauma because they can only tolerate intense feelings for a short period of time. Children may experience an emotion deeply, and then unconsciously back away from it until they again feel prepared to deal with its intensity. What may look like avoidance and denial to adults is an effective coping strategy for children. Take advantage of the opportunities to talk about the trauma when children present them. Children will be more alarmed if the adults in their lives seem upset and emotional and less affected if the adults react in calm, reassuring ways.

HELPFUL INTERVENTIONS AND RESOURCES

Focus on recovery efforts. In every disaster, you can see examples of courage and heroism in the way that people respond. Seek out these stories and use them in your classroom discussions. They provide balance to the tragedy as examples of the resiliency of the human spirit. Encourage students to consider ways to help those affected by the event. Active involvement in remediation counteracts the helplessness that is endemic to natural or provoked disasters. Community agencies offer disaster-related support services and are staffed with professionals trained in disaster response and recovery.

For both adults and children, recovery from trauma means putting the experience behind them and getting back to "normal life." For children, normal life consists of going to school and playing. Anything adults can do to create a safe and predictable environment will help children in trauma resolution. The structure and predictability of the school can create an island of stability for children during a crisis. The consistency of the rules and expectations of the school setting provide a sense of control and order, particularly when events in the environment seem out of control.

Maureen Underwood, LCSW, is a licensed clinical social worker in private practice in Morristown, NJ and co-author of Managing Sudden Traumatic Loss in the Schools: New Jersey Adolescent Suicide Prevention Project.

REFERENCE

Underwood, M., & Dunne-Maxim, K. (1997). *Managing sudden traumatic loss in the schools* (rev. ed.). Piscataway, NJ: University of Medicine and Dentistry of New Jersey (UMDNJ), University Behavioral HealthCare (UBHC).

ADDITIONAL RESOURCES:

www.counseling.org
Resources and links dealing with death, grief, and coping with national disasters

www.allkidsgrieve.org
Annotated bibliography and a section on "Overcoming Resistance to Loss and Death Curriculum in the Schools"

http://www.americanhospice.org/index.php
Article on writing a condolence note to a grieving child or adolescent as well as handouts

http://compassionbooks.com
Annotated bibliography of books for purchase dealing with types of deaths including a section for teachers and schools

www.crusebereavementcare.org.uk/
Information for schools and a brochure for children, "After Someone Dies"

www.dougy.org
Publications and information by respected center for grieving children and families

www.familymanagement.com
Article on children and grief written in English and Spanish

http://www.nasponline.org/
Information about children's grief and coping with large-scale disasters such as September 11 and Hurricane Katrina

www.sptsnj.org/
Information helpful in understanding and managing a student's reactions to suicide

http://teacher.scholastic.com/professional/bruceperry/child_loss.htm
Answers to questions about helping children deal with traumatic events from a national expert

http://smhp.psych.ucla.edu
Resources and presentations on children and grief from the UCLA School Mental Health Project

Intervening with School Students After Terrorist Acts

26

Gerald A. Juhnke

Elementary, middle, and high school students witnessing or experiencing terrorist attacks can experience negative residual psychological effects such as posttraumatic stress, generalized anxiety, and adjustment disorders.

Terrorists acts in New York City and Washington, DC, mass tragedies at Columbine High School, and shootings at Virginia Tech and Northern Illinois University, have led to the implementation of school crisis management plans to prepare for what counselors, teachers, and administrators hope will never happen again. Elementary, middle, and high school students are now accustomed to lockdown drills and evacuation practices in an increasingly unsafe world.

School counselors and mental health professionals working with these children need to be knowledgeable regarding interventions that provide opportunities for students to discuss openly immediate and future concerns, cumulative stressors resulting from ongoing terrorist threats, and post-terrorism psychopathology (e.g., anxiety, distress).

Thus, the intent of this chapter is to familiarize readers with basic Critical Incident Stress Debriefing (CISD), outline the distinct differences between CISD and the adapted family debriefing model for school students, and describe how mental health professionals can use this model as a post-terrorism response intervention.

CISD vs Adapted Family Debriefing Model

CISD is a widely recognized, small-group process originally developed to be used with adult emergency workers (e.g., firefighters, emergency medical technicians) who encounter particularly distressing situations (Mitchell & Everly, 1993). This seven-stage model uses adult peer facilitators. Some have cited CISD as a viable intervention with school-age children and adolescents who experience violence or suicide (O'Hara, Taylor, & Simpson, 1994; Thompson, 1990).

Yet, CISD originally was developed solely for adult use and did not take into account the special developmental cognitive, physical, and emotional needs of school-age children and their families. The adapted family debriefing model for school students, however, was developed as an assessment and intervention method specifically for elementary, middle, and high-school students exposed to violence (Juhnke, 1997).

Compared to CISD's single group experience, the adapted family debriefing model for school students requires two separate debriefing experiences. The first is with students' parents and does not include students. The second is a joint student-parent debriefing experience. Unlike the traditional adult CISD process, which utilizes nonprofessional adult peer facilitators, this model for school students requires the use of trained mental health professionals who have specific knowledge regarding children's developmental needs and an appropriate graduate degree that included clinically relevant courses and internship experiences. Mental health professionals using the model should be familiar with the social, intellectual, and psychological development stages corresponding to the students being served.

Description

Roles. The primary team member roles within the adapted family debriefing model for school students are leader, co-leader, and doorkeeper. The leader briefly explains the debriefing process, creates a sup-

121

portive milieu, identifies those experiencing excessive levels of emotional discomfort, and directs team members via hand signals to intervene with distraught students or parents.

In addition, the leader discusses with parents and students common symptom clusters experienced by children who: (a) have personally experienced terrorist acts or have suffered loss as a result of such acts (e.g., the death of a grandparent or sibling resulting from terrorism), (b) have witnessed (via the news media) terrorist acts or their aftermath, (c) understand the potential for continued terrorist acts, or (d) experience the cumulative effects of multiple terrorist acts.

Specifically, the leader discusses relevant depression, posttraumatic stress disorder (PTSD), adjustment disorders, and generalized anxiety disorder criteria. The leader normalizes symptoms and encourages parents to recognize more severe symptomatology, which may require additional counseling (e.g., recurrent encopresis, persistent outbursts of anger, chronic hypervigilance).

Co-leaders add relevant comments during the session and support the leader. Most importantly, co-leaders give immediate support to students and parents who become emotionally distraught. They also help prevent disruption that may otherwise inhibit group dynamics. The title of the third role is "doorkeeper." Persons performing this important role prevent nonparticipants from entering the session. Thus, journalists and others not seeking treatment are prevented from speaking with participants during the debriefing experience. Doorkeepers also prevent severely distraught students or parents from bolting from sessions.

Before the Debriefing. Before the debriefing, team members should be apprised of the circumstances surrounding the debriefing. For example, is the debriefing the result of a death of a fellow student or teacher who died as a result of a terrorist act or due to the fact that children reside within the same city or near the site of a terrorist act? Or, is the debriefing in response to cumulative effects of terrorist activities?

Additionally, teams should learn whether students' parents are at increased risk due to their occupations (e.g., firefighters, law enforcement) or have a greater probability of being activated into military service (e.g., National Guard, Army Reserves). These factors likely will have an influence upon participants' perceptions of terrorist acts and the moods with which the students and parents present.

Separate Debriefings for Parents and Students. Parent

and student needs are often different and cannot be addressed adequately through a single session. Thus, the first session is conducted with parents. It is important to keep the number of parents in these sessions small (i.e., fewer than 12). Parents most often express frustration and anger regarding their inability to adequately protect their children from terrorism. Many will perceive the situation as "hopeless" and feel the events and dangers are "out of their control."

Thus, it is imperative that the team keep parents focused on the immediate needs of their children and not make promises related to future student safety. Such promises cannot be guaranteed and they detract from the students' immediate reeds. Parents need to be reminded often that the primary goals of this session are to: (a) educate parents regarding possible symptoms their children may exhibit, (b) offer available referral sources, and (c) remind parents regarding their role in validating their children (which is not the same as validating possibly unfounded concerns their children may have) and normalizing their children's' concerns.

Student survivors of terrorism often are responding to their own perceived needs and concerns. Younger children especially are vulnerable emotionally and look to parents and teachers for protection. Often they require reassurances of safety and indications from parents that the crisis is over. Therefore, the team must encourage a sense of security and calmness during the joint student-parent session. Team members can foster this by slowing their speech rates and lowering their voice tones. Whenever possible, debriefings should occur in quiet rooms away from hallway and playground noise. Movable furniture that is comfortable for parents and children alike is helpful.

During this joint student-parent debriefing, two circles are formed. No more than five or six students of similar ages should sit in the inner circle with friends or familiar peers presenting with similar concerns. Parents should sit behind their children. This parental presence promotes a perception of stability, unity, and support, which can be heartening to students. An additional gesture of support is parents placing their hands on their child's shoulders. This should only occur when children are receptive to such gestures.

SEVEN STEPS OF THE MODEL

Introduction step. During this step, the team leader identifies members of the team and establishes rules for the debriefing experience. Participants are asked to identify persons who may not belong in the room. Identified persons not directly related to the children or debriefing process are then asked to leave. Confidentiality and its limits are explained in terms understandable to the students and participants are encouraged not to discuss what is said within the session outside the debriefing room. All participants are encouraged to remain for the entire debriefing. The leader states that the primary purpose of the debriefing session is to help student survivors of terrorism better understand their feelings about the specific terrorist act, increase their coping skills related to continued terrorist threats, and gain increased levels of solace.

Fact gathering step. The second step of the process is fact gathering. Typically if the debriefing is related to a specific terrorist act that team members did not experience but student survivors did, the leader will begin by reporting that the team was not present during the terrorist act and asking children to report what the experience was like for them. If the debriefing is related to recent terrorist acts that the students observed via news media coverage rather than directly experienced, the leader may begin by asking about what the students saw on television.

Those speaking are encouraged to give their name and state what they did when they first saw or heard about the terrorism. Emphasis is placed upon telling the facts of what each student saw or encountered, and team members do not push participants to describe their feelings about the incident. However, should students begin sharing feelings, the team leader and co-leaders should acknowledge emotions expressed and indicate that these feelings are normal.

Thought step. This step is transitional and helps participants move from the cognitive domain to the affective domain. The leader asks questions related to what students thought when the terrorism erupted (e.g., "What was your first thought when you saw the airplane fly into the Twin Towers?"). During this step, it is crucial to continue to validate and normalize each student's reported thoughts and perceptions.

Reaction step. The thought step can quickly give way to the emotionally charged reaction step. Here, the focus should be kept upon participants' sharing their reactions to the terrorism. Typically, the leader will start with a question such as, "What has been the most difficult part of seeing the airplane fly into the Twin Towers?"

Symptom step. During the symptom step, the leader helps direct the group from the affective domain back to the cognitive domain. As emotionally charged reactions begin to subside, the leader uses age-appropriate language to ask students about any physical, cognitive, or affective symptoms experienced since the violent episode. For example, "Have any of you felt kind of tingly in your tummies since you saw this on television?" Often the leader will discuss symptoms such as nausea, trembling hands, inability to concentrate, or feelings of anxiety.

Typically, the leader will ask those who have encountered such experiences to raise their hands. Such a show of hands helps normalize the symptoms and often helps survivors experience relief.

Teaching step. Symptoms experienced by group members are reported in age-appropriate ways as being both normal and expected. Possible future symptoms can be briefly described (e.g., recurring dreams of being attacked, restricted range of affect). This helps both parents and students better understand symptoms that they may encounter in the future and gives permission to discuss such symptoms should they arise. The group leader may ask, "What little things have you done or noticed your friends, teachers, and parents doing that have helped you handle this situation so well?" This question suggests that the students are doing well and helps them begin to look for signs of progress rather than continuing to focus upon past or future terrorist episodes. Sometimes older students will express feelings of support from peers, teachers, or parents.

Younger students may use active fantasy to help them better cope with their fears or concerns. An example of such active fantasy is a child pretending that he or she is a hero who disarms a terrorist and protects the other children from harm.

Re-entry step. The re-entry step attempts to place some closure on the experience and allows survivors and their parents to discuss further concerns or thoughts. The leader may ask students and parents to revisit pressing issues, discuss new topics, or mention thoughts that might help the debriefing process come to a more successful end. After addressing any issues brought forward by the students or parents, the debriefing team makes a few closing comments related to any apparent group progress or visible group support. A handout written at an age-appropriate reading level for students and another written for adults discussing common reactions and symptoms can be helpful.

Younger children may prefer drawing faces to depict

how they are feeling (e.g., anxious, sad, frightened). Later parents can use these pictures as conversation starters with their children at home. Handouts should list a 24-hour helpline number and include the work telephone number for the student's school counselor. Often, it is helpful to introduce parents to their child's school counselor at the debriefing.

POST-SESSION ACTIVITIES

After the session, team members should mingle with parents and children as refreshments are served. Team members should be looking for those who appear shaken or are experiencing severe distress. These persons should be encouraged to immediately meet with a counselor. The promotion of peer support (both parent and student) is important. Students and parents should be encouraged to telephone one another over the next few days to aid in the recovery process.

SUMMARY AND CONCLUSION

The described adapted family debriefing model for school students demonstrates promise for helping both student survivors of terrorism and their parents to cope with potentially negative residual psychological and social effects. The model has distinct differences from traditional CISD and was developed specifically for school-age students. It is relatively easy to implement and can be modified to meet the specific needs of students and parents alike.

Gerald A. Juhnke, PhD, LPC, MAC, is professor and doctoral program director at the University of Texas, San Antonio. Reprinted with permission from "Helping People Cope with Tragedy and Grief," published by ERIC Counseling and Student Services Clearinghouse.

REFERENCES

Juhnke, C. A. (1997). After school violence: An adapted critical incident stress debriefing model for student survivors and their parents. *Elementary School Guidance & Counseling, 31,* 163–170.

Mitchell, J. T., & Everly, C. S. (1993). *Critical incident stress debriefing (CISD): An operations manual for the prevention of traumatic stress among emergency services and disaster workers.* Ellicott City, MD: Chevron Press.

O'Hara, D. M., Taylor, R., & Simpson, K. (1994). Critical incident stress debriefing: Bereavement support in schools developing a role for an LEA education psychology service. *Educational Psychology in Practice, 10,* 27–33.

Thompson, R. (1990). *Post-traumatic loss debriefing: Providing immediate support for survivors of suicide or sudden loss.* Greensboro, NC: ERIC Clearinghouse on Counseling and Student Services. (ERIC Document Reproduction Services No. ED 315 708).

Section Six

Helping Children Cope with Tragedy

RING AROUND THE ROSIE: PLAY THERAPY FOR TRAUMATIZED CHILDREN

27

Jennifer Baggerly

Two months after Hurricane Katrina, Donny, a 5-year-old African American boy, repeatedly jumps off tables and says he is drowning in the rising water. Two months after her father was wounded and permanently disabled while serving in Iraq, Katelyn, a 7-year-old Latina girl, repeatedly throws dolls in the air and runs to them with a medical kit, but they die. What is the meaning of Donny's and Katelyn's play? How should counselors respond?

MEANING AND FUNCTION OF CHILDREN'S PLAY

Both Donny and Katelyn experienced a trauma defined as "an event that involves actual or threatened death or serious injury . . . or witnessing an event . . . or threat of death or injury experienced by a family member" (American Psychiatric Association, 2000, p. 463). Clearly, their play does have meaning. Counselors must recognize that toys are children's words, and play is their language (Landreth, 2002). Children often repeatedly reenact a specific traumatic event in their play, referred to as posttraumatic play (Terr, 1990). A poignant example of posttraumatic play was seen in England during the bubonic plague of the Middle Ages when children played "Ring Around the Rosie" (Terr, 1990). Reexamine the meaning of words in this familiar children's song:

Ring around the rosie: A red lesion circled the upper arm of people infected with black plague.

Pocket full of posies: Flower petals were placed in bubonic plague victims' pockets to reduce the odor of rotting flesh.

Ashes, ashes: Since burial of infected bodies was impractical, ashes from cremated corpses filled the air.

We all fall down: People drop dead.

Although an understanding of such traumatic play may be disturbing, it is essential that counselors understand the function of children's traumatic play. Essentially, children reenact trauma in their play in an attempt to transfer indelible images of disturbing events from their implicit memory into their explicit memory. (See Chapter 28 .) The "fight or flight" and "freeze or surrender" responses decrease children's language functioning (Perry, Pollard, Blakely, Baker, & Vigilante, 1995). In addition, children under 11 years old are in concrete cognitive functioning. Consequently, traumatized children often do not have the language to process frightening images out of their implicit memories. Yet, children use play to create a concrete narrative of traumatic events in an attempt to master these frightening images. According to Piaget (1962), this symbolic play helps children reconstruct their crisis experience and resolve internal conflicts. In fact, play has been called the "royal road" to recovery from trauma for preschoolers (Lieberman & Van Horn, 2008).

RATIONALE FOR PLAY THERAPY

Because children use play to process traumatic events, can they just play it out on their own without counseling? Not always. According to Terr (1990), posttraumatic play is repeated obsessively and does not relieve anxiety. Children with risk factors such as prior trauma, ethnic or racial minority, female gender, younger age, and intense and prolonged exposure to frightening events (La Greca, 2008) may need play therapy to prevent or treat symptoms (Gil, 2006; Lieberman & Van Horn, 2008). If children repeatedly reenact traumatic play and have other ongoing symptoms weeks after an event, then they need to be referred for play therapy. Why? Terr (1990) found that children do not

127

stop their posttraumatic play until they reach an emotional understanding. To reach this emotional understanding, children need therapeutic interventions to help them verbalize the cognitive, emotional, behavioral, physiological, and spiritual content of their narrative. (See Chapter 28.)

Play therapy helps children process their trauma narrative, aids in resolving symptoms, builds resiliency, and resumes the process of normal development (Gil, 2006). Play therapy goes beyond the play techniques and activities used in initial trauma interventions such as psychological first aid as described in the Chapter 28. Play therapy should be used in the *recovery* phase and *return to life* phase with children, ages 2 through 10 years old, who display ongoing trauma symptoms. Research demonstrates that play therapy has decreased symptoms in children who experienced various traumatic events such as domestic violence (Tyndall-Lind, Landreth & Giordano, 2001), sexual abuse (Reyes & Asbrand, 2005), homelessness (Baggerly, 2004), and natural disasters (Shen, 2002). A meta-analysis of 93 play therapy outcome research studies showed a large positive effect of .80 on treatment outcomes, indicating substantial change in children (Bratton, Ray, & Rhine, 2005).

PROCEDURES OF PLAY THERAPY AND TRAUMA RECOVERY PROTOCOL

Herman (1997) described a three-stage trauma recovery protocol in which therapists help clients establish safety, reconstruct the trauma story, and restore connection between the survivor and their community. For children, this trauma recovery protocol can be implemented within play therapy, providing children an opportunity to heal using their natural language of play (Baggerly, 2004; Gil, 2006). One humanistic play therapy approach that facilitates this three-stage protocol is child-centered play therapy, defined by Landreth (2002) as:

A dynamic interpersonal *relationship* between a child and a therapist *trained* in play therapy procedures who provides *selected* play materials and facilitates the development of a *safe* relationship for the child to fully express and *explore self* (feelings, thoughts, experiences, and behaviors) through the child's natural medium of communication, *play* [Italics added] p. 16.

Key words in this definition are (a) *relationship*, needed to develop trust for the trauma narrative; (b) *trained play therapist* who has developed specific knowledge and skills

in play therapy; (c) *selected play materials* to promote the child's story; (d) *safe*, so children can relax enough to tell the story, (d) *explore self*, in cognitive, emotional, behavioral, physiological, and spiritual realms; and (e) *play*, the language to communicate traumatic images "stuck" in the implicit memory. Child-centered play therapy principles and procedures that correspond with Herman's (1997) trauma protocol are described below.

Play Therapy Procedures to "Establish Safety"

Child-centered play therapists create a safe environment through a warm, inviting playroom with toys specially selected. Toys recommended by Landreth (2002) as well as toys related to the trauma healing process are: (a) real life toys such as ethnic doll families, puppets, cars, rescue vehicles, medical kits, and money; (b) acting out or aggressive release toys such as bop bag, toy soldiers, alligator puppet, gun, knife, and weapons that were used in a specific trauma; and (c) creative expression or emotional release toys such as sand, water, Play Doh, blocks, and dress-up clothes representing people related to the trauma. To create a safe relationship, child-centered play therapists implement Axline's (1969) eight basic principles including: (a) accepting children exactly as they are, symptoms and all; (b) allowing children to lead the process and pace of their trauma stories; (c) respecting children's ability to solve their own problems; and (d) not hurrying the trauma recovery process.

These principles to establish safety are facilitated by several procedures. Returning responsibility through statements such as, "In here you can decide what to do," and "That's something you can try," communicates confidence in children's self-direction and healing ability. Building self-esteem and providing encouragement through statements such as, "You did it on your own," and "You know a lot about doctoring others," build children's motivation for their healing process. Safety of self, others, and property is maintained through: (a) therapeutic limit setting through acknowledging the child's feeling, for example, "I know you are angry;" (b) communicating the limit, for example, "I'm not for hitting;" and (c) targeting an alternative, such as, "You can choose to hit the bop bag." This procedure also helps children develop self-control and realization that although they cannot control events, they can control their behavior.

In addition, play therapists can integrate cognitive behavioral therapy (CBT) procedures such as: (a) deep breathing through playful activities of blowing soap bubbles or pinwheels; (b) progressive muscle relaxation by tensing like a tin man and relaxing like a rag doll; (c) focusing on positive images by drawing happy places, meditating on peaceful places, or singing positive songs; (d) thought stopping by clapping hands and holding up a picture of a stop sign; and (e) identifying ways to ask for help from safe friends and adults (Baggerly, 2006; Cohen, Mannarino, & Deblinger, 2006; Gil, 2006). These CBT procedures help children increase their sense of safety and decrease hyperarousal, intrusive memories, and avoidance symptoms.

Play Therapy Procedures to "Reconstruct the Trauma Story"

Children will reconstruct their trauma stories, often unconsciously, during non-directed play. For example, 7-year-old Donny, who survived Hurricane Katrina, jumped off the table and pretended to drown but doctored himself back to life. Then he shot the dart gun around the room yelling "Stay away from me and my family!" Donny was attempting to master and make sense of events related to the Hurricane Katrina evacuation and violence in the Superdome. The medical rescue play of 5-year-old Katelyn, whose father was wounded in Iraq, was also her attempt to confront her fears, gain control over the overwhelming event, and maintain a safe distance through symbolic play.

To facilitate healing while children play out their trauma story, play therapists implement several procedures.

1. Play therapists *track children's behavior* and reflect play content through statements such as, "You fell in the water and need help," or "The doll flew up in the air and is hurt," to verbalize children's trauma narrative.
2. They *reflect children's feelings* during their play through statements such as, "You are very scared," or "The doll is worried," to help children reach an emotional understanding of an event and normalize their response.
3. Play therapists *facilitate understanding* through statements such as, "You are trying to protect your family," or "You know someone needs to rescue the doll and you wish you could," to provide children insight into their behavior.
4. They *expand the meaning* through statements such as, "You are relieved to get help for yourself and your family just like you did after Hurricane Katrina," or "You want to be caring and helpful to the doll just like you do for your father," to help children make connections between present, past, and future.

As children attempt to develop mastery over their trauma story, counselors should be mindful of typical play therapy stages. According to Landreth (2002), the four stages that children progress through are:

1. Exploratory and relationship building
2. Generalized expressions of aggression, anxiety, and other feelings
3. Specific symbolization in play and narrow expression of feelings
4. Mastery of specific situations, resolution, and closure

Thus, patience is needed for the process. If needed, play therapists can facilitate psychosocial education activities by: reading story books related to the child's trauma or to facilitate anxiety, stress, or anger management; helping the child write his or her own restorative trauma story; and creating memory boxes or other art projects (Baggerly, 2006; Gil, 2006). Offering children a snack and a comfortable beanbag chair is often a helpful transition between child-directed play and psychosocial education.

Play Therapy Procedures to "Restore Connections with Community"

For Herman's (1997) final stage of trauma recovery, play therapists can help children restore connections with their community through several procedures. First, play therapists provide *parent consultation,* informing them of expected symptoms and normalizing the process, teaching them to implement the therapeutic strategies described above (Guerney, 2000), encouraging them to reassure their children of their protection, and recommending they provide acceptance and comfort when their children experience symptoms (Shelby, 2000). Second, play therapists provide *teacher consultation* informing them of typical symptoms, asking them to communicate acceptance and protection to children, and encouraging the facilitation of friendships for children. Finally, play therapists may provide *group play therapy and psychosocial educational groups* for children who experienced the same or similar trauma, helping them develop a sense of belonging, universality, and connection with others (Sweeney & Homeyer, 1999).

RESILIENCY AND HOPE

The developmentally appropriate approach of play therapy helps children like Donny and Katelyn resolve their posttraumatic play and other ongoing symptoms and build resiliency to thrive in and for their communities. Counselors providing play therapy can help children transform posttraumatic play from a disturbing "Ring Around the Rosie" game into a more positive circle of people who give support and hope for a bright future.

Jennifer Baggerly, PhD, LMHC-S, RPT-S, is associate professor in the Counselor Education Program and is director of the Graduate Certificate in Play Therapy at the University of South Florida. She is also a field traumatologist.

REFERENCES

American Psychiatric Association. (2000). *Diagnostic and statistical manual of mental disorders* (4th ed., text rev.). Washington, DC: Author.

Axline, V. M. (1969). *Play therapy.* New York: Ballantine Books.

Baggerly, J. N. (2004). The effects of child-centered group play therapy on self-concept, depression, and anxiety of children who are homeless. *International Journal of Play Therapy, 13*(2), 31–51.

Baggerly, J. N. (2005). Ring around the rosie: Play therapy for traumatized children. In J. Webber, D. Bass, & R. Yep (Eds.), *Terrorism, trauma, and tragedies: A counselor's guide to preparing and responding* (pp. 93–96). Alexandria, VA: American Counseling Association Foundation.

Baggerly, J. N. (2006). Preparing play therapists for disaster response: Principles and procedures. *International Journal of Play Therapy, 15*(2), 59–82.

Bratton, S. C., Ray, D., & Rhine, T. (2005). The efficacy of play therapy with children: A meta-analytic review of treatment outcomes. *Professional Psychology: Research and Practice, 36*(4), 376–390.

Cohen, J. A., Mannarino, A. P., & Deblinger, E. (2006). *Treating trauma and traumatic grief in children and adolescents.* New York: Guilford Press.

Gil, E. (2006). *Helping abused and traumatized children: Integrating directive and nondirective approaches.* New York: Guilford Press.

Guerney, L. (2000). Filial therapy into the 21st century. *International Journal of Play Therapy, 9*(2), 1–17.

Herman, J. (1997). *Trauma and recovery: The aftermath of violence—from domestic abuse to political terror.* New York: Basic Books.

La Greca, A. M. (2008). Interventions for posttraumatic stress in children and adolescents following natural disasters and acts of terrorism. In R. G. Steele, T. D. Elkin, & M. C. Roberts (Eds.), *Handbook of evidence-based therapies for children and adolescents: Bridging science and practice* (pp. 121–141). New York: Springer Science.

Landreth, G. L. (2002). *Play therapy: The art of the relationship* (2nd ed.). Bristol, PA: Accelerated Development.

Lieberman, A. E., & Van Horn, P. (2008). *Psychotherapy with infants and young children: Repairing the effects of stress and trauma on early attachment.* New York: Guilford Press.

Perry, B., Pollard, R., Blakely, T., Baker, W., & Vigilante, D. (1995). Childhood trauma, the neurobiological adaptation and 'use-dependent' development of the brain: How "states become traits." *Infant Mental Health Journal, 16*(4), 271–291.

Piaget, J. (1962). *Play, dreams, and imitation in childhood.* New York: Norton.

Reyes, C. J., & Asbrand, J. P. (2005). A longitudinal study assessing trauma symptoms in sexually abused children engaged in play therapy. *International Journal of Play Therapy, 14*(2), 25–48.

Shelby, J. S. (2000). Brief therapy with traumatized children: A developmental perspective. In H. G. Kaduson & C. E. Schaefer (Eds.), *Short-term play therapy for children* (pp. 69–104). New York: Guilford Press.

Shen, Y. (2002). Short-term group play therapy with Chinese earthquake victims: Effects on anxiety, depression, and adjustment. *International Journal of Play Therapy, 11*(1), 43–63.

Sweeney, D. S., & Homeyer, L. E. (Eds.). (1999). *Group play therapy: How to do it, how it works, whom it's best for.* San Francisco: Jossey-Bass.

Terr, L. (1990). *Too scared to cry: Psychic trauma in childhood.* New York: Harper & Row.

Tyndall-Lind, A., Landreth, G., & Giordano, M. (2001). Intensive group play therapy with child witnesses of domestic violence. *International Journal of Play Therapy, 10,* 53–83.

Systematic Trauma Interventions for Children: A 10-Step Protocol

28

Jennifer Baggerly

For children, trauma is "an overwhelming, uncontrollable experience that psychologically impacts victims by creating in them feelings of helplessness, vulnerability, loss of safety, and loss of control" (James, 1989, p. 2). Thomas, a 5-year-old Latino boy dressed in a superhero costume, wildly runs around a small FEMA trailer pretending to fight off Hurricane Ivan 2 months after his family was forced to evacuate. Susanna, a 15-year-old Caucasian girl wearing all black clothing and heavy black eyeliner, cuts her forearm with a thumbtack in the back of the classroom on the 6-month anniversary of witnessing her father shoot her mother after years of ongoing domestic violence.

Impact of Trauma

Both children described above felt helpless, vulnerable, unsafe, and out of control. However, Thomas experienced Type I trauma, a single incident of terrorism, but Susanna experienced Type II trauma, domestic violence that was prolonged and repeated. Type II trauma can have a more severe impact because "repeated trauma in childhood forms and deforms the personality. The child . . . .must compensate for the failures of adult care and protection with the only means at her disposal, an immature system of psychological defenses" (Herman, 1997, p. 96).

Impact on Children's Brain

Recent research is revealing the profound impact that trauma can have on children's neurophysiology (Perry, 2001; Schore, 2003; Siegel, 2003; Silverman & La Greca, 2002). Both single and repeated traumatic incidents can cause the brain to activate either an arousal response of "fight or flight" or a dissociative response of "freeze and surrender" (Perry, Pollard, Blakely, Baker,

& Vigilante, 1995). During this time, brain functioning decreases in Broca's area, which controls ability to speak, and in Wernicke's area, which controls ability to comprehend language (van der Kolk, 1996). Children, like adults, can become "scared speechless." Children may not be able to formulate the words for a narrative of the traumatic event but they will encode an indelible picture of the event in their implicit memory (van der Kolk, 1996). Some children enter an altered state during a traumatic event to manage the terror and become fixated on one image such as a person's shoe. This terrifying mental picture may become a "fixed idea" in children's memory like a DVD stuck on pause.

If children do not process and integrate the traumatic event into their explicit memory through a restorative trauma narrative, they may: re-experience the trauma through intrusive images; attempt to avoid these frightening images and trauma related stimuli; and exhibit increased arousal such as hypervigilance, posttraumatic play, or outbursts of anger (Gil, 2006; Herman, 1997; Tinnin, 1996; van der Kolk, 1996). (Note that these are three of the criteria for the DSM-IV's diagnosis of posttraumatic stress disorder.) Along with these changes in memory, young children who experienced Type II trauma of prolonged ongoing events may have permanent changes in brain organization such as altered neurotransmitter pathways and responses (Perry et al., 1995).

Impact Within Five Realms

Trauma also has an impact on children's development and can cause symptoms within at least five realms (Kagan, 2004, Silverman & La Greca, 2002; Speier, 2000). The first realm is *cognitive*. Trauma alters children's beliefs and judgments, such as believing all people of a certain ethnic group are harmful. Children have difficulty concentrating or making decisions, and maintaining safety, trust, and morality; they also experience reoccurring visual images or intrusive thoughts and they develop negative attitudes about people, life, and the future (Terr, 1990).

The second realm is *emotional,* or *affective.* Traumatized children experience difficulty managing their feelings, connecting with others, feeling worthy of life, maintaining a healthy self-esteem, or developing intimacy.

The third realm is *behavioral.* Traumatized children experience social withdrawal, hypervigilance, aggressiveness, excessive use of drugs or alcohol, poor hygiene, or sexual acting out. They may engage in traumatic play reenactment such as being a scary wolf that chases and kills baby animals (Terr, 1990).

The fourth realm is *physiological.* Traumatized children experience muscle tension, nausea, headaches, sleeplessness, fatigue, or sustained blank "1000-yard" stares.

The final realm is *spirituality,* or *worldview.* Children may doubt their beliefs about God, their identity as a "good person," and their worldview (i.e., the world is a dangerous place). It is important for mental health professionals to recognize symptoms in all five of these realms in addition to avoidance, intrusion, and hyperarousal symptoms required for a formal DSM-IV diagnosis of PTSD.

Typical Responses and Guidelines at Different Developmental Levels

Children of any age may exhibit a range of short-term or long-term responses in the five areas as described above. However, children at different age levels tend to experience particular trauma responses. Table 1 summarizes Braden and Duchin's (2002) identification of typical trauma responses by children's age categories and suggested initial intervention guidelines. Most children's responses after a trauma are typical and temporary, and they recover within days or weeks after an event without professional interventions. Yet, some children develop more serious ongoing problems that result in acute stress disorder (less than 30 days), PTSD (over 30 days), other anxiety disorders, or depression.

For example, "in community studies, approximately 24% to 39% of children and adolescents exposed to

Table 1

Children's Trauma Responses by Age and Intervention Guidelines

Age	Typical trauma responses	Intervention guidelines

Preschool – 2nd Grade	• Believes death is reversible
	• Magical thinking
	• Intense but brief grief responses
	• Worries others will die
	• Separation anxiety
	• Avoidance
	• Regressive symptoms
	• Fear of the dark
	• Re-enactment through traumatic play
		• Give simple, concrete explanations as needed
		• Provide physical closeness
		• Allow expression through play
		• Read story books
		
		   – *A Terrible Thing Happened*
		
		   – *Brave Bart*
		
		   – *Don't Pop Your Cork on Monday*

3rd – 6th Grade	• Asks lots of questions • Begins to understand death is permanent • Worries about own death • Increased fighting and aggression • Hyperactivity and inattentiveness • Withdrawal from friends • Re-enactment through traumatic play	• Give clear, accurate explanations • Allow expression through art, play, journaling • Read story books
Middle School	• Physical symptoms of headaches, stomachaches • Wide range of emotions • More verbal but still needs physical outlet • Arguments, fighting • Moodiness	• Be accepting of moodiness • Be supportive and discuss when they are ready • Groups with structured art activities or games
High School	• Understand death is irreversible but believes won't happen to them • Depression • Risk-taking behaviors • Lack of concentration • Decline in responsible behavior • Apathy • Rebellion at home or school	• Listen • Encourage expression of feelings • Groups with guiding questions and projects

Note. Information from Braden and Duchin (2002).

destructive natural disasters have been found to meet criteria for a PTSD diagnosis in the first few weeks or months following the event" (La Greca, 2008, p. 124). This finding was confirmed by a study conducted 2 years after Hurricane Katrina, which also found that 31.5% of parents reported their child experienced clinically-diagnosed depression, anxiety, or a behavior disorder since the disaster (Abramson, Redlener, Stehling-Ariza, & Fuller, 2007). Children with risk factors, such as limited intellectual ability, female gender, younger age, unstable family life, and intense exposure to frightening events, often recover more slowly and may need professional intervention (La Greca, 2008).

Guiding Principles for Interventions

It is necessary to intervene as quickly as possible after a traumatic event to mitigate the deleterious effects of trauma on children. Before implementing interventions, counselors must be resolute in holding to emergency mental health guiding principles. The National Institute of Mental Health (NIMH, 2002) and later the National Child Traumatic Stress Network and National Center for PTSD (NCTSN, 2006) identified the following essential principles for emergency mental health trauma interventions with children:

1. Hold the expectation that most children will have a normal recovery so as not to over pathologize children's understandable and expected responses (Brymer et al., 2006).
2. Demonstrate a non-anxious presence by managing your own anxiety to a point of having a peaceful, calm demeanor (Rank & Gentry, 2003).
3. Maintain flexibility in your intervention protocol, allowing for variations to accommodate different environments, agencies, cultures, and personal characteristics.
4. Maintain a hardiness or fortitude to withstand demands and pressures.
5. Make every effort to reunite children with family members as quickly as possible.
6. Provide children with comfort and security through verbal reassurance, meeting physical needs of food, warmth, etc., and ensuring safety of children and their possessions.

In addition, mental health professionals must maintain a developmentally appropriate view of children. Landreth (2002) recommended being mindful of the following developmentally appropriate principles when interacting with children:

- Children are unique and worthy of respect
- Children are relational people
- Children are capable of positive self-direction
- Children are not miniature adults

Counselors must develop a relationship with children using children's natural language of play. Children often use toys as their words. To speak this language of play, counselors can make initial contact with children by using a friendly puppet or stuffed animal. Cohen, Berliner, and March (2000) also recommended incorporating play into cognitive behavioral approaches when treating traumatized children.

Protocol of Systematic Interventions with Children

Children's needs are different during various phases of disasters, therefore interventions must be specific to each phase (La Greca, 2008; Rosenfeld, Caye, Ayalon, & Lahad, 2005). According to NIMH (2002), the five phases of disaster are:

1. Pre-incident phase: communities plan and improve coping strategies
2. Impact phase (0–48 hours after the event): people focus on survival and communication
3. Rescue phase (0–1 week after an event): people adjust to changes
4. Recovery phase (1–4 weeks after an event): people conduct appraisal and plan
5. Return to life phase (2 weeks–2 years after an event): reintegration and return to pre-event level of functioning or better

Interventions offered during the Impact phase would not be appropriate during the Return to Life phase and vice versa.

A continuum of interventions should be offered beginning with brief, focused interactions and progressing to more intensive interventions such as small groups and individual counseling as needed after the incident (La Greca, 2008; Rosenfeld et al., 2005).

The following protocol provides a systematic approach of 10 interventions that may be used during specific phases of a disaster or traumatic event.

Pre-incident Phase: Primary prevention

1. *Pre-incident planning:* Develop children's protocol and specify roles of children's counselors with local public health and mental health agencies, Emergency Operations Centers, and schools (Mascari, 2005). Children's counselors should prepare "go packs" or kits of needed materials such as balloons, bubbles, puppets, Play-Doh, crayons, markers, paper, stuffed animals for children to keep, story books (Sheppard 1998; Holmes, 2000), water bottles, and snacks.

2. *Pre-incident training:* Join local emergency response teams such as Red Cross or Community Crisis Support Teams and participate in experiential systematic theory based interventions.

3. *Psychological immunization and stress inoculation:* Implement school-based curriculum to help all students develop coping strategies using the BASIC-Ph model (Lahad, 1997). Encourage families to develop and practice disaster plans.

Impact Phase

4. *Assessment:* Observe and ask local leaders what is needed. (This does *not* mean conducting formal psychological assessments). Inform leaders that children's counselors are available for deployment. Do not deploy to the site until authorized by an official agency.

Rescue Phase: Secondary intervention

5. *Psychological First Aid (PFA):* Provide a brief 5 to 10 minute one-on-one crisis intervention to "reduce the initial distress . . . and foster adaptive functioning and coping" (NCTSN, 2006). An extensive PFA field operations guide is available at www.nctsn.org. One helpful PFA model is C³ARE (Baggerly & Mescia, 2005):

Check – check the scene to make sure it is safe; check-in with the formal structure and people in charge; check self to make sure you are calm; check to see which child may need interventions the most.

Connect – connect with the child survivor and their support system through statements such as "Hi my name is Jennifer. This is my puppet Shep, the Sheepdog. I'm here with the team helping out today. What's your name? Who is here with you today? Who can you call?"

Comfort – calm and stabilize the child by asking "What can I do to help you feel more comfortable? Would you like some water or a snack? What do you usually do to calm yourself? I know some ways to help kids calm down. Would you like to learn?" Teach stabilization techniques such as "deep" breathing and progressive muscle relaxation.

Assess – monitor child survivor's physical and behavioral health status and assess coping and functioning through observation and asking "Is anything in your body hurting or feel strange right now?"

Refer – provide verbal and written referrals to formal support, specialized services, and resources. Help them connect with their own social support network.

Educate – teach common responses to trauma, stress management strategies, and resiliency skills; also, develop a plan of action to meet immediate needs. Say, "Many children, but not all, have uncomfortable feelings or thoughts after something scary happens. It is okay if you do. I can help with that. Let's look at this paper (or book) together and if you want, you can tell me if you have any of these things. What do you usually do to feel better? Would you like to look at the paper (or book) to learn new ways to feel better? Would you like to think of a plan together to do some things to help you feel better?"

Throughout these one-on-one and other interventions, be nonintrusive, sit at the child's eye level, match language to the child's developmental level, use simple feeling words, listen carefully, focus on the child's immediate concerns, and maintain confidentiality (NCTSN, 2006; Speier, 2000).

6. *Small group crisis interventions:* Peer groups allow children the opportunity for ventilation and validation to make sense of their trauma story while developing social supports (Rosenfeld et al., 2005). One approach is using the critical incident stress debriefing (CISD) seven step protocol (Mitchell & Everly, 2003), which usually lasts 1.5–2 hours. With children, the process can be facilitated by providing coloring books or implementing play therapy techniques for each stage (McPherson, 2003; amended by Baggerly, 2005):

- Introduction phase: Explain coach/athlete roles of leader/participant
- Fact phase: News broadcast (children pretend to be news reporters speaking into a toy microphone) or draw what occurred
- Thought phase: Puppet sentence completion or draw cartoon thought bubbles
- Reaction phase : Color your feelings or feelings faces
- Symptoms phase: Symptom charades or puppets demonstrate symptoms
- Teaching phase: Read *Brave Bart* (Sheppard, 1998) or *A Terrible Thing Happened* (Holmes, 2000); deep breathing by blowing bubbles or balloons; progressive muscle relaxation by "tensing like a tin-man and relaxing like a rag doll"
- Re-entry phase: Give "high fives" and group cheer

Kaduson and Schaeffer (2003) and Shelby (2000) described many of these activities as well as others. Other small group approaches for school settings include trauma and loss debriefing for kindergarten through 6th grade students (Steele, Malchiodi, & Klein, 2002), grief and trauma intervention for 7 to 12 year olds (Salloum, 2008), and cognitive behavioral intervention for trauma in schools (C-BITS) for 10 to 15 year old students (Kataoka et al., 2003).

7. *Family support and referrals:* Provide family members with reassurance, information on normal reactions of children to crisis, guidance on appropriate responses to their children, and referrals. Some helpful resources are *Parenting in a Challenging World* at www.nctsn.org and *After the Storm* (La Greca, Sevin, & Sevin, 2005) at http://www.psy.miami.edu/faculty/alagreca/after_the_storm.pdf

Return to Life Phase: Tertiary intervention

8. *Play therapy:* School and community counselors trained in play therapy should intervene with children whose symptoms persist several weeks after an event. (See Chapter 27.)

9. *Consultation with school staff and community leaders:* counselors should provide them with needed information outlined in this text and apprise them of needs and barriers.

10. *Compassion fatigue (CF) prevention and resiliency:* Counselors should participate in buddy systems to monitor CF, develop CF prevention and resiliency skills in trainings (Gentry, 2002), and seek individual counseling as needed.

This comprehensive 10-step protocol provides a range of interventions for mental health professionals working with children. As a result of these interventions, children such as Thomas and Susanna may recover faster and more fully, spared of disrupting symptoms. Counselors can control children's responses by providing empathic, systematic interventions to children who experience such events and help them develop resiliency to thrive in and for their communities.

Jennifer Baggerly, PhD, LMHC-S, RPT-S, is associate professor in the Counselor Education Program and director of the Graduate Certificate in Play Therapy at the University of South Florida. She is also a field traumatologist.

References

Abramson, D., Redlener, I., Stehling-Ariza, T., & Fuller, E. (2007). *The legacy of Katrina's children: Estimating the numbers of at-risk children in the Gulf Coast states of Louisiana and Mississippi.* Retrieved August 19, 2008, from http://www.ncdp.mailman.columbia.edu/files/legacy_katrina_children.pdf

Baggerly, J. N. (2005). Systematic trauma interventions for children: A 12 step protocol. In J. Webber, D. Bass, & R. Yep (Eds.), *Terrorism, trauma, and tragedies: A counselor's guide to preparing and responding* (pp. 97-102). Alexandria, VA: American Counseling Association Foundation.

Baggerly, J., & Mescia, N. (2005). *Disaster behavioral health: First aid specialist training with children (C-FAST).* Tampa, FL: Florida Center for Public Health Preparedness.

Braden, J. B, & Duchin, J. S. (2002). *Preparing for and responding to bioterrorism: Information for primary care clinicians. Psychological aftermath of crisis.* Retrieved from University of Washington, Northwest Center for Public Health Practice Web site: http://www.nwcphp.org/training/courses-exercises/courses/bttrain-phw

Cohen, J. A., Berliner, L., & March, J. S. (2000). *Treatment of children and adolescents.* In E. B. Foa, T. M. Keane, & M. J. Friedman (Eds.), *Effective treatments for PTSD* (pp. 106-138). New York: Guilford Press.

Gentry, J. E. (2002). Compassion fatigue: A crucible of transformation. *Journal of Trauma Practice,1*(3), 37–61.

Gil, E. (2006). *Helping abused and traumatized children: Integrating directive and nondirective approaches.* New York: Guilford Press.

Herman, J. (1997). *Trauma and recovery: The aftermath of violence—from domestic abuse to political terror.* New York: Basic Books.

Holmes, M. (2000). *A terrible thing happened: A story for children who have witnessed violence or trauma.* Washington, DC: Magination Press.

James, B. (1989). *Treating traumatized children. New insights and creative interventions.* Lexington, MA: Lexington Books.

Kaduson, H., & Schaeffer, C. (2003). *101 favorite play therapy techniques, Volume III.* Northvale, NJ: Jason Aronson.

Kagan, R. (2004). *Rebuilding attachments with traumatized children: Healing from losses, violence, abuse, and neglect.* Binghamton, NY: The Haworth Maltreatment & Trauma Press.

Kataoka, S., Stein, B. D., Jaycox, L. H., Wong, M., Escudero, P., Tu, W., . . . Fink, A. (2003). A school-based mental health program for traumatized Latino immigrant children. *Journal of the American Academy of Child and Adolescent Psychiatry, 42*(3), 311–318.

La Greca, A. M. (2008). Interventions for posttraumatic stress in children and adolescents following natural disasters and acts of terrorism. In R. G. Steele, T. D. Elkin, & M. C. Roberts (Eds.), *Handbook of evidence-based therapies for children and adolescents: Bridging science and practice* (pp. 121–141). New York: Springer Science.

La Greca, A. M., Sevin, S., & Sevin, E. (2005). *After the storm: A guide to help children cope with the psychological effects of a hurricane.* Coral Gables, FL: 7-Dippity. Available at http://www.psy.miami.edu/faculty/alagreca/after_the_storm.pdf

Lahad, M. (1997). BASIC Ph: The story of coping resources. In M. Lahad & A. Cohen (Eds.), *Community stress prevention* (Vols. 1 & 2, pp. 117–145). Kiryat Shmona, Israel: Community Stress Prevention Center.

Landreth, G. L. (2002). *Play therapy: The art of the relationship (2nd ed.).* Bristol, PA: Accelerated Development.

Mascari, J. B. (2005). The best laid plans: Will they work in a real crisis? In J. Webber, D. Bass, & R. Yep (Eds.), *Terrorism, trauma, and tragedies: A counselor's guide to preparing and responding* (pp. 97–102). Alexandria, VA: American Counseling Association Foundation.

McPherson, K. F. (2003, October). *Critical incident stress management (CISM) and play therapy.* Paper presented at the meeting of the Association for Play Therapy, Norfolk, VA.

Mitchell, J. T., & Everly, G. S. (2003). *Critical incident stress management (CISM): Basic group crisis intervention (3rd ed.).* Ellicott City, MD: International Critical Incident Stress Foundation.

National Institute of Mental Health. (2002). *Mental health and mass violence: Evidence-based early psychological intervention for victims/survivors of mass violence. A workshop to reach consensus on best practices.* NIH Publication No. 02-5138, Washington, DC: U.S. Government Printing Office.

NCTSN and NCPTSD (2006). *Psychological first aid: Field operations* guide (2nd ed.). National Child Traumatic Stress Network and National Center for PTSD. Available on www.nctsn.org and www.ncptsd.va.gov

Perry, B. D. (2001). The neurodevelopmental impact of violence in childhood. In D. Schetky & E. Benedek (Eds.), *Textbook of child and adolescent forensic psychiatry* (pp. 221–238). Washington, DC: American Psychiatric Press.

Perry, B., Pollard, R, Blakely, T., Baker, W., & Vigilante, D. (1995). Childhood trauma, the neurobiological adaptation and 'use-dependent' development of the brain: How "states become traits." *Infant Mental Health Journal, 16*(4), 271–291.

Rank, M. G., & Gentry, J. E. (2003). Critical incident stress: Principles, practices, and protocols. In M. Richard, W. Hutchinson, & W. Emener (Eds.), *Employee assistance programs: A basic text (3rd ed.)* (pp. 208–215). Springfield, IL: Charles C Thomas.

Rosenfeld, L. B., Caye, J. S., Ayalon, O., & Lahad, M. (2005). *When their word falls apart: Helping families and children manage the effects of disasters.* Washington, DC: National Association of Social Workers.

Salloum, A. (2008). Group therapy for children experiencing grief and trauma due to homicide and violence: A pilot study. *Research on Social Work Practice, 18,* 198–211.

Schore, A. N. (2003). Early relational trauma, disorganized attachment, and the development of a predisposition to violence. In M. F. Solomon & D. J. Siegel (Eds.), *Healing trauma: Attachment, mind, body, and brain.* New York: W.W. Norton.

Siegel, D. (2003). An interpersonal neurobiology of psychotherapy: The developing mind and the resolution of trauma. In M. F. Solomon & D. J. Siegel (Eds.), *Healing trauma: Attachment, mind, body, and brain.* New York: W.W. Norton.

Shelby, J. S. (2000). Brief therapy with traumatized children: A developmental perspective. In H. Kaduson & C. Shaefer (Eds.), *Short-term play therapy for children* (pp. 69–104). New York: Guilford Press.

Sheppard, C. (1998). *Brave Bart.* Groose Pointe Woods, MI: TLC.

Silverman, W. K., & La Greca, A. M. (2002). Children experiencing disasters: Definitions, reactions, and predictors of outcomes. In A. M. LaGreca, W. K. Silverman, E. M. Vernberg, & M. C. Roberts (Eds.), *Helping children cope with disasters and terrorism* (pp. 11–34). Washington, DC: American Psychological Association.

Speier, A. H. (2000). *Disaster relief and crisis counseling. Psychosocial issues for children and adolescents in disasters.* Rockville, MD: Center for Mental Health Services.

Steele, W., Malchiodi, C., & Klein, N. (2002). *Helping children feel safe: A debriefing program for children K–6th grade.* Detroit, MI: The National Institute for Trauma and Loss in Children.

Terr, L. (1990). *Too scared to cry: Psychic trauma in childhood.* New York: Harper & Row.

Tinnin, L. (1996). *Essential elements of narrative trauma processing.* Morgantown, WV: Trauma Recovery Institute.

van der Kolk, B. A. (1996). Trauma and memory. In B.A. van der Kolk, A. C. McFarlane, & L. Weisaeth (Eds.), *Traumatic stress: The effects of overwhelming experience on mind, body, and society* (pp. 279–302). New York: Guilford Press.

INTERVENTIONS WITH CHILDREN AFTER THE EARTHQUAKE IN CHINA

29

Emily Zeng

No one knows exactly how many children were killed in the earthquake that struck the Sichuan Province in Western China on May 12, 2008. Even at Beichuan High School, the only high school in Beichuan, which once housed 2,990 students and staff, one can only estimate that about 1,300 students died when the two 5-story buildings crumbled on that fatal day. The villagers, pointing to the vast wasteland between the main entrance, the girls' and boys' dorms, and the outdoor stadium, say that 300 bodies of children are still buried there.

THE TENT SCHOOL

Since the destruction of virtually every house in the area, tents became the practical substitute for classrooms, bedrooms, and kitchens. Brightly colored tents covered the place like mushrooms, rising above the side of *Xi Shanpo,* the Westside Mountain. The tent school where I was stationed was perched halfway up the mountain overlooking what was left of Beichuan High School. The school was a creative adaptation of the collapsed house of Captain Chen, who was in charge of the village. It consisted of two tents and was big enough to accommodate approximately 50 children who were divided into two classes, K–2 and Grades 3–7. The Grades K–2 class included 20 pupils, but there were surprise visitors such as the cute little 2-year-old boy who always carried a backpack much bigger than his torso. The Grades 3–7 class had about 30 students, five times as many boys as girls.

Despite the general unsanitary conditions of the quake zone, (shortage of electricity and clean water, swarms of flies and mosquitoes, etc.) our school was perhaps one of the best equipped of the tent schools. Thanks to the generosity of early volunteers, we had a

multi-functioning CD/SD/MP3/USB/radio/tape player with a projector that played DVDs when electricity was steady. The children learned new songs and English pronunciation from this ingenious machine. About 13 of them became excellent photographers, thanks to the child-friendly, digital minicameras donated by a friend in New York.

I worked with a small group of volunteers, mostly from Qingdao, Shandong, a province designated by the central government as the "partner" province for rebuilding Beichuan. In addition to teaching the upper grades, I visited the students' families and other villagers after school. The everyday life of the tent school resembled that of an ordinary Chinese school. The morning routine consisted of ancient poetry chanting, reading, writing, science, and English. The afternoons were composed of a review of the morning lessons, exercises, and play activities. Many opportunities were created for the children to play together: bubble blowing, Play-Doh, rope jumping, handicrafts, and board games such as Chinese chess.

Photo: Emily Zeng

Children in the tent school: three month anniversary.

Therapeutic Games

We had several special games such as *tumbling tower* that graphically depicted the issues of building up and falling down. The children were presented with collapsed structures that could be rebuilt with patience and collective effort, which paralleled the rebuilding process of their homes and school.

The children also created their own games. When they tired of Chinese checkers, they dumped all the marbles into a basin and used chopsticks to pick them up. To make the game even more challenging, they divided themselves into small groups with one child using a timer to oversee the competition. As anyone who has tried to pick up a marble with chopsticks can attest, this is a daunting task; the children created their own version of a challenging situation that, because of the timing pressure of the competition, needed to be accomplished quickly. This allowed them to "play through" the difficulties they faced in their lives outside of the classroom in a venue in which they had ultimate control.

The most popular games seemed to be those that required the most imagination. The *whisper game*, in which the children read the lips of one of their peers, cost nothing and was great fun. The metaphor that each child had the innate skills to decipher an environmental situation with only partial cues was not lost on them. *Noah's Ark*, the game the children enjoyed the most, required only a newspaper (a local scarcity then). The children divided themselves into groups, each group standing on an unfolded page of a newspaper. Then the paper was folded in half, and the group stood on it again. Then the paper was folded again. As the standing space diminished, the fun increased. The children arrived at creative solutions to maximize the space by taking off their shoes and socks or climbing on top of one another in all sorts of ways, trying to squeeze onto that tiny piece of paper. Xing, who had been buried for hours in her Beichuan High classroom, laughed aloud for the first time.

Therapeutic Group Projects

One of the books I used extensively as a practical guide for the tent school was Hart's (1992) *Children's Participation*, a participatory action approach for working with children. It provided excellent ideas for involving children in community development using a variety of methods such as drawings and collages, photography, mapping and charting the ways things looked before and after the quake, and interviews and surveys about their perceptions and reactions to the earthquake. Our first group project was to create a map showing where the stu-

dents lived in the village, which resulted in a village map scattered with the children's tents. The picture was clear: the tent school was the only center of the community. Another activity was about their former schools. One of the groups came up with the brilliant idea of making two drawings of their old school, the Beichuan Hope Primary School. The before-the-quake drawing was filled with color and the after-the-quake version was penciled with gloomy shades of gray.

Another extremely effective technique for helping the children come to terms with the impact of the earthquake turned out to be tiny digital cameras, which the children rotated among themselves (Hart, 1999). They mastered the basics of photography within days and began what turned out to be a fascinating visual journal. There was no access to a printer, so every day after school a small group of children would gather around my laptop to review their photos, sharing and critiquing each other's work. I was amazed that the children almost unanimously started with the familiar subjects: the tent school, family, and friends. Then they turned to the animals, plants, and the sky. After these safe subjects had been explored, they eventually ventured out, taking in the debris, the collapsed buildings, and the landslides. One of the most haunting images was from a sixth grader. "My grandpa was buried by this landslide. Now it is covered with grass."

Although the small camera offered a wonderful way for younger children to convey their thoughts and feelings, writing seemed more appropriate for the older ones. Changxin, a diligent fourth grader, took days to finish his "tent school dissertation," a series of "adventures" during the earthquake. In his eyes, the landslide looked like an elephant, and mountains crashed into one other, stopped the river, and formed a quake lake.

Photo: Emily Zeng

"Landslide, mud, blood." A child's drawing of the earthquake.

One of the most inventive things the children did was to show movies in the tent-filled stadium of Beichuan High School. Two children climbed up the metal fence to set up the screen. One child brought a DVD player from home, and another borrowed a power extension cord from his uncle. The rest of us set up tables and chairs, inviting parents and villagers to come. The children also generously loaned the DVD equipment to another village, so the children there could enjoy the show. Their ability to recreate one of their favorite pre-earthquake pastimes and then share it with others was, to me, a sign of their underlying resiliency and strength.

Reading was also an important part of the tent school regime. One of the stories the children enjoyed the most was a Chinese version of *The Snow Globe* (Underwood & Clark, 2005). The original story, which had been widely used after September 11, was about two friends who learned to deal with the loss of a birthday present through a taleidoscope. "A taleidoscope is similar in construction [to a kaleidoscope] but instead of looking at a container with brightly colored things inside, you look through the lens at everyday objects that are multiplied and transformed into miraculous treasures" (p. 11). I shortened the story so that even the youngest child could follow it. I also used two bears to make it into a mini puppet show. Here is the version of the story I translated into Chinese.

THE STORY: *THE SNOW GLOBE*

Once upon a time, there were two friends. They were the best friends in the world.

One was called Creep Face. He was a boy. The other was called Maggie. Maggie was a girl.

Maggie's birthday came soon. Creep Face was so excited. He shopped for days, and found a special birthday present for Maggie, a giant globe! It was not an ordinary globe. It was a very special one. Inside the globe, there was a girl sitting on a rock, surrounded by a bunch of animals. There was a sun in the sky with a rainbow behind it. But when you shook it up, the sun became the moon, the rainbow turned into the Milky Way and a million stars.

So the day came when it was Maggie's birthday. Creep Face went to Maggie's house, carrying the giant globe. When Creep Face saw Maggie, he ran to her. Maggie ran to him. Maggie's puppy, Dirt Ball, also ran along. "Ruff! Ruff!"

All of sudden, Creep Face bumped into Dirt Ball, and tripped over him. Oh no! The globe flipped out of his hand. It went into the air, and crashed onto the floor. The

giant globe broke into pieces. The little girl's dress broke off. The animals were shattered. The sun disappeared.

Creep Face was so sad. "I'm sorry," he said to Maggie.

Maggie felt sorry, too. But she looked at the broken pieces for a moment, stood up, and ran off. In a minute she returned, holding a small tube with a glass marble stuck in one end.

"This is another present I got for my birthday," she said, "From my grandmother. It's called a taleidoscope."

Maggie rolled the taleidoscope around for a few seconds, and then put it up to her eye. Something happened! A thousand suns! A thousand stars. Everything was transformed! Creep Face was so astounded. He and Maggie took turns admiring the wreckage on the floor for a really long time. Through the taleidoscope, the snow globe looked even more beautiful!

Many years passed. Maggie and Creep Face are now in high school. They are still the best friends in the world. Life is going fast. Sometimes it changes to a degree that it doesn't make much sense. But Maggie and Creep Face both know that the goodness and beauty of life are always there.

The children loved the story so much that they retold it without missing a single detail. When I explained that it had been written to help children in America deal with the impact of September 11, I was stunned to learn that none of the children had heard of the terrorist attacks. When I used Legos to demonstrate the plane crashing into the World Trade Center and the Pentagon, they stared at me in disbelief. Liang was the first one who raised his hand and said, "Teacher, the pilot must be so poorly trained! He was perhaps sleeping!" The whole class broke out laughing, unable to comprehend the paradox of intentional destruction. Each child received a taleidoscope as a special gift from the authors of the story.

The collective life of the tent school culminated in a memorial trip to Beichuan city. On the day of the 3-month anniversary of the earthquake, the children decorated the classroom with balloons, wrote special messages to their loved ones, and made a remembrance box. It was the first time we took a trip as a class. Passing the military checkpoint and troops of soldiers, we went up Jinjiashan Mountain and buried our remembrance box in the cave overlooking Beichuan city. I was surprised to see one of the students bent over near a pile of rubble; as I approached, however, my heart flooded with understanding. He was looking at the destruction through his taleidoscope.

Aftershocks

Although the earthquake itself was over, the danger was not. I was quick to learn the practical meaning of local seismological terms such as *yuzhen* (aftershock), *huapo* (landslide), along with other secondary environmental threats such as floods. The treacherous Tangjiashan Quake Lake, which is within 10 miles walking distance, had caused an evacuation of more than 250,000 residents from the downstream Mianyang Municipality. After the initial magnitude 8 quake and the thousands of aftershocks that followed, the children had been sensitized or habituated in various ways. In the middle of class proceedings, a student would swiftly stand up, reporting, "Teacher, I just sensed an aftershock," and sit down as if nothing had happened. Then the whole class ran a quick check, discussing whether he was right. I stood aside watching, baffled by my own inability to detect even the slightest sign from the ground below.

As the summer wore on, even I began to experience the aftershocks at a frequency of almost once a week. One of the first aftershocks came on an exceedingly humid afternoon when even the most exuberant child was listless. I was sitting at a desk typing my journal when, suddenly, the wind began to blow and the trees and tents began to shake loudly. The desk wobbled back and forth so much that I could not steady it. Chen and Wang, two sixth graders who had been playing marbles, jumped in the air and called out, "Aftershock!" The village became instantly noisy, adults calling, children crying, dogs barking, cocks crowing, as if it were early in the morning. Captain Chen, the leader of the village, came by and told us not to worry. Because we were now officially residing in tents, he reassured us that even if they did fall upon us, they were likely to cause more fun than harm. On August 14, 2008, two aftershocks woke me up about 5 a.m. The kitchen utensils next door made tingling sounds, as things fell on the floor. Strangely, I developed a fever that lingered around all day and my nose was bleeding for the first time.

The K–2 class had two girls who cried whenever it rained; they worried that an aftershock was coming. Other children often teased them. In trying to find a more productive way to help them cope with their fears, I read them the story *Me* by Waechter (2007), which is a preschool picture book about the adventures of a bear. I wanted to introduce the idea of dealing with the things that frighten us. Then I asked the youngsters what they were most afraid of. Some children said snakes (a local regular); some said dinosaurs. It was not until I took out *Earthquake* (Collier, 2006) featuring buildings falling upon each other, that everyone shouted out, "Earthquake!" They all admitted that they were afraid of aftershocks. Then I roamed around holding the book pretending to be a quake monster. The class, acting like they were the tents and houses, engaged in a whole body game of shaking and moving. There was, however, a lullaby-like ending that captured for us all, the resiliency skills we were all learning from the steadying forces in the universe:

> Shake, shake, shake the house,
> Here comes the earthquake.
> Shake, shake, shake the tent,
> Here comes the aftershock
> [hold up hands and shake in rhythm].
> Oops, it stops! [the class freezes]
>
> [After a few seconds, whispering, slowly]
> Here come the stars,
> Here comes the moon,
> Everyone falls asleep,
> All children of Beichuan.

Postscript

So many things have happened since I returned to New York. In late September, a landslide caused by nonstop rain buried the village. We lost four children who had been students in the tent school, two mothers, and 20 other adults. The village was forced to move out. The Westside Mountain, which the children once charted and mapped so enthusiastically, no longer exists.

Since then, I received more disturbing news. Local officials killed themselves one after another. Survivors dropped out of the windows of hotel or hospital buildings out of despair. More children were left orphaned. More aftershocks.

A new Beichuan High School was established. The old town of Beichuan was relocated to An County, now part of Beichuan. While the villagers are living in prefab houses, a world-class earthquake museum, which encompasses Beichuan High School, the Beichuan City, and the quake lake, is being built.

I stay in touch with a few children but it is difficult because their cell phones are frequently turned off. One of my students dropped out of school and began selling quake photos in front of Beichuan High School. Several other children also joined him in their spare time. Life goes on. In my heart, I hope that the children remember the lesson from *The Snow Globe*. No matter what happens, the goodness and beauty of life are always there.

Emily Zeng, PhD, is expanding the Yeshiva China project into a long-term participatory action research. She is a native of Sichuan, China, and was a doctoral student at Yeshiva University when she volunteered in the quake-prone Beichuan. She returned to Beichuan in August 2009.

Editor's Note: After the devastating earthquake on May 12, 2008, Emily, a native of Sichuan, China, felt compelled to return home to provide support and relief. Through the Yeshiva China Earthquake Relief Project, a model that fostered and encouraged community participatory involvement, Emily brought a child-centered, resiliency-focused perspective to the Beichuan tent school. Her interventions were also informed and guided by the work of Maureen Underwood from the Going on after Loss Center for Families and Dr. Suzanne Phillips of the American Group Psychotherapy Association. Emily's narrative of her experience highlights the interplay of personal perspective with a theoretical underpinning that was developed after September 11, 2001 to help families deal with the aftermath of that trauma.

REFERENCES

Collier, B. (2006). *Time for kids: Earthquakes.* New York: Harper Collins.

Hart, R. (1992). *Children's participation: From tokenism to citizenship.* Retrieved from http://web.gc.cuny.edu/che/cerg/documents/Childrens_participation.pdf

Hart, R. (1999). *Children's participation: The theory and practice of involving young citizens in community development and environmental care.* UNICEF. London: Earthscan.

Underwood, M., & Clark, C. (2005). Using metaphor to help children cope with trauma: An example from September 11th. In J. Webber, D. Bass, & R. Yep (Eds.). *Terrorism, trauma, and tragedies: A counselor's guide to preparing and responding* (2nd ed.) (pp. 33-36). Alexandria, VA: American Counseling Association Foundation.

Waechter, P. (2007). *Me* (Y. H. Zhao, Trans.). New York: Handprint Books. (Original work published 2005).

VIOLENCE TOWARD CHILDREN IN OUR NATION'S CAPITAL

30

Pat Schwallie-Giddis and Kelli Jones Sannes

Violence against children seems to be the rule rather than the exception in Washington, DC. Unfortunately, Washington, DC has had a reputation as one of the nation's leaders in violent crime. The 1980s and early 1990s suggested that the city would not see a reprieve in such hostile acts within the community. By 2001, 126 per 100,000 teens ages 15 to 19 died due to homicide, suicide, or accident; the national average is 50 per 100,000 teen deaths under these parameters (Annie E. Casey Foundation, 2004). By the end of September 2004, 21 children and youth had already fallen victim to violent crime since the beginning of the year in comparison to a total of 12 victims by the close of 2003, according to local news reports. Although these statistics represent a dramatic 47% decline in teen deaths in DC since 1996, our community still has much work to do.

So in a city wrought by community violence and the threat of potential terrorist attacks what can we, as counselors, do to make a difference? How can we contribute as individuals and as professional counselors to help our children? As professional counselors, we may sometimes feel bound by confidentiality and ethical duty not to extend our services in innovative ways, or we may lack confidence that we could make a difference.

As Washington, DC faces a state of continued heightened security, recognizing the possibility of being at the center of future terrorist attacks, we must pay close attention to the additional stress placed on our children. The terror of September 11th continues to haunt our city as we remember the losses of family members, friends, and members of our community. Schools have implemented crisis intervention plans not only in preparation for such events, but also because our schools already have been a site of violence including the sniper shootings in 2002, school shootings, and gang activity.

SIGNS OF TRAUMA AND EXPOSURE TO COMMUNITY VIOLENCE

Exposure to community violence includes falling victim to or witnessing a violent act. In 1993, Richters and Martinez reported that approximately 40% of children in DC manifested posttraumatic stress disorder (PTSD) symptoms due to community violence. Inner-city children often experience repetitive trauma, and they experience multiple stressors – both physical (noisy or crowded environments) and psychological (family disorder or family violence), putting them at greater risk for socio-emotional problems (Evans & English, 2002). As children try to make sense of traumatic events, serious developmental, cognitive, intellectual, social, behavioral, psychosomatic, and emotional consequences ensue. The child also may experience some developmental regression (Aisenberg & Mennen, 2000; Overstreet, 2000). Cognitively, a child strives to make sense of and create meaning for a traumatic event, and, in the case of repetitive trauma, the memories of such events may be unclear (Fivush, Hazzard, Sales, Sarfati, & Brown, 2003). Also, prior exposure to violence may lead to normative beliefs regarding aggression and an increase in aggressive fantasy (Guerra, Huesmann, & Spindler, 2003). Children exposed to violence will likely have academic difficulties, may have poor concentration on tasks or assignments, and may lose the ability to perform previously acquired skills, thus negatively affecting intellectual functioning (Aisenberg & Mennen, 2000; Margolin & Gordis, 2000). Inability to form and maintain positive peer relationships, substance use, and withdrawal are only a few of the social ramifications of exposure to violence (Aisenberg & Mennen, 2000; O'Donnell, Schwab-Stone, & Muyeed, 2002). Behaviorally, children exposed to violence display higher levels of aggression and anti-social behavior including fighting and gang involvement (Overstreet, 2000).

Children who have experienced traumatic events may present several physical and psychosomatic symptoms such as difficulty sleeping, nightmares, headaches, and stomachaches (National Institute of Mental Health, 2004; O'Donnell et al., 2002). Extreme emotional consequences such as depression, anxiety, and low future expectations can also occur (Aisenberg & Mennen, 2000; Margolin & Gordis, 2000). Other signs of post-traumatic stress include:

- Intense psychological distress upon exposure to similar situations
- Intrusive thoughts
- Avoidance of reminders of traumatic events
- Exaggerated startle response
- Feelings and/or actions associated with the belief that the trauma is occurring in the present (Aisenberg & Mennan, 2000; Overstreet, 2000)

Other signs of trauma due to exposure to community violence include:

- Refusal to attend school (National Institute of Mental Health, 2004)
- Suspension from school
- Placement in special education due to academic failure (O'Donnell et al., 2002)
- Internalized distress
- Feeling unsafe at school
- Reduced ability to delay self-gratification and cannot delay as long (Evans & English, 2002)

POTENTIAL BARRIERS TO HELPING CHILDREN

Children who are most at risk of being exposed to violence are already living in high-risk environments, and the risk becomes cumulative (Garbarino, 2001). It is important to acknowledge these risks and understand the following potential barriers to assisting these children:

- Inability of the parent or caregiver to respond to child's needs because of their own PTSD

symptoms (Aisenberg & Mennen, 2000), mental impairment, or substance abuse
- The parent or caregiver's underestimation of the violence to which the child has been exposed (Overstreet, 2000)
- Fractured family system
- Poverty
- Cultural variables
- Mental health centers that do not assess for exposure to community violence
- Lack of sufficient assessment tools measuring exposure to community violence
- Children not receiving treatment in a timely or appropriate manner (Aisenberg & Mennen, 2000)
- Comorbidity with ADHD, depression, or other anxiety disorders (Overstreet, 2000)
- Lack of support in the school system
- Lack of community support
- Counselor frustration and feelings of helplessness in trying to untangle a systemic issue

THE IMPACT OF TRAUMA ON CHILDREN

Traumatic events and experiences have lasting consequences for children especially due to their age and developmental status (Cohen, Mannarino, & Deblinger, 2006; Ford & Cloitre, 2009; Nader, 2004). Age and development affect children's ability to understand the degree and nature of the threat, their ability to report experiences and symptoms; and emotional, cognitive, and psychological coping (Nader, 2004). Cohen et al. described affective, behavioral, and cognitive trauma symptoms, and the psychobiological impact of trauma. Affective trauma symptoms include fear, depression, anger, and inability to regulate affect via mood swings. Behavioral trauma symptoms include avoidance of people, places, thoughts, and feelings that remind them of the traumatic event. Cognitively, children try to integrate a horrific traumatic event into their schema. When there is not an "answer" to why the event happened to them, children create their own world of understanding. Self-blame, the child's claiming responsibility, guilt, and other misguided justifications are predominant ways children explain bad things that happen to them.

Extensive research substantiates that traumatic experiences organically affect the body and brain (Cohen et al., 2006; Ford & Cloitre, 2009; van der Kolk, 2005). Blood pressure, increased heart rate, altered brain chemistry leading to poor academic functioning, inability to focus and concentrate, lowered immune system, and decreased brain size are all related to traumatic experiences (Ford & Cloitre, 2009; Cohen et al., 2006).

Understanding traumatic reactions in childhood is convoluted and confusing due to a lack of understanding regarding: information about the child pre-event; mediating variables such as family, culture, and socioeconomic status; how to incorporate the changing nature of traumatic symptoms over time; and the lack of research studies looking at children pre, during, and post traumatic events (Nader, 2004). As a result, assessing children's posttraumatic reactions is problematic. Type of assessment, the nature of the measure and traumatic event, and the child's specific issues and background are difficult to capture. Moreover, externalizing symptoms are often more accurately measured by adults, but internalizing symptoms are often misunderstood and/or unreported by the child because of the impact of the trauma. As a result, Nader suggests multiple assessments that consider the source of the information, the event factors, childhood characteristics and development, family history, culture, socioeconomic status, type of traumatic experience, manner of the trauma (intensity, duration, the relationship to the perpetrator), degree of threat to the child's person and psychological integrity, and the support the child receives.

Community violence may easily be categorized as creating a sufficient environment whereby complex posttraumatic stress is experienced. Complex posttraumatic stress occurs when an individual or group of individuals is entrapped and conditioned over time. Complex psychological trauma results from "exposure to severe stressors that (1) are repetitive or prolonged, (2) involved harm or abandonment by caregivers or other adults, and (3) occurred at developmentally vulnerable times in the victim's life, such as early childhood or adolescence" (Ford & Courtois, 2009, p. 13).

Originally, complex posttraumatic stress described adult reactions to trauma over the lifespan (Courtois, 2004). However, children display symptoms of complex posttraumatic stress when they are trapped in an environment of violence and/or abuse. They display symptoms previously mentioned and will more than likely carry the impact of multiple traumatic experiences into adulthood. Van der Kolk (2005) suggested a new DSM diagnosis of development trauma disorder that identifies the impact of multiple traumatic experiences throughout a child's life.

Ford and Cloitre (2009) stated that there have been no new best practice guidelines for mental health prac-titioners for the treatment of children with PTSD in the past decade. Cohen et al. (2006) outlined trauma-focused cognitive behavioral therapy for children (TF-CBT) with PTSD that utilizes psychoeducation, skill building, and CBT attuned to trauma symptoms previously mentioned. Ford and Cloitre developed best practices for psychotherapy for children with complex traumatic stress that specifically target those trauma symptoms that develop as a result of multiple traumatic experiences, which likely occur in communities of repeated violence. Ford and Cloitre used empirically supported treatments as well as evidence-based practice as a foundation for the following goals that mirror Courtois' (2004) description of problem areas experienced by adults with complex posttraumatic stress:

- Increase affect regulation and impulse control by helping children to manage and modulate emotions, behavior, and impulses in a way that is manageable enhances the child's sense of self control.
- Understand and target altered information processing by assessing and treating problems with attention, memory, and executive functioning that have developed as a result of altered brain chemistry and functioning.
- Understand and target dissociation and dysregulation of motivation and consciousness because children will dissociate or detach their emotions, thoughts, and perceptions of their self and others as a way to survive a traumatic situation.
- Understand somatization and dysregulation of bodily functioning because traumatized children will often report chronic physical ailments, illness, distress, and discomfort as a result of the physical effects of trauma on the body.
- Understand disorganized attachment and relational dysregulation, as defined by Bowlby's attachment theory, because the child's relationship to the perpetrator(s) may cause significant problems in relating to others and creating meaningful, trusting relationships in their lives.

STRATEGIES AND SUGGESTIONS FOR WORKING WITH CHILDREN

Children's exposure to community violence is a systemic and multidimensional problem that requires a multidimensional strategy. A counselor must consider the treatment of the child, family, and community environment to promote resilience (O'Donnell et al., 2002). Furthermore, a counselor should identify interactions and relationships among these three variables (Lynch & Cicchetti, 2002) in order to understand the larger picture.

For the child, cognitive behavioral therapy is widely known to be effective. Use assessment tools that have some focus on exposure to violence and assess the child's level of distress. Gather information from multiple sources including parents, teachers, and other significant persons in the child's life. Also, obtain a history of community violence in the neighborhood and assess the repetitive nature of the trauma. Allow the child to tell the story of what has happened to them in order to assist the child in recalling negative experiences and to begin to make sense of them (Fivush et al., 2003). Help the child to develop new ways of thinking about the traumatic event in order to give it meaning and give the child a sense of control through cognitive restructuring (Aisenberg & Mennen, 2000). However, be extremely careful not to dispose of adaptive cognitions that are helpful to the child and his or her safety should they experience repetitive trauma.

The role of the family is crucial; it is important to determine how much support a child is receiving at home and to assess potential dangers in the home environment that may further disable the child. The counselor must assess potential posttraumatic symptoms in the parent and determine whether the counselor can work with the parent or if it is more appropriate to refer the parent elsewhere. It is important to remain sensitive to various cultural variables within the family system and make appropriate adjustments in the counseling process that can better meet the needs of that particular family. Invite parents and other vital family members to counseling sessions, as long as these family members are non-offending toward the child.

Community involvement is essential in addressing the broader picture of community violence and assisting a child who has been exposed to violent acts. An innovative way to expand the counselor's role is to use a more community-focused approach to counseling. Counseling has traditionally been practiced primarily using one-to-one interventions that focus on the internal experiences of clients. Most counseling models have paid little attention to factors within the child's environment. A more proactive approach would involve the counselor in becoming an integral part of the community in which they serve. This approach will encourage more active involvement among the counselor, the parents, and the community at large. This preventive approach could lead to advocating for local policy changes and to reaching larger numbers of individuals in need of counseling who would never receive services under the traditional model of counseling.

Thus, community-focused counseling could improve the counselors' ability to serve individuals from marginalized groups such as ethnic minority children and those from low socioeconomic backgrounds. In summary, using a community-focused counseling approach will expand the role of the counselor to promoting activities and interventions that will have an impact not only on the individual child but on the total community as well.

Pat Schwallie-Giddis, PhD, is an associate professor and Chair of the Counseling Department at The George Washington University in Washington DC.

Kelli Jones Sanness, LPC, is a doctoral candidate at The George Washington University, and is the staff counselor/lead clinical supervisor for the GW Community Counseling Services Center. She is also a private practitioner in Washington DC.

REFERENCES

Aisenberg, E., & Mennen, F. E. (2000). Children exposed to community violence: Issues for assessment and treatment. *Child and Adolescent Social Work Journal, 17*(5), 341–360.

Annie E. Casey Foundation. (2004). *Kids 2004 databook online.* Retrieved from http://www.aecf.org

Cohen, J. A., Mannarino, A. P., & Deblinger, E. (2006). *Treating trauma and traumatic grief in children and adolescents.* New York: Guilford Press.

Courtois, C. A. (2004). Complex trauma, complex reactions: Assessment and treatment. *Psychotherapy: Theory, Research, Practice, Training, 41*(4), 412–425.

Evans, G. W., & English, K. (2002). The environment of poverty: Multiple stressor exposure, psycho physiological stress, and socioemotional adjustment. *Child Development, 73*(4), 1238–1248.

Fivush, R., Hazzard, A., Sales, J. M., Sarfati, D., & Brown, T. (2003). Creating coherence out of chaos? Children's narratives of emotional positive and negative events. *Applied Cognitive Psychology, 17,* 1–9.

Ford, J. D., & Cloitre, M. (2009). Best practices in psychotherapy for children and adolescents. In C. A. Courtois & J. D. Ford (Eds.), *Treating complex traumatic stress disorders: An evidence-based guide* (pp. 59–81). New York: Guilford Press.

Ford, J. D., & Courtois, C. A. (2009). Defining and understanding complex trauma and complex traumatic stress disorders. In C. A. Courtois & J. D. Ford (Eds.), *Treating complex traumatic stress disorders: An evidence-based guide* (pp.13–30). New York: Guilford Press.

Garbarino, J. (2001). An ecological perspective on the effects of violence on children. *Journal of Community Psychology, 29*(3), 361–378.

Guerra, N., Huesmann, R., & Spindler, A. (2003). Community violence exposure, social cognition, and aggression among urban elementary school children. *Child Development, 74*(5), 1561–1576.

Lynch, M., & Cicchetti, D. (2002). Links between community violence and the family system: Evidence from children's feelings of relatedness and perceptions of parent behavior. *Family Process, 41*(3), 519–532.

Margolin, G., & Gordis, E. B. (2000). Effects of family and community violence on children. *Annual Review of Psychology, 51,* 445–479.

Nader, K. O. (2004). Assessing traumatic experiences in children and adolescents: Self reports of DSM PTSD criteria B-D symptoms. In J. P. Wilson & T. M. Keane (Eds.), *Assessing psychological trauma and PTSD* (pp. 513–537). New York: Guilford Press.

National Institute of Mental Health. (2004). *Helping children and adolescents cope with violence and disasters.* Retrieved from http://www.nimh.nih.gov/publicat/violence.cfm

O'Donnell, D. A., Schwab-Stone, M. E., & Muyeed, A. Z. (2002). Multidimensional resilience in urban children exposed to community violence. *Child Development, 73*(4), 1265–1282.

Overstreet, S. (2000). Exposure to community violence: Defining the problem and understanding the consequences. *Journal of Child and Family Studies, 9*(1), 7–25.

Richters, J. E., & Martinez, P. (1993). The NIMH community violence project: I. Children as victims and witnesses to violence. *Psychiatry: Interpersonal and Biological Processes, 56*(1), 7–21.

van der Kolk, B. A. (2005). Developmental trauma disorder. *Psychiatric Annals, 35,* 439–448.

Children of First Responders: Outreach and Counseling Strategies

31

George M. Kapalka

First responders provide an invaluable service to our society. When disasters strike, police officers, firefighters, medical rescue personnel, or members of the armed forces are usually the first to arrive to respond to the crisis or trauma. They witness serious injury, death, and destruction, often risking their own lives to assist the victims. Consequently, first responders always have presented a special challenge within the larger context of trauma victims and are at high risk for personal, familial, occupational, and social problems. As their functional problems spill over into the home, they affect all family members, including spouses and children who are likely to be affected by changes within the family.

Spouses of first responders can access resources and support systems to get help. The children within the home usually do not have the ability to do so and are most vulnerable to secondary effects of domestic problems. When children need help, their ability to obtain support and assistance on their own is very limited, and they must rely on their parents to do so. However, dynamics within the home may interfere and outreach may be needed to sensitize parents to their children's needs and the assistance that they may require.

The 2001 attacks on the World Trade Center present an example of the unique factors that place children of first responders at risk. New York City's search, rescue, and recovery teams witnessed a massive instant loss of life; the magnitude of the clean-up operation and the atrocities they faced along the way are still difficult for many to comprehend. Our follow-up with 600 New York City police officers who were first responders revealed that many first responders brought this stress home and experienced depression, anger, anxiety, and disillusionment 18 months later. More

than half of them still exhibited significant problems with their physical health, and about 40% presented with at least one DSM-IV diagnosis, mostly PTSD, Major Depression, and Generalized Anxiety Disorder (Kapalka et al., 2004). Almost 14% of officers surveyed admitted that their family life did not return to normal after September 11 and that significant family discord was evident. This may be a conservative estimate because officers tend to underestimate the degree to which their family life is affected (asking the spouses may have rendered a more accurate result). However, these findings suggested that 18 months after the trauma, about 14,000 New York City police officers' families were in need of assistance.

Six months later, 28% of New York City children in Grades 4 through 12 met the criteria for any anxiety disorder, and 10% met the diagnostic criteria for PTSD (Hoven et al., 2005). By contrast, at the same time, children of first responders sampled from the same population exhibited nearly twice (18.9%) the rates of PTSD (Duarte et al., 2006).

Why Children of First Responders Have Problems

When assessing a family, several factors must be considered.

Fear of loss of parent or injury to parent. Most children whose parent has been traumatized suddenly become aware of the parent's mortality and the fragility of human life. Children whose parents were traumatized by a single event (accident, victim of crime) may come to recognize that this was an event that is unlikely to reoccur. However, children of first responders become acutely aware of how dangerous their parent's job really is and that the parent risks death or injury every day. Consequently, they will begin to fear the loss of that parent every time the parent goes to work.

This feeling of fear may be compounded by several factors. First, the parent's own attitude toward the job, and how tentative or fearful the parent may be to return to work will greatly magnify the child's reaction. Even when the parent does not exhibit obvious reaction problems, the child still may have difficulties accepting the danger. For example, when the parent is regarded as a hero and given some recognition for bravery, the child may be caught in a double-bind: being proud of the parent's accomplishment but fearful for the parent's safety. The child may not know how to handle these feelings. In our follow-up, one 7-year-old child of a police officer commented, "I wish my dad was just a mechanic." Yet this child stated that she was very proud when her father's name appeared in the local paper.

First responder health and personal adjustment problems. Children tend to mirror the parents' behaviors and reactions. A child of a police officer who continues to enjoy his or her job is likely to have an easier time adjusting to the dangers inherent in that job. However, a child may become fearful if the parent dislikes going to work and exhibits significant posttraumatic reactions. When the child sees a parent having difficulties handling the stress, the child is much more likely to exhibit similar reactions and they may become even more pronounced than the parent's.

Children who are exposed to a parent who became injured or exhibits other health problems since the traumatization also may exhibit a strong reaction. First responders are individuals generally known for their physical strength and prowess, and their children are likely to expect that the parent will continue to exhibit good physical health and significant physical acumen.

Parental relationship problems. When officers become traumatized, the stress that they endure is greater than that experienced in most other occupations, and the reactions to it are likely to be more pronounced and intense. Consequently, the family may be affected to a more significant degree. Indeed, some suggest that "extraordinary stress [inherent in the job of an officer] makes police officers more prone than average citizens to alcoholism, domestic violence, divorce, and suicide" (Lott, 1995).

Changes in work and socioeconomic status. Nearly 30% of the New York City police officers reported that their work life did not return to normal after the trauma of September 11. When the officers experience problems at work, they may cut back their hours, refuse overtime, utilize more sick time, take a leave of absence, or quit. About one-third of New York City's police officers moved

or retired in the 3 years since September 11. These officers, as well as others who remain employed but miss opportunities for advancement and promotions, are likely to experience a decrease in income, which may have an adverse impact on the family's socioeconomic status.

The child's age. Young children (age 5 or younger) may have difficulties understanding the trauma that the parent experienced and may present with special challenges for the counselor because of their limited ability to express themselves verbally and match their feelings with words. Counselors must remember that although young children may not be able to say what they feel or tell their parents that they are in distress, they may have more difficulty in understanding and coping with those feelings. Older children may present with different challenges and are more likely to understand the continued danger that the parent may face.

OUTREACH TO CHILDREN

In order to reach the children, it is usually necessary initially to reach the first responder. Children of first responders usually do not become the target of initial clinical intervention within the family; the primary recipient of counseling services is likely to be the first responder, perhaps referred by a supervisor or self-referred through an employee assistance program (EAP). Individuals in distress are likely to spend the time during the counseling session discussing their own difficulties; therefore, the counselor needs to make a conscious effort to ask questions along the way to assess the children.

During treatment, the counselor needs to balance the needs of the first responder and the family by asking about the relationship between the first responder and the spouse/partner and the adjustment of the children. Moreover, it is important to educate the first responder about how the children may have been exposed to the trauma through media, as well as how children may be affected by conflict and stress within the family. The first responder may be aware of behavioral and academic problems, but may not be aware of the emotional changes that children also exhibit. In addition, the first responder may not recognize that these changes may be secondary to the trauma and its ripple effects on the family.

COMMON PROBLEMS

When working with first responders, counselors should help them recognize the signs of secondary traumatization that their children may exhibit. The following suggestions may be helpful.

Emotional problems and symptoms. Children who are under emotional distress commonly experience any combination of these symptoms: crying, clinginess, fears (especially at bedtime), nightmares and night terrors, problems separating from parents when dropped off at school or day care, loss of interest in some play activities, and general withdrawal. The counselor and the first responder must work together to identify these signs of emotional distress and determine the degree to which these behaviors have changed after the parent was traumatized.

Behavior problems. Distressed children often exhibit behavior problems that include acting out such as argumentativeness and defiance, difficulties handling frustration—particularly with siblings—problems controlling their anger, temper tantrums, and general crankiness. Children present with difficult personalities that make them prone to more outbursts and behavioral problems. In addition, parents sometimes utilize child management skills that exacerbate these problems.

Peer problems. Children exposed to significant family stress also may behave differently with their peers. These changes include increases in withdrawal and shyness, or the reverse—increased bossiness and difficulties in sharing.

Academic problems. Common school problems that may be related to parental trauma include reluctance to do homework, becoming more forgetful and distractible, decreased interest in school, a drop in grades, an increase in missing assignments, and acting out behaviors that lead to detention or suspension. In the more severe cases, youngsters may begin to present with truancy.

Alcohol and drug problems. Counselors must be aware that teenagers of traumatized parents may be at particularly high risk for developing substance-related problems. Teens may use alcohol or drugs to mask their feelings of discomfort or to seek kinship with others.

Criminal problems. Adolescents (as well as some younger children) who feel stressed and misunderstood may turn to mischief and criminal behaviors such as shoplifting. Although this may be an expression of anger and a "cry for help," it also may be another example of behaviors seeking acceptance into a counterculture that, in their estimation, is better equipped to understand their anger and frustration.

COUNSELING THE FIRST RESPONDER

Reaching the children usually begins with counseling the first responder, but first responders may resist seeking treatment. During their training, police officers learn to suppress their emotions and control any emotional arousal. For a police officer, a rush of emotions often means that danger is approaching, and the officer must learn to control fear and other emotions in order to remain calm and respond appropriately under pressure. Police officers are usually unable to "turn on and off" such a stance, and consequently they are likely to work hard to keep their emotions under control even in counseling settings where open expression of emotions in counseling would promote health and adjustment.

This has two implications for counselors. First, officers are less likely to recognize that they are under psychological distress, especially when to them the immediate situation does not seem to involve clear and present danger. Consequently, officers are less likely to seek treatment and may instead work hard to deny (consciously or not) that anything is wrong. Psychoeducation and outreach efforts are necessary to help officers recognize the internal signs that they need help (e.g., sleeping poorly, loss of appetite, irritability, or anhedonia).

Second, even when officers do present in treatment, they may have difficulty disclosing emotional or other symptoms, feeling that admitting to psychological distress is a sign of weakness. Counselors must be sensitive to the subtle signs that the officers may be under emotional duress in order not to miss opportunities to pursue self-disclosure. In addition, counselors must help them reframe emotional reactions to sensitize the officers to the effects the reactions have on their life and general functioning. In our follow-up, almost 80% of the police officers were male, which is typical of most police departments across the country. Conversely, counselors are disproportionately female. Gender, however, did not have a direct impact on the utilization of counseling, and married individuals were as likely to exhibit difficulties as single officers were.

Although there is some symptomatic overlap among various diagnostic categories—PTSD, anxiety, depression, adjustment disorders—counselors must refrain from automatically expecting PTSD. Our follow-up data revealed that New York City police officers are very heterogeneous with regard to diagnosis and symptom presentation. However, symptoms can evolve and change over time, and the counselor must remain sensitive to these variations. It can be difficult to determine if an individual's chest tightness and shortness of breath is a symptom of anxiety and panic or the result of exposure to environmental hazards. Sleep disorders are commonly seen with PTSD, depression, and anxiety, but they also can stem from breathing difficulties associated with environmental hazards.

COUNSELING THE CHILDREN

If the outreach effort is successful and the child is brought to treatment, the counselor will need to employ treatment approaches that address the children's needs and the underlying family dynamics. Young children who are unable to express their feelings adequately must be given assistance to do so; adjunct nonverbal therapies such as play therapy and art therapy can be helpful. Those who are better able to verbalize will likely benefit from individual and group counseling approaches aimed at assisting them with developing necessary coping strategies. Children of first responders must come to terms with the dangers inherent in the parent's occupation, especially if the parent plans to remain in that line of work. Group treatment—when children of first responders come together and share their feelings and coping strategies—may be beneficial.

Job stress of the parent is likely to change family dynamics significantly and family discord is a common consequence. Outreach may be necessary to enlist the participation of all family members of primary significance to the child.

If the child is experiencing problems in school, contact with the teacher, school counselor, or administrators may be necessary, or, when more extreme problems are present, the child could be referred to the child study team for an evaluation. The counselor can help the family navigate the educational system that so many parents find confusing and intimidating.

Parents may need assistance if their adolescent is engaging in more serious acting out such as substance abuse and criminal behavior; a multimodal approach may be necessary. If the counselor can establish that these problems are at least, in part, secondary to the family trauma and resulting adjustment problems, appropriate family interventions may be utilized. Counselors know how to treat traumatized children and adolescents. However, children of first responders may not always get the counselor's attention. By increasing their awareness and vigilance, counselors will reach the children and provide much needed services.

George Kapalka, PhD, is associate professor in the Department of Psychological Counseling at Monmouth University, West Long Branch, NJ.

REFERENCES

Duarte, C. S., Hoven, C. W., Wu, P., Bin, F., Cotel, S., Mandell, D. J., . . . Markenson, D. (2006). Posttraumatic stress in children with first responders in their families. *Journal of Traumatic Stress, 19,* 301–306.

Hoven, C. W., Duarte, C. S., Lucas, C. P., Wu, P., Mandell, D. J., Goodwin, R. D., . . . Susser, E. (2005). Psychopathology among New York City public school children 6 months after September 11. *Archives of General Psychiatry, 62,* 545–551.

Kapalka, G. M., Letizia, G., Bascom, R., Quian, Z., Buyantseva, L., Young, M., & Roberts, A. (2004). *Physical and mental health of New York City police officers 18 months after the World Trade Center attacks.* New York: International Society for Environmental Epidemiology.

Lott, L. D. (1995). Deadly secrets: Violence in the police family. *FBI Law Enforcement Bulletin, 64.*

Section Seven

Self Care for Counselors and First Responders

GROUND HERO: A STORY OF COMPASSION FATIGUE AFTER SEPTEMBER 11

32

Tom Query

I stood in the rubble and the dirt of the fallen Trade Centers, which was not just dirt, and peered into the pit. The Caterpillars moved piles of metal and debris with paradoxical care as the smoke from still burning fires wafted upward.

"They are looking for heavy rubber turnout gear," stated Captain Frank McGlocklin, a retired FDNY firefighter. "When they find that, they know where to start digging. By the markings on the gear, they know which station to call down here so they can dig with us and carry the remains out if we're that lucky. You tell folks to call this Ground Hero, not ground zero," he emphasized. "We know we got at least 25,000 people out of the towers that morning."

The scene was overwhelming, a surreal mixture of destruction, confusion, and smell. The odor was acrid, metallic, and burning and when it arrived unannounced on a breeze anywhere in Manhattan or Brooklyn, we would look at each other and know.

I had arrived in New York a week before my pilgrimage to Ground Hero. Like all Americans, I had wanted to do something after the attacks. I got an e-mail from Bill Harkins, an Atlanta marriage and family therapist colleague, that the Red Cross was looking for licensed mental health workers to go to New York. I told my wife and daughter about the e-mail.

My daughter exclaimed, "Oh, Dad! You have to go! All of us want to go and do something. Go for all of us." My wife said wryly, "You can go, but you can't fly." Within 2 weeks, I had taken all the required courses that the Red Cross needed. With no advanced notice, I received a call at my office stating that I had been "called up" and would leave the next day! I had a full practice, but after a whirlwind of preparation, I was on a plane 2 days later.

The Red Cross headquarters in Brooklyn was lo-

cated in a closed school building. There was a flurry of urgent activity. On the mental health floor, there were hundreds of tiny yellow stickers hung on a wall representing the volunteers at the different sites. There were Respite Centers in the "hot zone" working directly with the rescue workers. There were eight Service Centers where families and survivors could come for assistance and help. Pier 94 on Westside Highway was one of them. It was a one-stop shop for a multitude of agencies and where the urns, filled with dust from the site, were presented to the families. I was assigned to Service Center 6 on Staten Island. Most of the individuals affected did not live in Manhattan—they lived in the boroughs in and around New York City.

Service Center 6 was located at the picturesque Mt. Manresa Catholic spiritual retreat center overlooking Ground Hero from Staten Island. Father Ryan was the undisputed leader in the midst of the chaos. Along with Service Center 6, Mt. Manresa also hosted the rescue dogs and handlers, the FDNY Counseling Center, DNA collection from family members, and lodging for workers at Ground Hero and the landfill. When the courier dropped me off at this location, a crazed-looking woman ran up to the van, flung open the door and said, "Are you mental health?" "Yes," I answered. "Welcome to hell" she moaned. She was the other mental health worker.

Service Center 6 could process 50 people a day if pressed to the limit; 150–300 individuals would line up on the doorstep each day, sometimes arriving as early as 3 a.m. Everyone was evaluated for need: widows, survivors from the buildings, displaced workers and families, and, those described as—for lack of a better word—collateral damage. About 80,000 persons who had worked in and around the Trade Centers were now out of work; many were traumatized from the sights of

September 11. Individuals returned day after day until they could be helped. My predecessor was burned out. No, that is too mild a phrase. She was "deep fried." She had been banned from entering the building where the individual and family work was being done due to her distracting PTSD behavior. It was "Mental Health's" job to triage needs and determine priorities for assistance. The parking lot was the "waiting room" where triage took place. It was a giant debriefing zone. It took a day or two to gain the trust of the workers who then started calling me into the building to talk to distraught people. From that time on, I was deluged with requests for assistance as well as having to manage the multitudes.

People of like ethnicity would group together and tell their stories, reexperiencing the event through memories, reminders, reactions, and feelings. Asians, Czechs and Slovaks, Serbs, Russians, Italians, Arabs, Israelis, Muslims, and Christians gathered. There was an attitudinal separation between those who had been "there," in and around the towers, and those who had watched from afar. Those who had been present considered themselves survivors. The clinical "group work" that took place was one of the most important therapeutic interventions I made as a therapist, and it just occurred by accident and necessity, not design. In such a chaotic environment, a clinician can make an intervention by utilizing what is naturally occurring and structuring the interaction so as to encourage each individual to examine their reactions and beliefs in relation to the event. I facilitated the sharing of anger, shame, or guilt, which is common among survivors of sudden trauma and promoted the idea of seeking further help.

We worked 18-hour days. Each morning we arrived at 6 a.m. to a new list of names taped to the door in the order that they had arrived. Often someone who was in line would come up to me as I opened the door and tell me the most important need. One experience involved a Russian man who approached me and said in a deep accent, "Tom, there is a woman over here...see, she is pregnant and she lost her husband in the towers...she needs to go first." In New York, your place in line means something. I went over, placed my arm around the shoulder of the woman, and led her to the front of the line. The crowd parted. No one said a word.

One day, a Chinese man who had waited several days for help and whom I had gotten to know well, made it into the building for assistance. When he came out, he assumed I had pulled strings to get him in and thanked me, saying he owed me. I assured him that he owed me nothing, but he persisted. Having just seen the movie Pay It Forward, I recounted the premise that you don't pay

back but pay forward by doing something good for someone else. He agreed to this and went off into the crowd.

Later that day a Cantonese woman arrived, and there were no translators. To make matters worse, this woman did not trust us, as was the case with many of the non-English speakers. In fact, many ethnic groups exhibited a tremendous amount of paranoia about letting agencies help them. The Red Cross would request documentation (such as a lease or cancelled check) to assist, for example, in providing rent money for those unemployed by the attack. In some communities, a person might have a bed in a room of a "cousin's friend's place" and the transaction might be in cash. There were no documents to provide. Bending the rules, we would ask for a name of someone to call to corroborate the information. This made them anxious. Late in the evening, while we were struggling to communicate with the Cantonese woman, the Chinese man who had been in earlier reappeared and asked if he could help. I was delighted and grateful. They began to talk. Then it escalated into shrill shouting.

He turned to me after a while, and with tears in his eyes stated, "This is a stubborn woman. She will not trust you. She is going to go away even though she needs your help. I am sorry. I failed you in trying to repay you."

After a moment of silence I replied, "No, you did as I asked. I did not say you had to succeed, just try." He collapsed into my arms sobbing.

There was no formal therapy to speak of at Service Center 6. There was just a tremendous amount of assessment, catharsis, and brief intervention that we called "debriefing and defusing." We saw 1,000 people in 15 days. Categories like posttraumatic stress, dissociation, grief, and depression did not apply. The books and theories were useless. We did not have a referral list of local therapists at our disposal. In particular, we needed referral sources skilled in multicultural work, and we had none. When I returned to Georgia, I spoke to as many therapist groups as I could, advising that if this happened in our community we would need to have a drop-in center where the Red Cross and others could simply hand out addresses and say, "Go there!"

In one incident, a 13-year-old girl whose father died in the towers was suffering greatly. She was estranged from him at the time of his death. I asked if there was anyone she would talk with. She reported that in the past she had gone to a particular counselor and agreed to talk to her. I called the counselor. "Does she have insurance?" the counselor asked. "Did you hear what I just said?" I exploded. "Give me an appointment time tomorrow, see this girl, and ask that asinine question later."

I made three journeys away from Service Center 6. One was with the firefighters who took me to Ground Hero. A second trip was to the Rescue Five FDNY station on Staten Island that lost 11 of 22 men and had buried nine of them. The third trip came when Father Ryan approached me one day. He looked at the documents we were required to wear around our neck—our Red Cross ID and a copy of our professional license. I also inserted my ministerial credentials. I am ordained, though I confess, I normally carry my collar "in my back pocket."

Father Ryan said, "You need to take a trip with me to the south side of the island." We rode to the Fresh Kills landfill, which had been closed but was reopened to receive the remains of Ground Hero. Hundreds of men in white "space suits" and respirators were toiling on top of this barren hill. They were sorting and filtering the debris and remains from the Trade Center being brought over by barge. Everything was screened for human remains, going so far as to sift the dust. There were several trailers with body bags for each part found. It was cold and blustery on top of this hill with no fires covering the smell as there had been in Manhattan. It was a horrible, putrid smell of death and decay. We visited with the workers as chaplains.

It was here that I lost my ability to feel. My main tool as a therapist is my intuition, which is fueled by my emotions. I lost them that day on top of that barren mountain. The rest of the time there, I worked as hard as I had before but could not feel sad, angry, scared, or happy. I returned to Georgia without my feelings; they were left in the dirt of Fresh Kills. I came home to a family who said I was different. I sat in my office and went through the motions of therapy. It was good to be back where not everything seemed like a process of bailing the ocean with a thimble. One good friend, who is Native American by faith, came up to me after he heard that I had stopped feeling. Ed Taylor told me that in some Native American thought, when there is a great tragedy like the 3,000 murders in New York, they believe the spirits remain there waiting for a good heart to attach to so they can go on their way. He touched his hand to my chest and said, "Maybe you are just all full up. Let's find a way to let them go on their way."

This chapter was developed from the author's presentation at the ACAF/Argosy University First Annual Winter Counseling Symposium entitled "Responding to Tragedy, Trauma, and Crisis," in Sarasota, Florida, February 2004.

Eight Years Later: An Update from Tom Query

I came back home from New York to a changed world; my emotions were locked up inside me. My wife had received a letter from the Red Cross for her to be prepared that I would not come home the same, and I did not. She will say I never came home from New York. I felt that I came home with a new way of looking at life. I did not want to live life in the same way—life is too short.

It took a couple of months for my feelings to resurface. We know that my reaction was a symptom of post-traumatic stress disorder. Some Native American friends of mine held a sweat lodge for me so that I could release the "spirits" inside of me. I spoke at a couple of churches about my experience and I began to develop a continuing education workshop for therapists and counselors. I saw that Argosy University was providing a Traumatology Symposium on September 11 and I did not see any speakers that had worked in New York on the program. I contacted them and they suggested I come. I ended up presenting this program numerous times over the next year and a half, which allowed me to "debrief" my experience and to work through the trauma by telling my story over and over. I still feel that it was a major mistake for the Red Cross not to provide such assistance to me after my discharge.

Music is a wonderful healer. I first felt my feelings return while listening to a song—James Taylor's "Fire and Rain." Bruce Springsteen's album "The Rising" was a remarkable piece of art arising from the dirt of Ground Hero and his phraseology seem to come directly from the mouths of the victims and survivors. I sought out other workers who had been in the dirt and we told each other our stories. I sought out any family member or survivor in the Atlanta area and provided therapy to two such families. I saw one man for over 2 years pro bono as he struggled with his brother's murder. I collected books on September 11. There are some marvelous ones particularly *Report From Ground Zero*, *Brotherhood*, and *This is New York*. I cherish drawings I kept from the kids I worked with; they are deeply poignant and moving. I still have my Red Cross vest and security tags.

In my personal life, I came home to my family, particularly my wife, and began to work on some problems we had; our marriage had stalled and was dead. While in New York, I realized I had some gifts and talents and wishes for living, and that I had some deep personal needs that I had to address in our marriage. I began to ask for changes in our relationship and this deepened our problems. After a couple of years of therapy and painful work, we separated and eventually divorced.

I am an amateur photographer and my art suddenly transformed as people started telling me they could feel my images. I developed a class called Emotional Photography that I teach at the Cedar Heights Wellness Center in North Georgia.

My practice was different. For the couple of months that I had no "feelings," it was a strange environment. Not having my emotions as a ground and compass left me feeling lost. I am a very intuitive therapist and I am trained in experiential psychotherapy. I went through the motions and said all the right words, but I did not feel anything. My clients were very patient with me, and I felt they were caring for me for a while. I did not sit as long with people as they whined or were not moving on in their work and wanted them to "get on with it" as life is too short. I was not as harsh as those words sound, but my style did change, for the better, I think.

I write this just before the eighth anniversary of the attack. We are still at war in Afghanistan, the anthrax killers have never been found, and we have a new President and a new country. They are erecting the first pole of the buildings that will sit on the 16 acres we call Ground Hero. Many lives were lost or changed on that day and thousands have died since from the same cause. Mine is a very small story. I feel I am a better person, a better therapist, and a better father from my experience. And I still feel life is too short to wait.

Tom Query, LPC, is a counselor in private practice in Roswell and Dawsonville, GA.

Compassion Fatigue: Our Achilles Heel

J. Eric Gentry

On the afternoon of August 20, 2004, I sat in the front seat of a Florida Power & Light utility truck conducting an Individual Defusing (Gentry, 2003; Myers, 1987; Young, Ford, Ruzek, Friedman, & Gusman, 2003) with a lineman who had, literally, looked Hurricane Charley in the eye and survived. The employee suffered the complete devastation of his home and barely escaped death as he and his wife were pummeled with debris from 145+ mile-per-hour winds of the Category IV storm. This was my sixth long day of employee assistance for those men and women who were urgently and effectively restoring power to the one-quarter million homes across Florida darkened by Charley. I was working in Charlotte County the area that has come to be known by the emergency service and disaster relief workers as "Ground Zero," which bears a striking resemblance to the New York site, where I had worked almost 3 years before.

I listened to this employee's narrative describing a narrow escape from his crumbling home, fleeing with his wife to the relative safety of his SUV, escalating fear as the malevolent wind ripped at his vehicle, and the uninterrupted assault of debris from neighbors' homes, each an ongoing perceived threat to survival. As he reached a pause in the telling of his story, he sat mute for several seconds. I watched his eyes become fixed in the near distance, his leg begin shaking, and his eyes reddened. From having heard thousands of trauma narratives throughout my career, I knew we had entered the crux of his telling—the recounting of his memory of the micro-events surrounding the time in which he thought he was going to die. He pointed out the front windshield of the truck toward the tangle of wires and steel lattice of a power relay station that was bathed in sunlight. I knew he was no longer seeing with his eyes

in the present but was instead fully transfixed by the intrusive internal vision and was transported to 7 days earlier—seeing those sights and hearing those sounds.

"The roof came clean off my neighbor's house and headed right for us," he whispered. He tightly gripped the steering wheel as he braced for the impact of this structure slamming into the front of his vehicle, which would have certainly resulted in severe injury if not death. With a grunt, he described the cracking sound of a falling tree—a tree that he had planted 25 years earlier—as it collided with the neighbor's roof, which was careening toward him at more than 100 miles per hour.

"As soon as that tree fell, I knew we were going to be OK…don't ask me how, I just knew," he said. He continued his narrative, describing the lightening of the sky from black to grey to brilliant sunlight and unnatural calm. "We were in the eye," he said matter-of-factly. Emerging for the first time from the trance of this nightmare, he looked me in the eye with a quizzical expression as if to say, "Where did you come from and how long have you been here?" When the eye of the hurricane passed, the winds became even more violent, blowing now in the opposite direction, with rain so heavy he could no longer see outside his vehicle. "But I knew we were going to be OK," he said once again.

In 1 hour, it was all over. Lesser winds and rain remained but Charley had already moved on to wreak havoc in other areas of Florida. The employee and his wife finally left the safety of their vehicle and found that their home, which had been built on stilts, had crumbled to the ground. It was completely destroyed and uninhabitable. He said that they were staying with extended family until they decided whether to rebuild or buy another home. He is working with the Federal

Emergency Management Agency (FEMA) to acquire assistance for both the short-term and for rebuilding. He said his insurance would not cover the costs of rebuilding.

"You want to know the worst part?" he asked. I responded with silence and continued my self-regulated, non-anxious presence that I learned in my years of training and experience. "The worst part of this whole thing," he said as tears filled his eyes, "is when I get done working an 18- or 20-hour day...I just want to go home...."

When he completed his narrative, I helped him normalize some of the responses and symptoms that he had experienced (e.g., anxiety, difficulty sleeping, irritability, headaches) and let him know that I would be following up with him over the next few weeks. He requested that I speak with his wife, who also was experiencing some of the same responses and symptoms; I agreed. I told him that I predicted a complete recovery for him that might include support from his employee assistance program. I helped him identify his supports and agreed to get information for him on assistance from FEMA and the Small Business Administration on low-interest loans for rebuilding. I gave him my card and told him that he and his wife did not need to endure this difficult process alone. He agreed to follow up with me.

As we shook hands and he left the cab of the truck, walking across the futuristic landscape of a power relay station, I was left in a whirlwind of profound emotions and images. For the next several days, I continued to re-experience images and emotions associated with my interaction with this employee. Balancing these difficult feelings and insights was the comforting knowledge that I had done all that could be done for this employee—I had witnessed his story, conducted an informal triage/assessment, helped him stabilize his emotions, normalized his responses, connected him with support, and predicted positive outcomes for his recovery. Even while wrapped in this awareness, I was acutely aware of my own powerlessness in the face of so much devastation, loss, and suffering.

Psychological first aid, like emergency medical services, requires a special set of skills and a shift in orientation for many mental health professionals. The specific training and skill requirements for this work have been discussed elsewhere (Myers, 1994; Rank & Gentry, 2003; Young, Ford, Ruzek, Friedman, & Gusman, 2003), but one of the most important elements of critical incident intervention is the development and maintenance of resiliency on the part of the caregiver. Compassion fatigue can be effectively treated (Baranowsky, Gentry, & Schultz, 2010; Gentry, Baggerly, & Baranowsky, 2004;

Gentry & Baranowsky, 1999) but more important, it can be prevented by developing specific skills, orientations, and practices that augment our resiliency and mature us as caregivers.

Fatigue, environmental destruction and damage, work demands, previous experiences of personal trauma, previous work in disaster contexts, and secondary traumatic stress can have a negative effect on the physical and psychological health of caregivers working in any high-demand situation. These negative effects—including physical, emotional, psychological, behavioral, and spiritual symptoms—have come to be known as compassion fatigue.

For those of us who have chosen traumatology as a professional path, there is no sweeter experience than witnessing a survivor emerge transformed and fortified from the dark jungle of posttraumatic symptoms. There is also little doubt that serving these survivors exacts a toll, which may be minimal for some caregivers, but devastating for others. As Viktor Frankl, one of the twentieth century's greatest traumatologists, warns and encourages simultaneously: "That which is to give light must endure burning" (Frankl, 1963, p. 129).

Professionals who listen to reports of trauma, horror, human cruelty, and extreme loss can become overwhelmed and may begin to experience feelings of fear, pain, and suffering similar to that of their clients. They also may experience PTSD symptoms similar to that of their clients, such as intrusive thoughts, nightmares, avoidance and arousal, as well as changes in their relationships with themselves, their families, friends, and communities (Figley, 1995; McCann & Pearlman, 1990; Salston, 1999). Therefore, they may eventually need assistance in coping.

Vicarious traumatization (McCann & Pearlman, 1990) refers to the transmission of traumatic stress through observation or hearing others' stories of traumatic events and the resultant shift and distortions that occur in the caregiver's perceptual and meaning systems. Secondary traumatic stress occurs when one is exposed to extreme events directly experienced by another and then becomes overwhelmed by this secondary exposure to trauma (Figley & Kleber, 1995). It has been hypothesized that the caregiver's level of empathy with the traumatized individual plays a significant role in this transmission (Figley, 1995). Figley also proposed that the combined effects of the caregiver's continuous visualizing of clients' traumatic images added to the effects of burnout could create a condition of progressive debilitation of the caregiver; he called this *compassion stress*.

We have augmented Figley's definition to include pre-existing and concomitant primary posttraumatic stress and its symptoms, finding that many caregivers enter the service field with a host of traumatic experiences in their past (Baranowsky, Gentry, & Schultz, 2009; Gentry, 1999). In addition, we have discerned an interactive, or synergistic, effect among primary traumatic stress, secondary traumatic stress, and burnout symptoms in the life of an afflicted caregiver. This seems to lead to a rapid onset of severe symptoms that can become extremely debilitating to the caregiver within a very short period.

TREATMENT AND PREVENTION: ACTIVE INGREDIENTS

No one who chooses to work with trauma survivors is immune to the potential deleterious effects of this work. However, in our work, either individually through the Accelerated Recovery Program for Compassion Fatigue (ARP) or in Certified Compassion Fatigue Specialist Training (CCFST) (Gentry & Baranowsky, 1998, 1999), we have identified some enduring principles that consistently lead to positive treatment outcomes and enhanced resiliency. The CCFST was the first conceptualization of the "training-as-treatment" model (Gentry, 2000) for addressing the participants' symptoms of compassion fatigue.

We strongly urge the caregiver who specializes in working with trauma and trauma survivors to develop a comprehensive self-care plan that addresses and meets the caregiver's individual needs. With a self-care plan in place, the caregiver can practice with the assurance that they are maximizing resiliency and preventing the symptoms of compassion fatigue; this protection is akin to wearing a seatbelt.

Care providers responding onsite to crisis situations, such as those caused by the Florida hurricanes or the events of September 11, may be limited in their ability to employ habitual self-care activities. They may not have access to exercise facilities or to their traditional support network, and nutritious food and water may be scarce. Although most trauma responders are a hardy and resilient breed, we simply cannot sustain the rigors of this depleting and intensive work without intentional concern for our own health and welfare. Making best use of available resources to establish respite and sanctuary for ourselves can have an enormous effect in minimizing our symptoms and maximizing our sustained effectiveness. Many responders have reported acts of kindness as simple as the gift of a bottle of water, a pat on the back, or an opportunity to share a meal with another responder as having a powerful impact on their morale and energy.

The creation of a time-line narrative of a caregiver's career that identifies the experiences and the clients from which the caregiver developed primary and secondary traumatic stress is invaluable in the resolution of compassion fatigue symptoms. In the ARP, we instruct the participant/caregiver to "tell your story…from the beginning—the first experiences in your life that led you toward care giving—to the present." We use a video camera to record this narrative and ask the caregiver to watch it later that same day, taking care to identify the experiences that have led to any primary and secondary traumatic stress (intrusive symptoms) by constructing a time-line. In the CCFST, we utilize dyads in which two participants each take a 1-hour block of time to verbalize their narrative while the other practices non-anxious "bearing witness" of this narrative.

The caregiver is now ready to resolve these memories. In the ARP, we have utilized Eye Movement Desensitization and Reprocessing (Shapiro, 1989, 1995) and in the CCFST, we utilize a hybrid version of an Anchoring Technique Neuro-Linguistic Programming (Revised) (Gentry & Baranowsky, 1998). Any method that simultaneously employs exposure and relaxation (i.e., reciprocal inhibition) is appropriate for this important cornerstone of treatment. This often comes with a concomitant sense of rebirth, joy, and transformation.

In our work with the responders of the Oklahoma City bombing, none reported experiencing intrusive symptoms of secondary or primary traumatic stress until days, weeks, months, and sometimes years after their work at the site. According to an incident commander for a team of mental health responders who worked with more than 2,700 victims in New York City during the first month after the attacks (Norman, personal communication, 2002), at least one certified compassion fatigue specialist was available to provide daily debriefing services for every 10 responders. If a responder began to report symptoms or show signs of significant traumatic stress, they were provided with acute stabilization services by the team and arrangements were made for transportation back home with a referral to a mental health practitioner in the worker's hometown. With the intense demands of critical incident work and the paramount importance of worker safety, attempts to desensitize and reprocess a provider's primary and secondary traumatic stress while onsite seem counterproductive because they draw from the often already depleted resources of the intervention team. The worker should engage in resolving the effects of accumulated traumatic memories only after safely returning to the existing resources and support offered by their family, friends, churches/synagogues, and healthcare professionals in their hometown.

Caregivers recovering from the symptoms of compassion fatigue will need to soften their critical and coercive self-talk and shift their motivational styles toward more self-accepting and affirming language and tone. We have employed an adapted elegant and powerful technique called video-dialogue (Holmes & Tinnin, 1995). It challenges the participant to write a letter to themselves from the "Great Supervisor," lavishing upon themselves all the praise, support, and validation that they wish from others and then reading it into the eye of the camera. The cognitive therapy triple column technique (Burns, 1980) also helps identify particular cognitive distortions and challenges a client to rewrite these negative thoughts into ones that are more adaptive and satisfying. As caregivers suffering from compassion fatigue develop some mastery in resolving these internal polarities, they are challenged to identify and resolve polarities with significant others.

THE CRUCIBLE OF TRANSFORMATION

As we embarked upon the formidable task of sitting across from our peers who were suffering with these symptoms, many of whom were demoralized, hopeless, and desperate, we began to understand that recovery from compassion fatigue required significant changes in the fundamental beliefs and lifestyles of the caregiver. As we navigated through the five sessions of the ARP, we found that most underwent a significant transformation in the way in which they perceived their work and, ultimately, themselves.

Instead of viewing the symptoms of compassion fatigue as a pathological condition that requires some external treatment agent or techniques for resolution, we began to see these symptoms as indicators of the need for the professional caregiver to continue his or her development into matured caregiving and self-care styles and practices. From this perspective, the symptoms of compassion fatigue can be interpreted as messages about what is right, good, and strong within us, rather than indicators of shameful weaknesses, defects, or sickness.

We have been able to identify two primary principles of treatment and prevention that lead to a rapid resolution of symptoms and sustained resilience: (a) the development and maintenance of intentionality, through a non-anxious presence, in both personal and professional spheres of life; and (b) the development and maintenance of self-validation, especially self-validated caregiving. When these principles are followed in our own practices and with the caregivers whom we have treated, not only do negative symptoms diminish, but also quality of life is significantly enhanced and refreshed as new perspectives and horizons begin to open. It is humbling to participate in this healing, on any level.

From our experience with the emergency service workers and professional caregivers who served the survivors of the Oklahoma City bombing since 1995, we also know that there will be casualties in this effort. Many kind and good-hearted emergency service professionals, caregivers, friends, and family members who have witnessed the pain, grief, and terror in their service to survivors will themselves end up wrestling with encroaching intrusive images, thoughts, and feelings in the future.

The good news is that the symptoms of compassion fatigue seem to be very responsive to treatment and are ameliorated rapidly (Gentry & Baranowsky, 1998; Pearlman & Saakvitne, 1995). Moreover, we have witnessed that for numerous caregivers, the symptoms of compassion fatigue become a powerful catalyst for change. With skilled intervention and determination, care providers with compassion fatigue can undergo a profound transformation, leaving them more empowered and resilient than they were previously. As such, they are better equipped to act as "givers of light."

J. Eric Gentry, PhD, LMHC, is in private practice in Sarasota, Florida. He is the owner of Compassion Unlimited, an international training and consulting company, and he is a compassion fatigue specialist and traumatologist.

The author wishes to acknowledge support for this article from **Anna Baranowsky, PhD,** *private practice, Toronto, Canada.*

Part of this article takes excerpts from J. Eric Gentry, PhD, "Compassion Fatigue: A Crucible of Transformation" from *Journal of Trauma Practice, 1*(3/4), 37–61. Reprinted with the permission of The Haworth Press, Inc.

REFERENCES

Baranowsky, A., Gentry, J. E., & Schultz, D. F. (2010). *Trauma practice: Tools for stabilization & recovery* (2nd ed.). Cambridge, MA: Hogrefe & Huber.

Burns, D. (1980). *Feeling good: The new mood therapy.* New York: Morrow.

Figley, C. R. (1995). *Compassion fatigue: Coping with secondary traumatic stress disorder in those who treat the traumatized.* New York: Brunner/Mazel.

Figley, C. R., & Kleber, R. (1995). Beyond the "victim": Secondary traumatic stress. In R. J. Kleber & C.R. Figley (Eds.), *Beyond trauma: Cultural and societal dynamics. Plenum series on stress and coping* (pp. 75–98). New York: Plenum Press.

Frankl, V. E. (1963). *Man's search for meaning.* New York: Washington Square Press.

Gentry, J. E. (1999). *The trauma recovery scale (TRS): An outcome measure.* Poster presentation at the meeting of the International Society for Traumatic Stress Studies, Miami, FL.

Gentry, J. E. (2000). *Certified compassion fatigue specialist training: Training-as-treatment.* Unpublished doctoral dissertation, Florida State University.

Gentry, J. E. (2003). Initial trauma intervention. In J.E. Gentry, D. Fojt & J. Baggerly (Eds.), *Bioterrorism trauma intervention specialist training: Building trauma preparedness and response capacity for community resiliency and recovery training manual.* Tampa, FL: University of South Florida.

Gentry, J. E., Baggerly, J., & Baranowsky, A. (2004). Training-as-treatment: Effectiveness of the Certified Compassion Fatigue Specialist Training. *Emergency Mental Health, 6*(30), 147–155.

Gentry, J., & Baranowsky, A. (1998). *Treatment manual for the Accelerated Recovery Program: Set II.* Toronto: Psych Ink.

Gentry, J. E., & Baranowsky, A. (1999, November). Accelerated recovery program for compassion fatigue. Preconference workshop presented at the 15th annual meeting of the International Society for Traumatic Stress Studies, Miami, FL.

Holmes, D., & Tinnin, L. (1995). The problem of auditory hallucinations in combat PTSD. Retrieved from http://www.fsu.edu/~trauma/art1v1i2.html

McCann, I. L., & Pearlman, L. A. (1990). Vicarious traumatization: A framework for understanding the psychological effects of working with victims. *Journal of Traumatic Stress, 3*(1), 131–149.

Myers, D. (1987). *Prevention and control of stress among emergency workers. A pamphlet for team managers.* DHHS Publication No. (ADM) 90-1496).

Myers, D. (1994). Psychological recovery from disaster: Key concepts for delivery of mental health services. *National Center for PTSD Clinical Quarterly, 4,* 3–5.

Pearlman, L. A., & Saakvitne, K.W. (1995). *Trauma and the therapist: Countertransference and vicarious traumatization in psychotherapy with incest survivors.* New York: W.W. Norton.

Rank, M., & Gentry, J. E. (2003). Critical incident stress: Principles, practices, and protocols. In M. Richard, W. Hutchinson, & W. Emener (Eds.). *Employee assistance programs: A basic text* (3rd ed.). New York: Charles C Thomas Publisher.

Salston, M. (1999). *Compassion fatigue: Implications for mental health professionals and trainees.* Defended critical review, Florida State University.

Salston, M. (2000). *Secondary traumatic stress: A study exploring empathy and the exposure to the traumatic material of survivors of community violence.* Unpublished dissertation, Florida State University.

Shapiro F. (1989). Efficacy of the eye movement desensitization procedure: A new treatment for post-traumatic stress disorder. *Journal of Traumatic Stress, 2*(2), 199–223.

Shapiro, F. (1995). *Eye movement desensitization and reprocessing: Basic principles, protocols and procedures.* New York: Guilford Press.

Young, B., Ford, J. D., Ruzek, J. I., Friedman, M. J., & Gusman, F. D. (2003). *Disaster mental health services. A guidebook for clinicians and administrators.* Menlo Park, CA: The U.S. Department of Veterans Affairs, The National Center for PTSD Website: http://www.ptsd.va.gov/

APPENDIX
SYMPTOMS OF COMPASSION FATIGUE

Intrusive Symptoms	Avoidance Symptoms	Arousal Symptoms
• Thoughts and images associated with client's traumatic experiences	• Silencing response (avoiding hearing/ witnessing client's traumatic material)	• Increased anxiety
• Obsessive and compulsive desire to help certain clients	• Loss of enjoyment in activities/ cessation of self care activities	• Impulsivity/reactivity
• Client/work issues encroaching upon personal time	• Loss of energy	• Increased perception of demand/ threat (in both job and environment)
• Inability to "let go" of work-related matters	• Loss of hope/sense of dread working with certain clients	• Increased frustration/anger
• Perception of survivors as fragile and needing the assistance of caregiver ("savior")	• Loss of sense of competence/ potency	• Sleep disturbance
• Thoughts and feelings of inadequacy as a caregiver	• Isolation	• Difficulty concentrating
• Sense of entitlement or "specialness"	• Secretive self-medication/addiction (alcohol, drugs, work, sex, food, spending, etc.)	• Change in weight/appetite
• Perception of the world in terms of victims and perpetrators	• Relational dysfunction	• Somatic symptoms
• Personal activities interrupted by work-related issues		

Self Care for Disaster Mental Health Workers: Force Health Protection Strategies

34

Rob T. Yin and Marjorie Bagwell Kukor

Disaster mental health (DMH) workers are trained to understand the importance of self care while on a disaster assignment—taking breaks, getting exercise, and staying connected to loved ones and support systems. Yet, as with all disaster relief workers, DMH workers consistently struggle to engage in adequate self care. Mendenhall (2006) identified the need for mental health practitioners to transition successfully from office work to disaster fieldwork, and noted that interpersonal relationships on a relief operation can be obstacles. Pre-deployment training and boundary- and goal-setting are ways to promote worker self care (Aten, Madson, Rice, & Chamberlain, 2008; Rosser, 2008).

American Red Cross (ARC) DMH teams composed of more than 8,000 master's level state-licensed mental health professionals deploy annually to more than 70,000 disasters. These teams provide triage, assessment, and crisis intervention to both survivors and responders. Although disasters vary from single-family fires to large hurricanes, they all put disaster responders at risk for vicarious trauma and compassion fatigue.

Chaotic work environments, highly vulnerable clients, and pressure to view all tasks as "mission critical" (immediate) have been identified as obstacles to worker self care in the crisis environment of child protective services (Perry, 2003; Yin, 2004). These obstacles were resolved successfully through the use of supervisory strategies dividing work into mission critical and non-mission critical elements, prioritizing the worker's health ahead of the client's, and resisting the urge to micro-manage the workers.

Force Health Protection Obstacles and Stragedies

The United States military, recognizing the importance of having their workforce in the best possible condition during times of need, developed a strategy called Force Health Protection (FHP) (TRICARE, 2009), which transfers well to disaster settings. This program emphasizes the need for all service members to maintain optimal physical and mental health in order to respond to any event. Obstacles (threats) were identified and solutions developed to assist leaders and service members in this process. The FHP program also emphasizes pre-deployment assessment and training activities (Force Health Protection, 2004) involving organization-wide solutions to put service members in a better position to protect and care for themselves. The FHP concept broadens the focus from an individual worker struggling to engage in self care to organizational strategies necessary for the entire workforce to succeed. Drawing on experience from 25 disaster relief deployments and 500 days on assignment, we have identified FHP obstacles and strategies to overcome them.

Obstacle 1: It is difficult to find the time for worker self care.

On many disaster relief operations, the number and size of shelter, feeding, and other service delivery sites will stretch the capacity of your DMH team. These service delivery sites open, close, and consolidate frequently, with a significant amount of time spent reassigning staff and changing service delivery plans. An average day for a DMH worker is 12–16 hours and the workload makes it difficult to find time for self care.

Supervisory Strategies

Develop DMH service delivery plans that include emotional support provided by all disaster workers. Offer Red Cross Psychological First Aid (PFA) training to new workers who are not yet trained. PFA training teaches workers to provide realistic reassurance, encourage good coping, connect survivors to their natural support systems, and know when to refer to DMH. PFA-trained workers are a "force multiplier," freeing up the DMH team to focus on tasks requiring greater professional expertise (e.g., triage, assessment, crisis intervention, training, consultation, and public mental health messaging).

Utilize evidenced-based triage tools to assign DMH workers where they are most needed. The PFA curriculum includes a triage system, PsySTART (Schreiber, 2009), utilizing evidence- and exposure-based risk factors (e.g., saw or heard someone injured or killed, death of a family member or pet), and enhances efficient use of DMH workers. All disaster workers should utilize PsySTART to triage and identify survivors that need to be seen first and to make more appropriate referrals to DMH.

Utilize on-call support strategies if a team is too small to provide 24-hour onsite coverage, allowing workers to take turns providing remote support.

Maximize the use of state and local mental health partnerships to coordinate DMH service delivery plans and avoid duplicating services. Engage local mental health agencies who are familiar with social demographics and community resources as early as possible.

Worker Strategies

Provide support to your non-DMH co-workers as they apply their PFA skills. Remind them of their ability to provide support to survivors and other workers and to handle emotional survivors on their own. Discourage DMH workers from referring individuals to you who are tearful or slightly anxious.

Encourage others to use the PsySTART triage system so that you receive appropriate (and fewer) referrals. Non-DMH workers should check their PsySTART wallet-sized reminder card to determine whether to refer a survivor. Respond first to survivors with acute symptoms and utilize the PsySTART triage system to prioritize your work according to exposure-based risk factors.

Remember that your skills and your time are valuable and taking time for self care maintains those skills.

Obstacle 2: Everything seems "mission critical."

Amid the profound loss and chaos of a disaster relief setting, all tasks seem urgent. DMH workers may struggle to make time for self care because they feel that their needs pale in comparison to the needs of survivors. Supervisors can be tempted to increase control over their workers, or when feeling overwhelmed, spend too little time with them.

Supervisor Strategies

Help workers distinguish between mission critical and non-mission critical DMH tasks by reminding them of priorities when they start feeling overwhelmed. The Red Cross DMH Manager's Toolkit (to be available on the Red Cross Intranet—CrossNet) identifies the core DMH mission critical tasks that "must be accomplished under an umbrella of protection that first prioritizes the well-being of all DMH workers…." (ARC, 2008a, p. 8).

Take care of yourself first by reminding yourself of the obligation to be in the best condition to do the tasks before you.

Triage the survivors and begin by providing support to those with the most acute needs—those few who are threatening harm to self or others or who are non-responsive, inconsolable, psychotic, or delusional.

Set achievable goals by utilizing the PsySTART exposure-based risk factors to provide support to survivors at greater risk for developing post-disaster mental disorders (Schreiber, 2009). Stay in contact with your team and follow DMH intervention and ethical standards (do not do Critical Incident Stress Debriefing (CISD), counseling, Eye Movement Desensitization Debriefing (EMDR), or psychotherapy).

Put self care at the top of the mission critical list. Bumping self care out of the first priority position will start you on a slippery slope as you are drawn to the urgent requests of others.

Resist the urge to micro-manage workers. Provide oversight and quality control over mission critical work and let workers decide how to tackle non-mission critical tasks (distribute psycho-educational materials, choose outreach routes, decide how much time to spenwith a client).

Worker Strategies

Find out what the supervisor sees as most important and as non-mission critical.

Know your limits and convey them to the supervisor. Is working in excess of 12 hours a day or working an entire morning or afternoon without a short break beyond your mental and physical capabilities?

Elevate self care to priority #1 before deployment. It is unlikely that you will make a significant shift in behavior while on a disaster relief assignment. Your success at self care will be influenced by prior success at home and work.

Be prepared for "push-back" from other disaster workers who don't view self care as priority #1. Anticipate pressure from other workers to change your priorities or to work beyond your limits.

Obstacle 3: Disaster teams are hastily assembled and constantly in flux, making structure and predictability difficult.

It is likely that you will be working with people you have met for the first time. With workers arriving and departing on a daily basis, it is difficult for supervisor/worker teams to develop rapport and cohesiveness. Personality differences that might normally be tolerable can become exaggerated and problematic.

Supervisor Strategies

Spend time supporting workers. Schedule time to meet every day. Develop a staggered day off schedule by the third or fourth day and give workers advance notice of time off so they can plan relaxing or rejuvenating activities (Red Cross policy is for workers to get 1 day off every 7 days).

Be collaborative. Solicit input from your workers, encourage feedback, and follow recommendations whenever possible. Short overlapping shift meetings will help you avoid duplication of efforts and mitigate potential problems.

Address conflicts as soon as they begin. The needs of disaster survivors can distract you from addressing conflicts with workers, allowing problems to fester and take more of your time later.

Be a flexible supervisor. Don't blame workers for being inflexible when your management style is rigid.

Worker Strategies

Work to develop a collaborative environment. Work relationships are established quickly in a disaster setting; however, your supervisor and coworkers may be from disciplines other than yours. Be open to direction, willing to try different assignments, and constructive in suggestions and feedback. (Roberts & Yeager, 2009).

Be a flexible and positive disaster worker. Anticipate that today's service delivery plans and work assignment will change tomorrow. Disaster settings are not the place for rigid work styles. When you see work well done, compliment the person responsible.

Do an end of day shift review. Hand off information to the arriving worker(s) in a short meeting to provide closure. Do not dwell on difficulties of the day once your shift is over.

Provide your own structure on a daily basis. Develop a schedule to increase control, even if you don't keep to it perfectly.

Assert yourself and get help if needed. Voice concerns to your supervisor if the relationship between the two of you becomes strained (feeling your supervisor is rigid, non-supportive, or micromanaging). Identify concerns, listen to responses, offer solutions, and be prepared to offer changes to your own actions. If problems persist or worsen, consider requesting support from a staff relations worker (disaster relief human resources).

Accept what belongs to you and tolerate what does not. Projection, personality conflicts, and getting pulled into other people's problems can occur during disaster relief operations. The Red Cross has a zero tolerance policy for intimidating and abusive behavior, which should be reported to human resources. Identify your behaviors that may be contributing to the difficulty and make adjustments to reduce the conflict. Be cognizant of your own reactions and be patient with others.

Obstacle 4: Disaster supervisors and workers are not always thoroughly prepared

With an emphasis on rapid response, disaster workers' pre-deployment preparation and training can get short-changed. A lack of experienced DMH supervisors can lead to field promotions of inexperienced workers who are unprepared to be supervisors. With pressure to deploy quickly, new workers may bypass key orientations. Sometimes workers deploy at times when they are emotionally unprepared and distracted by family needs or problems at home.

Supervisor Strategies

Spend more time preparing workers early in their deployment. Take time to: (a) assess worker capabilities, communication styles, and interests; match them to tasks and teams for which they are well suited; (b) conduct job inductions that show the workers' role within the broad service delivery plan; (c) clarify the tasks and expectations of assignments; and (d) let workers know how their assignment will fit into the broader service delivery plans (ARC, 2008b). Resist the urge to bypass worker orientations in order to deploy them quickly.

Assign experienced supervisors to visit service delivery sites. A few hours of support from an experienced counselor supervisor can provide inexperienced counselor supervisors the guidance they need to succeed in leading the team. Use your phone for additional consultation and support.

Find a supervisor buddy if you are an inexperienced DMH supervisor or ask for a mentor when you first arrive on the relief operation.

Overlap newly arriving and outgoing workers for 2-3 days to get oriented to their surroundings, culture, and expectations.

Worker strategies

Think carefully about whether now is the time to deploy. If family matters, health reasons, or work issues are looming, it may be better to stay home.

Call home. Make plans before you deploy to stay in touch with your loved ones and professional peers.

Inform the supervisor of your experience, skill sets, and interests so that you are adequately prepared and appropriately assigned.

Take training courses offered during a disaster relief operation to increase your preparedness level.

Find a buddy if you are an inexperienced DMH worker or ask for a mentor at the beginning of your assignment and touch base every day.

Ask the supervisor if you're having trouble getting necessary information, resources, or guidance. Your supervisor's primary job is to provide you with the support needed to do your job

You must successfully get past all four FHP obstacles to maximize opportunities for DMH worker self care. For example, if you succeed in identifying mission critical tasks (Obstacle 2), you will still need to have sufficient time to tackle those mission critical tasks (Obstacle 1). These strategies will reduce the tendency for disaster leaders and supervisors to place the blame for inadequate self care on the worker. FHP requires coordinated effort from everyone—workers, supervisors, and the organization deploying them. By attending to the needs of workers, a stronger response can be offered to those in need.

Rob Yin is Manager of the Disaster Mental Health program of the national American Red Cross and he provides oversight to the activities of 8,000 DMH volunteers.

Marjorie Bagwell Kukor, a licensed psychologist in private practice in Columbus, Ohio, is a community crisis responder for NetCare. She is also a volunteer disaster mental health manager for the American Red Cross.

REFERENCES

American Red Cross (ARC). (2008a). *Disaster mental health manager's toolkit.* Unpublished document. Washington, DC: American Red Cross.

American Red Cross (ARC). (2008b). *Frontline supervisor.* Retrieved from www.crossnet.redcross.org

Aten, J. D., Madson, M. B., Rice, A., & Chamberlain, A. K. (2008). Post disaster supervisor strategies for promoting supervisee self-care: Lessons learned from Hurricane Katrina. *Training and Education in Professional Psychology, 2*(2), 75-78.

Force health protection. (2004). Retrieved from http://fhp.osd.mil/pdfs/fhpcapstone2004.pdf

Mendenhall, T. J. (2006). Trauma-response teams: Inherent challenges and practical strategies in interdisciplinary fieldwork. *Families, Systems & Health, 24*(3), 357-362.

Perry, B. (2003). *The cost of caring: Secondary traumatic stress and the impact of working with high-risk children and families.* Retrieved from http://www.childtrauma.org/ctamaterials/SecTrma2_03_v2.pdf

Roberts, A., & Yeager, K.R. (2009). *Pocket guide to crisis intervention.* New York: Oxford University Press.

Rosser, B. R. S. (2008). Working as a psychologist in the Medical Reserve Corps: Providing emergency mental health relief services in Hurricanes Katrina and Rita. *Professional Psychology: Research and Practice, 39*(1), 37-44.

Schreiber, M. (2009, January). Managing the psychological impact of mass casualty events: The PsySTART™ Disaster Systems of Care Incident Management Model. Presentation to Idaho State University, Idaho Bioterrorism and Preparedness Program. Retrieved from: http://www.isu.edu/irh/IBAPP//documents/Schreiberjan18.pdf

TRICARE. (2009). *About force health protection.* Retrieved from http://www.ha.osd.mil/forcehealth/about/main.html

Yin, R. T. (2004). Innovations in the management of child protection workers: Building worker resilience. *Social Work, 49*(4), 605-608.

THE CLEARNESS COMMITTEE: A PEER SUPERVISION MODEL FOR TRAUMA AND CRISIS COUNSELORS

35

Michael Dubi and Samuel Sanabria

Supervision for counselors working in trauma and crisis events is almost nonexistent despite the continually increasing demand for professionals in crisis and disaster situations. Compared with traditional models of counseling, crisis, trauma, and disaster counseling is unique. Although there is considerable professional literature on clinical supervision for traditional counseling, it is difficult to apply the principles of supervision to unique events in the field or in chaotic situations far from the counseling office. In addition, all professional counselors must receive thousands of hours of supervision before becoming licensed, yet few counselors have the opportunity for supervised experience in trauma, crisis, and disaster response.

TRADITIONAL SUPERVISION FOR COUNSELORS

Traditionally, the supervision of counselors has paralleled conventional counseling in its look and function. Supervision typically occurs in an office where supervisors attempt to teach and model the best clinical practices and then remediate what they believe to be ineffective practices. They then recommend corrective interventions, most often in accordance with a particular theoretical model. Supervisors usually assume the roles of teacher or counselor within this hierarchical relationship (Bernard & Goodyear, 2009). Most professionals assume that this is the most effective method for clinical supervision. However, in many cases, the busy supervisor uses supervisory sessions as client case conferences, in which case the supervisee has little exposure to current best practices.

Over the past decade, even though new clinical intervention strategies have been developed and supervisors have begun applying these models in sessions with supervisees, no new models for crisis or disaster supervision have emerged. Current popular models include solution-focused supervision and strength-based supervision. These models, although less hierarchical and more supervisee sensitive, are often not useful to trauma counselors who need more timely and relevant supervision interactions (Briggs & Miller, 2005; Edwards & Chen, 1999). They are certainly not appropriate for disaster situations that can be intense and frequently chaotic.

THE NEED FOR A SUPERVISION MODEL FOR CRISIS COUNSELORS

Crisis and trauma are unpredictable and indeterminate, therefore a model better suited to these situations was needed. In the 1980s, Critical Incident Stress Management (CISM) was developed to provide crisis intervention by peers and trained mental health professionals to emergency service workers and victims. Although popular, there is conflicting research regarding the efficacy and effectiveness of these interventions. In addition, they are not generally supervision oriented because CISM was not developed as a supervision model—it was developed to provide crisis victims with psychological first aid (Everly & Mitchell, 1997).

The following case illustrates the need for counselors working in disaster or crisis situations to have a supervision resource available that is effective and timely.

Nicole and September 11

Nicole, a Florida licensed mental health counselor, Red Cross-certified disaster mental health worker and, at the time, a supervisee with one of the authors, was visiting her family in New York City on September 11,

2001. She saw the planes crash into the Twin Towers on TV and witnessed the chaos that followed. Nicole immediately volunteered to provide mental health services to victims, their families, and responders. She worked 12-hour days for almost 3 weeks without a day off while providing services to various volunteers, mainly traumatized morgue workers who brought up events such as the processing of unidentified body parts, some as small as a thumb. She slept in a makeshift dormitory when she was able to sleep, ate in a temporary cafeteria with scores of other volunteers, showered when she was able, and had scant phone contact with her family. There were no formal opportunities to provide for her own mental health needs. Although there were many clinicians working alongside Nicole, there were few clinical supervisors and few opportunities for supervision to help her understand and resolve some of the intense clinical situations she experienced daily. Most of the time, she simply processed the daily events with other workers before bedtime if she was not too exhausted.

Nicole's case demonstrates the need for more timely supervision onsite for counselors involved in crisis and disaster events. The need for an effective and more immediate approach to supervision that can be applied both in the field and in the office is urgent as more counselors engage in this type of practice.

A MODEL FOR TRAUMA COUNSELORS

The Clearness Committee is one method of group clinical supervision that can be utilized in working with trauma and crisis counselors. The supervision model was adapted from the book *The Courage to Teach* (Palmer, 1998) which, in turn, was adapted from a traditional and successful Quaker technique for problem solving. Having no clerical leaders, the Quakers use this technique to help each other solve problems. As a clinical supervision model, the technique is also leaderless.

This model has been described as an approach to help develop the counselor-as-self and to help counselors resolve problems rather than focusing on teaching appropriate counseling techniques and interventions. Therefore, the Clearness Committee approach can be effective when working with trauma or crisis counselors to help reduce problems such as vicarious traumatization.

In this approach, the counselor with the presenting problem becomes the focus of the committee. The facilitator acts as timekeeper and makes sure that the questions asked are appropriate. If questions are not appropriate, they are not permitted; the members cannot argue with the facilitator's decision. In addition, there are three to four committee members who are involved in the process. The focus of this approach is on the development of the counselor-as-self and problem solving beginning with the case presentation. The case should include the following:

Statement of the counselor's problem. This should deal with the case and not a client's problems. This helps the counselor process through his or her own struggles in resolving the problem. It can include a range of counseling issues such as transference/countertransference, uncertainties regarding appropriate interventions, and secondary traumatization. (Secondary or vicarious traumatization issues are especially important to trauma counselors.)

Relevant background. The counselor may choose to discuss previous professional and personal experiences when the presenting problem had caused distress.

Sought after outcomes. The counselor should be able to articulate the goals toward which he or she is striving.

Time of centering. Once the problem has been established, the facilitator calls for a time of centering silence for the entire committee. The counselor is then invited to break the silence by introducing the problem at hand. The committee may engage in dialogue with the counselor but is not allowed to give any advice, suggestions, or interpretations. Nothing is allowed except open, honest questioning that allows the counselor to access his or her own inner truth. This is more difficult than it sounds. The committee cannot guide the counselor in any way, which means that questions such as, "Have you considered …?" or "Why don't you …?" are not allowed. The idea behind this approach is that the counselor is the only one who can resolve his or her problem. There is no advice or input that the committee can give that could be of any value at any point in the process.

Asking questions that will get the counselor to the heart of the problem is not easy. Questions such as these may work: "Did you ever feel like this before?" or "What makes this situation special for you?" The best indicator of an open, honest question is that the questioner could not anticipate an answer. Members should ask questions that refer to the counselor as well as to the problem.

The counselor responds to the questions as they are asked, in the presence of the committee. The responses should generate deeper questions; however, the counselor has the right not to answer questions.

The process should be gentle, relaxed, and humane, and it should never become a cross-examination. Silence needs to be respected; it is frequently a source of new insights.

The committee must be totally attentive to the counselor. There should be no chitchat, joking, or laughter. The counselor should be surrounded by quiet, loving space. The committee needs to resist the urge to comfort or reassure the counselor.

The committee should run for one full hour and not end early. Approximately 10 minutes prior to the end of the committee, the facilitator should ask the counselor if he or she wants to suspend the "questions only" rule and invite members to mirror back what they have heard the counselor say. If the counselor says no, the questions continue. If he or she says yes, mirroring can begin. Mirroring is not an excuse to give advice or fix the problem. In the final 5 minutes, the facilitator should invite all members to celebrate and affirm the counselor and his or her strengths.

Members should not confront the counselor after the meeting. What is said in the committee remains in the committee.

If there are any ethical or legal issues that arise, the committee will continue to function. The facilitator will discuss the matter with the counselor immediately after the meeting.

Nicole, Post September 11

Nicole subsequently learned about the Clearness Committee shortly after returning to Florida in October 2001. She organized and led several committees in Mississippi after Hurricane Katrina. They were not only effective for problem solving but they were also instrumental in building morale among mental health workers. Some members of Nicole's "Katrina Kommittees" brought this method back to their agencies and practices. This method of peer supervision is being taught in several universities and has been for several years. In addition, it is practiced in various agencies in the United States.

THE CLEARNESS COMMITTEE TODAY

Although Quakers have been using the Clearness Committee since the 1660s, there is a need for research to determine the effectiveness of this model in clinical supervision and disaster work. Both authors, who have been trained in this model by Eric Gentry through the International Traumatology Institute, are engaged in research on it.

The Clearness Committee is a simple, effective, and powerful method used to help trauma and disaster counselors engage in problem solving. It is especially helpful in resolving the negative effects of vicarious traumatization.

For further information, visit http://www.couragerenewal.org/parker/writings/clearness-committee

Michael Dubi, EdD, LMHC, is associate professor, an approved Clinical Supervisor, and he is certified in acute traumatic stress management and compassion fatigue.

Samuel Sanabria, PhD, LMHC, is assistant professor and program chair.

Both are in the School of Psychology and Behavioral Sciences at Argosy University, Sarasota, Florida.

REFERENCES

Bernard, J. M., & Goodyear, R. K. (2009). *Fundamentals of clinical supervision* (4th ed.). Upper Saddle River, NJ: Merrill/Pearson.

Briggs, A., & Miller, G. (2005). Success enhancing supervision. *Journal of Family Psychotherapy, 16*(1–2), 199–222.

Edwards, J., & Chen, M. (1999). Strength-based supervision: Frameworks, current practice and future directions: A Wu-wei method. *The Family Journal, 7*(4) 349–357.

Everly, G. S., & Mitchell, J. T. (1997). *Critical Incident Stress Management (CISM). A new era and standard of care in crisis intervention.* Ellicott City, MD: Chevron Publishing.

Palmer, P. J. (1998). *The courage to teach.* San Francisco: Jossey-Bass.

CRITICAL INCIDENT STRESS DEBRIEFING AND THE PROCESS OF CRISIS GROUP WORK

36

Debra Pender

Critical Incident Stress Debriefing (CISD) is a small-group structured psychoeducational meeting consisting of seven distinct phases "designed to mitigate the psychological impact of a traumatic event, prevent the subsequent development of a post-traumatic syndrome, and serve as an early identification mechanism for individuals who will require professional mental health follow-up" (Mitchell & Everly, 2006, p. 81). For more than 20 years, I have been a part of CISD circles with emergency responders, teachers, and factory workers after explosions and after a worker shot and killed his co-workers. The CISD process is about resilience, and about normal people having normal reactions to life's most horrible sights, sounds, tastes, smells, and feelings.

PLANNING ELEMENTS IN THE CISD PROCESS

The process starts the moment a call comes in to the critical incident stress management team (CISM). Sometimes the caller is sure that a CISD is needed, but often the caller is unsure whether to ask for assistance. The task is to establish a working relationship with the caller in order to understand and assess what happened, who is affected, and how the caller knows that the impact is there.

Group work best practice guidelines require pre-screening members prior to the beginning of a group (Association for Specialists in Group Work, 2008; Pender & Prichard, 2009). In CISD work, this pre-group process occurs in the first contact between the group needing services and the CISM team. Clarity about the event is essential, as is the question, "Is what happened beyond the range of normal work experiences for this unit?"

The team coordinator and clinical director determine what CISM team intervention is most appropriate for the situation. A CISD must be about a significant event that occurred within the last 24 hours to 7 days. It involves only personnel (emergency responders, teachers, mental health workers, or hospital staff) who were directly involved in the incident (Mitchell & Everly, 2006) and who know that the process will be interactive. This rule is often violated as well-meaning fire chiefs, police chiefs, and emergency management services or emergency room coordinators invite people who should not be included (e.g., city aldermen, family of the deceased, spouses of injured coworkers, and risk managers). Although these individuals may need assistance, it is not appropriate for them to attend the responder CISD.

The CISD should be held in a neutral, private site. The team members are selected by profession (e.g., firefighters for firefighters) and location, as well as who is ready to respond on that level. CISM team size is based upon the size of the group to be debriefed. It is important to be aware of recent personal experiences of the CISM peers and mental health providers in the event they may need some time away from the CISD circle.

STAGES OF THE CISD

Introduction Stage

The CISD begins by establishing ground rules/norms, discussing confidentiality limits, and clarifying the purpose for the group. It is important that all members of the CISM team speak in the opening moments to get acquainted with the group members, establishing contact, and conveying openness. This minimizes the awkwardness of "that stranger in our midst looking at us" and models to all participants that the team has shared power (i.e., the mental health person is accepted by CISM team peers).

Confidentiality is critical for a safe atmosphere. The CISM team enters a world that already exists: subgroups, likes/dislikes, and social isolation/connections already abound. Even though the CISD facilitators share what confidentiality means and ask participants to agree to follow the rule, they cannot guarantee it will be respected. If participants demonstrate that something is wrong (e.g., crossed arms, glares, looking at the floor, shifting uncomfortably in their chairs), facilitators repeat the rule that everyone is encouraged to speak about the incident, but only in a manner that seems safe to each individual. If body language does not improve as cohesion and trust in the CISD process develop, facilitators reduce the level of self-disclosure in the next phases.

Facts Phase

During the facts phase, participants are invited to share their roles in relation to the event and to describe what happened. Two strategies for facilitating this cognitive process are rounds to ask everyone to speak in turn, which enhances early participation, and, asking individuals to tell the facts in order, providing greater clarity about the event. Not pointing out uncomfortable memories makes the task easier. Individuals can pass, but most want to tell what happened. Peers should not get lost in shoptalk or discussions about protocols or procedures; the focus is the event itself, not the management of the event.

In the more than 200 CISD groups I have been involved in, 10 involved human-error that contributed to a death. These groups are emotionally charged. Clear boundaries must be in place to focus on the human element, rather than protocol issues, because in each human-error case, a piece of information was missing that led to the error.

Thoughts Phase

In this phase, participants are asked to share their thoughts about what happened, providing a transition from the report of the event (detail knowledge) into a personal recount of the cognitive aspects (cognitive appraisal). The thoughts phase begins the deepening into the personal viewpoint and internal processes. Answers range from "I was totally focused on doing my job," to "This isn't going to end well." It is important to listen for the cognitive element that will frame potential meaning for the upcoming emotional response phase (identifying their affective interpretation).

Using first names links common thoughts, identifies and honors differing thoughts, and enhances the CISD group cohesion. It is also important to pace the disclosures because moving too quickly into reactions can overwhelm everyone. Listen for time distortion that may signify some level of dissociation, making the person more vulnerable to a maladaptive stress reaction.

Reactions Phase

The most challenging section begins when participants transition from the recall and initial appraisal of the event and share their deepest personal disclosure and affective response to the event (meaning making). A pivotal decision by the CISD facilitators is how much graphic detail to allow; it is vital to monitor nonverbal reactions in relation to what is being shared and listen to the style of the speaker in order to shape disclosure and avoid excessive discussion of gore. The person may have a dramatic style or could be communicating a deeper level of struggle with the event stimuli. Participants will roll their eyes, turn their shoulders away, vacantly stare, or glare at the speaker. "Drama of the trauma" disclosure needs to be cut off and redirected. After the CISD meeting, do individual follow-up. Follow the rule of good group work—to protect the person from doing harm to self or others in the group.

In one case, a coroner did not want the CISD to take place and insisted on attending in order to sabotage it. The incident involved the brutal, extremely violent murders of a mother and four children under the age of 5 by the husband/father. The coroner leaned back in his chair with fingers under his suspenders and shut down every participant's attempt to share even the facts. He quickly went into gross but accurate descriptions. Then he described a ritual of going out to dinner with the state police investigator after every autopsy. Adding to the graphic burden was his description of the restaurant they went to and the food that was eaten.

CISD honors reactions as normal reactions to abnormal events; it is not about personal growth through feedback. The coroner was essentially telling the CISM team, "I have figured out a ritual to allow me to do this horrendous task, to deal with the destruction of these precious lives, and I do not want you telling me that what I am doing is wrong." I said, "I appreciate how truly hard your tasks were that night, and I want to honor that, while not many of us in this room would handle it the way you do, you have found what works for you by always doing the ritual of eating out at the same place with your colleague when the work is over. Thank you for sharing that with us." He sat speechless for a few moments, stood up, and declared that everyone had talked about it enough. He left, but told the participants in the debriefing that they should listen; this is a good process. The CISM team started over with everyone else. More than 15 years later, I met him and he reported that he was still "doing his thing" after the tough deaths.

Ultimately, the purpose of the reaction phase is to identify aspects of the event that may remain in the conscious and unconscious processes of the first responders. In the culture of first responders, it is not easy to admit that their work is painful and distressing. The personal bar for a successful mission is to save every life, every time, no matter what it takes. The reality of the event actually sets the bar for what can or cannot be done on that day, at that moment. The space between what the responders wanted to do and what reality allowed them to do is the worst part of the experience. The successful CISD helps responders verbalize that "space" through their reactions to it, thus separating the difference in mission failure (not being able to stop the outcome of the event) and personal failure (not able to handle the job).

It is helpful for the debriefers to acknowledge the various reactions by voicing that the participants have identified elements that are important to discuss: "I am glad that you brought out that point. What other details stand out?" By saying this, it shifts the emphasis from seeing a weakness to creating a common task for everyone to figure out why this event had an impact. This can be empowering.

Symptoms Phase

The process moves to the symptoms phase in which facilitators encourage participants to identify changes they have noticed since the event occurred (normalization of reactions). The "figuring this out" element helps participants share their stress reactions. Peers are vital here. When a firefighter peer points to his temple and says, "Sometimes the image gets stuck right here," others nod their heads. A firefighter talking to another firefighter conveys permission—something that mental health providers rarely achieve.

Teaching Phase

During this phase, facilitators encourage sharing coping strategies, offering normalization of reactions and symptoms, and providing stress education. The data gathered during the thoughts, reactions, and symptoms phases shape the content of this phase. It is important to communicate that the team does not assume everyone

is struggling; this can be accomplished by asking what strategies participants already employ. The debriefers then share this basic set of techniques:

- Remember to breathe (in 4, hold 4, out 4, hold empty 4); this clears the mind and slows the heart rate.
- Use water to cleanse the stress hormones (crying and/or drinking water to flush the body).
- Work out for at least 30 minutes to sweat the stress out, or soak or swim for 30 minutes to wash it away.
- Engage in everyday tasks that are separate from "the job" to reconnect with everyday life.

Re-Entry Phase

The final phase completes the CISD process. Facilitators and participants co-summarize what was accomplished and acknowledge the humanness of serving under extraordinary circumstances. During wrap-up, I often use my hands to describe what I heard could be done in this event (low hand) and the desired outcome of everyone in the room (high hand). This visual is well received but should not be used if responder error was involved. Identify acts that responders made during the efforts to save victims when they seem unaware that these efforts may have mattered. For example, responders often share that they try to shield a surviving family member from the graphic vision of a loved one's injuries; this is protective and respectful. When appropriate, thank them for agreeing to carry the burden of sadness and disappointment in order to serve others.

A firefighter had witnessed the death of a lifelong friend but made eye contact with him just as the friend was covered in a trench collapse. During the CISD, he was clearly depressed, with the affect of a person who might be considering suicide and shared that he could not close his own eyes without seeing those of his friend. Everyone in his department and the peers on the team tried to help him feel better for a long time. Finally, it was stated that there is a difference between a mission failure and a personal failure. This resonated with the firefighter, and he showed signs of improvement. I said to him, "I respect how hard it is to be there and see what you saw. I invite you to realize that while you feel the pain of that image, what your friend saw at the last moment of his life was that he mattered, and you were busting your (firefighter language) to save his. Not many people leave this life with such a gift." The firefighter then understood, as did everyone in the room, that caring is worth it, even if it hurts. In fact, the hurt is there because what happened was, and may always be, significant.

Debra Pender, PhD, LCPC, is assistant professor in the Department of Counseling, Administration and Higher Education at Northern Illinois University in DeKalb, IL. She is also clinical director, Southern Illinois Critical Incident Stress Management Team.

REFERENCES

Association for Specialists in Group Work. (2008). Association for Specialists in Group Work best practice guidelines. *Journal for Specialists in Group Work, 33*(2), 111–117.

Mitchell, J. T., & Everly, G. S. (2006). *Group crisis intervention* (4th ed.). Ellicott City, MD: International Critical Incident Stress Foundation.

Pender, D. A., & Prichard, K. K. (2009). AGSW best practice guidelines as a research tool: A comprehensive examination of the critical incident stress debriefing. *Journal for Specialists in Group Work, 34*(2), 175–192.

Section Eight

Current Issues in Disaster Mental Health

INTERNATIONAL DISASTER COUNSELING: TODAY'S REFLECTIONS, TOMORROW'S NEEDS

37

J. Scott Hinkle

The primary goals of disaster mental health services are to avert further harm, relieve distress, support effective coping, and help people regain an adequate level of autonomy (Reyes, 2006a; Reyes & Elhai, 2004). Disasters often result in the loss of property, resources, and life; however, political, economic, and social disruptions also are common consequences. Although survival behavior and adaptations to change can lead individuals to question their fundamental beliefs, the ancient medicines of love, faith, and compassion all too often are an inadequate match for the misfortune and grief following a disaster (Reyes, 2006b).

This is particularly true when human rights abuses have occurred in cases of human-caused disaster (Holtz, 1998). For example, ongoing violent conflicts in the former Yugoslavia (Kapor-Stanulovic, 2006), Uganda (Agger, 2006), and Rwanda (Neugebauer, 2006) have a disastrous emotional impact that spills across, national, cultural, civic, or tribal borders (Reyes, 2006b).

NATURAL DISASTERS: THE HAITI EARTHQUAKE

Unfortunately, for every country that has prepared for a disaster—natural or human-caused—there are many more that lack the resources to limit its impact. As this book goes to press, the impact of natural disasters is tragically evidenced in Haiti. Developing countries have fewer resources to prepare for disasters before they strike and consequently have more difficulty effectively dealing with disasters after they occur. Resource-poor countries have fewer healthcare opportunities and invest minimally in mental health services. Moreover, without a functioning community-based mental health system, post-disaster mental health

counseling responses are extremely difficult to organize (Saraceno, 2006).

The latter part of the twentieth century revealed a sharp escalation of natural disasters, human-caused disasters, as well as a host of complex humanitarian crises such as forced international migration of refugees (Reyes, 2006a, 2006b). Such crises include bombings in southern Lebanon leading to a disintegration of local communities (Lahad, 1999) and natural disasters such as earthquakes in Pakistan and Latin America that stressed already weak local capacities (Khan, 2006; Reyes, 2006a).

Humanitarian organizations began to recognize the increased need for emotional support at disaster sites in the 1990s (Barron, 2004). However, considering today's great needs, limited resources, and significant challenges, this has proven to be an extremely difficult task (Reyes, 2006b). In addition, nongovernmental and religious organizations attempt to provide assistance in the aftermath of disasters. The International Federation of Red Cross/Red Crescent Societies (IFRC) is one example. The National Board for Certified Counselors, which is a nongovernmental organization maintaining operational relations with UNESCO, assists with disaster-related efforts by training mental health facilitators around the globe.

Although the majority of individuals adapt following a disaster, symptoms associated with post-traumatic stress disorder (PTSD), anxiety, depression, and somatic complaints can be found (Bolton, Hill, & O'Ryan, 2004; Reyes, 2006b). Even though idiosyncratic symptoms are observed, international disaster mental health interventions typically favor a community-based model over a clinical model (North & Hong, 2000; Petevi, Revel, & Jacobs, 2001; van Ommeren, Saxena, & Saraceno, 2005), making professional counselors a good fit for providing disaster mental health services. Moreover, community intervention models that focus on restoring personal resiliency are globally appealing in that they do not emphasize pathology and seem less stigmatizing (Dodge, 2006). This helping approach places confidence in the community's capacity to support itself (Pupavac, 2006; Reyes & Elhai, 2004; Tuicomepee & Romano, 2008) and encourages local communities to take the lead in implementing assistance that is consistent with local norms. Innovative, culturally sensitive counseling programs have been developed that involved integrating individual and community interventions (Silove, 2006). Furthermore, intercultural partnerships foster improvement in local communities' capacities for meeting needs and sustaining this capacity once temporary, external helpers are withdrawn (Beech, 2006).

Obviously, due to the increase in natural and human-caused disasters (Goodman & West-Olatunji, 2008), the need for international disaster mental health counseling is rising. However, while trauma expertise has grown in the past 20 years (Campbell, Brown, Amato, & Sharma, 2008) and national and international trauma training guidelines have been produced (Marotta, 2000; Weine et al., 2002), there is a gap between the data and the training. Although crisis interventions associated with disasters can be found in some social work training programs (Reyes & Elhai, 2004), the majority of graduate students within the helping professions receive cursory disaster counseling instruction. In addition to trauma counseling skills, trainees need a thorough understanding of local, regional, national, and international agencies and organizations that aid in disaster relief (Campbell et al., 2008). Fortunately, after tragedies have occurred, organizations may take preventive actions, including increases in disaster mental health training. For example, in the United States, the Council for Accreditation of Counseling and Related Education Programs (CACREP, 2009) has revised its educational standards to include emergency response training and the American Counseling Association has published this text, now in its third edition, and has added a new topic category—Disaster Mental Health—to its programming for the ACA Annual Conference.

Most people will demonstrate resilience in the face of a disaster (Reyes & Elhai, 2004) but adjusting and adapting to intense stress and painful loss can exceed the normal coping mechanisms of some individuals, regardless of where in the world they live. For some, more assistance is needed rather than relying only on personal re-

silence and the passage of time (Reyes, 2006b). Effective interventions have included drama therapy in Lebanon (Goldberg & Green, 1986; Lahad, 1999), eye movement desensitization reprocessing (EMDR) with earthquake victims in Turkey (Konuk et al., 2006), and supportive counseling for airplane crash witnesses in Italy (Fernandez, Gallinari, & Lorenzetti, 2004).

It is clear that mental health support during and after a disaster is helpful, but it is not clear exactly what this support should entail and who should provide it. For example, *debriefing* has its supporters and detractors; PTSD focuses on individuals but often deemphasizes more community-oriented approaches (Gist & Devilly, 2002). Although the discipline of counseling is cited in the disaster literature, it is generally referred to in terms of "crisis counseling." A broader look at entities affected by disasters, including family, community, and employment reveal a wealth of issues that can be effectively managed by professional counselors. Additionally, counselors are well trained to help people in two major forums: dealing with loss and assisting with community change in culturally appropriate ways.

Professional counselors, however, do need training and experience that are consistent with effective work at a disaster site, especially one on foreign soil (Reyes & Elhai, 2004). Disaster mental health counselors with the following characteristics will be better suited for this type of work: life experience, poise, extreme flexibility, quick mental reflexes and tenacity, ability to delay gratification, and having courage under fire. Optimism, good reality orientation, calmness under stress, effectiveness in low control, unpredictable environments, objectivity, good self-concept, and a strong belief that people can overcome insurmountable odds are helpful traits (Gilliland & James, 1993; Reyes & Elhai, 2004). Moreover, innovative approaches often are needed in order to adapt to cultural and sociopolitical disaster conditions encountered in various areas of the world (Armstrong, Boyden, Galappatti, & Hart, 2006).

Counselors performing international disaster mental health work should exercise caution in applying Western helping frameworks as though they were universally valid because this can exacerbate the situation (Summerfield, 1999; Reyes, 2006a). Cultural differences (e.g., language, customs, and beliefs) are major considerations when applying counseling interventions outside the counselor's culture of origin (Stamm & Friedman, 2000). Most mental health techniques are designed for use in controlled environments such as counseling centers, clinics, and hospitals, which are a far cry from the chaos of a disaster setting. Furthermore, the burden of proof that Western methods are effective in disaster situations outside of the Western world lies on the individuals and institutions that perform the services. Fortunately, the core elements of support, protection from further harm, assistance with emotional distress, compassionate care, encouragement and hope, and respect for human dignity are not necessarily values that span every culture (Reyes, 2006a), but applying them is generally a good strategy regardless of the international setting.

Once physical safety is secured, disaster mental health counseling essentially consists of a compassionate presence, normalization of the event, provision of accurate information, facilitation of support systems, enhancement of coping skills, connection to higher levels of care when necessary, and follow-up (Brymer et al., 2006). Conventional talking approaches are less advantageous and effective than crisis counseling methods that focus on immediate problems and practical coping strategies (Reyes, 2006b). Essentially, disaster counseling is aimed at stabilization, not change.

Broad stages of crisis and trauma recovery include establishing safety, remembrance and mourning, and reconnection (Herman, 1997). Similarly, Ranier and Brown (2007) presented a remembering, reorganizing, and restoration model of helping. These processes rarely follow a clear linear path but are interconnected stages along the road to recovery (Phillips, 2009). A limited but important checklist of counseling issues and concerns when working at an international disaster site follows:

- Always practice within the limits of expertise and training (Reyes & Elhai, 2004).
- Indigenous infrastructures are often damaged or destroyed by disasters and conflict, whereby aid is not distributed equally due to political interests (Wessells, 1998).
- Local understanding and customs should not be deemphasized while services offered by international organizations are emphasized (Wessells, 1998).
- Assess the needs and resources of the affected population (Reyes, 2006a) and make optimum use of community and media resources (Kuriansky, 2006; Ronan, Finnis, & Johnston, 2006).
- Do not inadvertently encourage personal passivity and disengage people from taking social action to deal with *their* disaster situation (Pupavac, 2006).
- Integrate immediate disaster counseling with

long-term developmental goals and programs (Beech, 2006).
- Exposure methods that focus on potentially stress-inducing details are often not well suited for disaster situations (Bryant & Harvey, 2000).
- Be aware of the entire clinical picture and utilize multimodal, team outreach approaches (Kapalka, 2005).
- Be aware of the various symptoms associated with mental health issues including stress and trauma (Dubi & Sanabria, 2005).
- PTSD is steeped in Western culture and has limitations for use in global contexts (Pupavac, 2006).
- Normalize the crisis response by using distraction for refocusing, disruption to reduce the emotional reaction, and diffusion to pace and lead the person in a supportive direction (Dubi & Sanabria, 2005).
- Use psychoeducation to mobilize disaster-affected communities to reduce negative psychosocial impact (Reyes & Elhai, 2004).
- Implement developmentally appropriate interventions for children and adolescents (Baggerly & Exum, 2008).
- Children often need recreational activities, art therapy, and family assistance to become more resilient and to develop coping skills (Burnham, 2009; Tuicomepee & Romano, 2008; Wells, 2006).
- First responders can be helpers *and* victims; don't overlook the needs of disaster services providers (Center for Mental Health Services, 2003; Pupavac, 2006).
- Be familiar with local mental health laws (Reyes & Elhai, 2004).
- Be aware of the barriers to success—they will be everywhere (Dingman, 1996).
- Keep "rescue fantasies" to yourself (Miller, 2004).
- Provide follow-up as well as aftercare (Reyes & Elhai, 2004).

Professional counselors can utilize churches, temples, and mosques because they are natural gathering places for people in crisis who feel panic and grief (Phillips, 2009). For example, establishing survivors' self-help groups at religious sites is a constructive and empowering postvention method. Additionally, providing community education and awareness can help reduce the incidence of mental health related issues, including suicide (World Health Organization, 2006).

Disasters strain the limits of human capacity for coping with stress (Somasundaram, 1996) and counseling interventions may need to extend for some time after the disaster. For example, adolescents who experienced the 2004 tsunami continued to be affected significantly more than 1 year later (Tuicomepee & Romano, 2008).

Response to Haiti

In the aftermath of the Haiti earthquake many American disaster mental health counselors have opportunities to volunteer to deploy to Haiti through national and international agencies, organizations, and religious groups. Training, preparation, identification with a specific response unit, and credentials/licenses are essential to being eligible and ready for deployment to Haiti or other international sites. Keeping Western ideas about counseling in perspective in international disaster situations is critical. With the infrastructure nearly destroyed and few resources available in the country, disaster mental health providers face interpersonal, political, and cultural challenges. Responders also need to keep in mind that they are guests of the Haitian government and people and they are collaborators with many other units and volunteers in the recovery process (see Chapters 6 and 40).

J. Scott Hinkle is the clinical training coordinator at the National Board for Certified Counselors in Greensboro, NC.

The author wishes to thank Gayle McCorkle and Joyce DiBacco for their editorial comments.

References

Agger, I. (2006). Approaches to psychosocial healing: Case examples from Lusophone Africa. In G. Reyes & G. A. Jacobs (Eds.), *Handbook of international disaster psychology*, Vol. 2. (pp. 137–155). Westport, CT: Praeger.

Armstrong, M., Boyden, J., Galappatti, A., & Hart, J. (2006). Participatory tools monitoring and evaluating psychosocial work with children: Reflections on a pilot study in Eastern Sri Lanka. In G. Reyes & G. A. Jacobs (Eds.), *Handbook of international disaster psychology*, Vol. 2. (pp. 157–175). Westport, CT: Praeger.

Baggerly, J., & Exum, H. A. (2008). Counseling children after natural disasters: Guidance for family therapists. *The American Journal of Family Therapy, 36,* (1)79–93.

Barron, R. A. (2004). International disaster mental health. *Psychiatric Clinics of North America, 27* (3), 505–519.

Beech, D. R. (2006). Peace-building, culturally responsive means, and ethical practices in humanitarian psychosocial interventions. In G. Reyes & G. A. Jacobs (Eds.), *Handbook of international disaster psychology*, Vol. 1. (pp. 93–112). Westport, CT: Praeger.

Bolton, D., Hill, J., & O'Ryan, D. (2004). Long-term effects of psychological trauma on psychosocial functioning. *Journal of Child Psychology and Psychiatry, 45*(5), 1007–1014.

Bryant, R. A., & Harvey, A. G. (2000). *Acute stress disorder: A handbook of theory, assessment and treatment,* Washington, DC: American Psychological Association.

Burnham, J. J. (2009). Contemporary fears of children and adolescents: Coping and resiliency in the 21st century. *Journal of Counseling & Development, 87*(1), 28–35.

Campbell, C. L., Brown, E. J., Amato, M., & Sharma, K. (Spring/Summer, 2008). A developmental perspective on trauma training. *Trauma Psychology, 3*(2), 15–17.

Center for Mental Health Services. (2003). *Mental health all-hazards disaster planning guidance*. Rockville, MD: Author.

Council for the Accreditation of Counseling and Related Education Programs (CACREP). (2009). 2009 *Standards.* Alexandria, VA: Author.

Dingman, R. L. (1996). The mental health counselor's role in Hurricane Andrew. *Journal of Mental Health Counseling, 17*(3), 321–335.

Dodge, G. R. (2006). Assessing the psychosocial needs of communities affected by disaster. In G. Reyes & G. A. Jacobs (Eds.), *Handbook of international disaster psychology*, Vol. 1. (pp. 65–92). Westport, CT: Praeger.

Dubi, M., & Sanabria, S. (2005). Understanding and working with acute stress disorder. In J. Webber, D. Bass, & R. Yep (Eds.), *Terrorism, trauma, and tragedies: A counselor's guide to preparing and responding* (pp. 113–114). Alexandria, VA: American Counseling Association Foundation.

Fernandez, I., Gallinari, E., & Lorenzetti, A. (2004). A school-based EMDR intervention for children who witnessed the Pirelli Building airplane crash in Milan, Italy. *Journal of Brief Therapy, 2,* 129–136.

Gilliland, B. E., & James, R. K. (1993). *Crisis intervention strategies* (2nd ed.). Pacific Grove, CA: Brooks/Cole.

Gist, R., & Devilly G. J., (2002). Post-trauma debriefing: The road too frequently travelled. *The Lancet, 360*(9335), 741–742.

Goldberg, R. L., & Green, S. A. (1986). A learning theory perspective of brief psychodynamic psychotherapy. *American Journal of Psychotherapy, 40*(1) 70–82.

Goodman, R. D., & West-Olatunji, C. A. (2008). Transgenerational trauma and resilience: Improving mental health counseling for survivors of Hurricane Katrina. *Journal of Mental Health Counseling, 30,* 121–136.

Herman, J. (1997). *Trauma and recovery.* New York: Basic Books.

Holtz, T. H. (1998). Refugee trauma versus torture trauma: A retrospective controlled cohort study of Tibetan refugees. *Journal of Nervous and Mental Disease, 186*(1), 24–34.

Kapalka, G. M. (2005). First responders and their families outreach and treatment strategies. In J. Webber, D. Bass, & R. Yep (Eds.), *Terrorism, trauma, and tragedies: A counselor's guide to preparing and responding* (pp. 131–135). Alexandria, VA: American Counseling Association Foundation.

Kapor-Stanulovic, N. (2006). Implementing psychosocial programs in the Federal Republic of Yugoslavia: Was it really mission impossible? In G. Reyes & G. A. Jacobs (Eds.), *Handbook of international disaster psychology,* Vol. 2. (pp. 37–52). Westport, CT: Praeger.

Khan, M. M. (2006). When mountains weep: Psychological care for those affected by the earthquake in northern Pakistan. *Psychiatric Bulletin, 30*(12), 454–456.

Konuk, E., Knipe, J., Eke, I., Yuksek, H., Yurtsever, A., & Ostep, S. (2006). The effects of eye movement desensitization and reprocessing (EMDR) therapy on posttraumatic stress disorder in survivors of the 1999 Marmara, Turkey earthquake. *International Journal of Stress Management, 13,* 291–308.

Kuriansky, J. (2006). Working effectively with the mass media in disaster mental health. In G. Reyes & G. A. Jacobs (Eds.), *Handbook of international disaster psychology,* Vol. 2. (pp. 127–146). Westport, CT: Praeger.

Lahad, M. (1999) The use of drama therapy with crisis intervention groups following mass evacuation. *The Arts in Psychotherapy, 26*(1), 27–33.

Marotta, S. A. (2000). Best practices for counselors who treat posttraumatic stress disorder. *Journal of Counseling & Development, 78*(4), 492–495.

Miller, L. (2004). Psychotherapeutic interventions for survivors of terrorism. *American Journal of Psychotherapy, 58*(1), 1–93.

National Child Traumatic Stress Network. (2006). *Psychological first aid: Field operations guide,* 2nd ed. Rockville, MD: Center for Mental Health Services.

Neugebauer, R. (2006). Psychosocial research and interventions after the Rwanda genocide. In G. Reyes & G. A. Jacobs (Eds.), *Handbook of international disaster psychology,* Vol. 2 (pp. 125–136). Westport, CT: Praeger.

North, C. S., & Hong, B. A. (2000). Project CREST: A new model for mental health intervention after a community disaster. *American Journal of Public Health, 90,* 1057–1058.

Petevi, M., Revel, J. P., & Jacobs, G. A. (2001*). Tool for the rapid assessment of mental health needs of refugees, displaced and other populations affected by conflict and post-conflict situations.* Geneva: World Health Organization.

Phillips, S. B. (2009). The synergy of group and individual treatment modalities in the aftermath of disaster and unfolding trauma. *International Journal of Group Psychotherapy, 59*(1), 85–107.

Pupavac, V. (2006). Humanitarian politics and the rise of international disaster psychology. In G. Reyes & G. A. Jacobs (Eds.), *Handbook of international disaster psychology,* Vol.1 (pp. 15–34). Westport, CT: Praeger.

Ranier, J. P., & Brown, F. F. (2007). *Crisis counseling and therapy.* New York: Haworth.

Reyes, G. (2006a). International disaster psychology: Purposes, principles, and practices. In G. Reyes & G. A. Jacobs (Eds.), *Handbook of international disaster psychology, Vol.1* (pp. 1–13). Westport, CT: Praeger.

Reyes, G. (2006b). Overview of the international disaster psychology volumes. In G. Reyes & G. A. Jacobs (Eds.), *Handbook of international disaster psychology, Vol.1* (pp. xxi–xxxiv). Westport, CT: Praeger.

Reyes, G., & Elhai, J. D. (2004). Psychosocial interventions in the early phases of disasters. *Psychotherapy: Theory, Research, Practice, Training, 41*(14), 399–411.

Ronan, K. R., Finnis, K., & Johnston, D. M. (2006). Interventions with youth and families: A prevention and stepped care model. In G. Reyes & G. A. Jacobs (Eds.), *Handbook of international disaster psychology,* Vol. 2 (pp. 13–36). Westport, CT: Praeger.

Saraceno, B. (2006). Foreword. In G. Reyes & G. A. Jacobs (Eds.), *Handbook of international disaster psychology,* Vol.1 (pp. xiii–xiv). Westport, CT: Praeger.

Silove, D. (2006). The impact of mass psychological trauma on psychosocial adaptation among refugees. In G. Reyes & G. A. Jacobs (Eds.), *Handbook of international disaster psychology,* Vol. 3 (pp. 1–18). Westport, CT: Praeger.

Somasundaram, D. J. (1996). Post-traumatic responses to aerial bombing. *Social Science & Medicine, 42*(11), 1465–1471.

Stamm, B. H., Friedman, M. J. (2000). Cultural diversity in the appraisal and expression of traumatic exposure. In A. Shalev, R. Yehuda, & A. McFarlane (Eds.), *International handbook of human response to trauma* (pp. 69–85). New York: Plenum.

Summerfield, D. (1999). A critique of seven assumptions behind psychological trauma programmes in war-affected areas. *Social Science & Medicine, 48*(10), 1449–1462.

Tuicomepee, A., & Romano, J. L. (2008). Thai adolescent survivors 1 year after the 2004 tsunami: A mixed methods study. *Journal of Counseling Psychology, 55*(3), 308–320.

van Ommeren, M., Saxena, S., & Saraceno, B. (2005). Mental and social health during and after acute emergencies: Emerging consensus? *Bulletin of the World Health Organization, 83*(1), 71–76.

Weine, S., Danieli, Y., Silove, D., Van Ommeren, M., Fairbank, J. A., & Saul, J. (2002). Guidelines for international training in mental health and psychosocial interventions for trauma exposed populations in clinical and community settings. *Psychiatry, 65*(3), 156–164.

Wells, M. E. (2006). Psychotherapy for families in the aftermath of a disaster. *Journal of Clinical Psychology: In Session, 62*(8), 1017–1027.

Wessells, M. (1998). Humanitarian intervention, psychosocial assistance, and peace-keeping. In H. J. Langholtz (Ed.), *The psychology of peacekeeping* (pp. 131–152). Westport, CT: Praeger.

World Health Organization. (2006). *Preventing suicide: A resource for counsellors.* Geneva: Author.

Responding to Pandemics: Preparing Counselors

J. Barry Mascari and Jane Webber

38

At 8 years old, I was at the cemetery with my maternal grandmother. She was caring for gravestones with the names of her parents and two brothers, both of whom died under the age of 20 in 1918. I asked, "Did they die in the war? She replied, "No, they died of the flu." I said, "Ma, no one dies of the flu." She never spoke of the flu again, and, like many who remember 1918, the horror was once again buried inside. We can only imagine what pain and traumatic memory remained and how, without the benefit of intervention, those memories took a toll on a generation (Mascari, 2009).

Much to our surprise, as of the writing of this chapter, the Swine Flu (H1N1) pandemic is on its second wave, appearing first as rare spring flu and then as a declared pandemic. On June 11, 2009, the World Health Organization (WHO) (2009) declared it the first pandemic in 41 years. It returned in the fall with widespread outbreaks in 48 states and serious outbreaks around the world, raising fears of the possibility that the strain might mutate and become more lethal. Many counseling colleagues—shocked by WHO's declaration—sought direction on how to prepare. For traumatologists, and other counselors who will be called upon to respond in times of crisis, knowledge about pandemics and influenza is vital.

Our approach to managing our own anxiety over the Avian Flu in 2006 was to read and learn as much as possible. During a trip to Barcelona, where street vendors on Las Ramblas were selling domestic birds as pets, we watched wild birds land on cages and were struck with the startling reality that a possible jump from bird to human was very real. This led to an even more frightening realization: the world is overdue for a pandemic, defined as when an epidemic spreads rapidly across many geographic locations, countries, or continents. Pandemic is not to be confused with an epidemic, when the observed number of cases exceeds the expected number of cases of a given disease in a defined time period. In brief, a pandemic is an epidemic gone wild, spreading beyond borders.

To respond to the threat of a pandemic, we monitored the worldwide H5N1 flu outbreaks (more commonly referred to as Avian Flu) and SARS. Attendees at the 2007 American Counseling Association Annual Conference and the Argosy University Symposium on Trauma, Tragedy and Crisis (Webber, Mascari, & Dubi, 2007) reacted to our concerns with a combination of fear and concern, but lacked a sense of urgency. The final chapters on H1N1 and H5N1 are yet to unfold.

Pandemic History

There have been 10 known pandemics in 300 years, occurring approximately three to four times every 100 years. The Bubonic Plague (The Black Death) of 1348 killed 25%–50% of the European population in 3 years; the next pandemic was the Spanish Flu of 1918. Infection estimates for the Spanish Flu ranged from 200 million to 1 billion people and number of deaths from 50 million to 100 million (Billings, 2005). The 20- to 40-year-old population suffered the most deaths, instead of elderly and children—who are usually the most at risk. In 2 years and three waves, nearly half the world was infected. Although these two pandemics were separated by centuries, one commonality is that the fields of public health and medicine had limited understanding, and crude forms of disease control were practiced.

Unlike world wars that have celebrated veterans and honored the dead with stories shared by parents and grandparents, pandemics have no such history. Instead, what most people know comes from history books or children's rhymes ("*Ashes, ashes, we all fall down*") (see Chapter 31) or the children's jump rope rhyme ("*I had a little bird, its name was Enza, I opened the window and in-flu-enza*") (Crawford, 1995). *The Plague* (Camus, 1947) was a novel about a fictional plague in Algeria, although few people make the connection between Camus' existential world-view and pandemic.

Modern pandemics include the Asian Flu of 1957 (H2N2 strain) and the Hong Kong Flu of 1968 (H3N2 strain) that led to 1 to 4 million deaths. Recent outbreaks with pandemic potential include HIV/AIDS, SARS, the West Nile Virus, and Avian Flu (H5N1).

Pandemic is Not Seasonal Flu

Most people have experienced a seasonal flu, often minimizing it as a bad cold, despite its ability to kill. Pandemics are different—they infect 15% to 50% of the population, placing all ages at-risk and producing severe illness and a high death rate. The US Department of Health & Human Services (2009) noted:

> It is the sheer scope of influenza pandemics, with their potential to rapidly spread and overwhelm societies and cause illnesses and deaths among all age groups, which distinguishes pandemic influenza from other emerging infectious disease threats and makes pandemic influenza one of the most feared emerging infectious disease threats.

Each seasonal flu vaccine is an educated guess based on the strains that have been identified the previous year. In a pandemic, new strains may emerge or old ones may reappear, with no effective vaccine available for 4–6 months after onset. Antiviral drugs such as Tamiflu have been effective, but their impact on a new or reappearing strain is largely unknown. Drugs will likely be in short supply and government stockpiles are limited. Preliminary data from the H1N1 outbreak in fall 2009 indicated shortages in Tamiflu and vaccine--production has not met demand (MSNBC, 2009).

In most pandemic outbreaks, unlike seasonal flu, the healthiest individuals are at greatest risk, ironically, because they have the most robust immune system. Non-seasonal flu is devastating because of the cytokine storm, an extreme immune system overreaction that results in a ferocious assault on the lungs by immune cells. The inflamed lungs can become congested with dead cells and fluids, resulting in serious respiratory distress and suffocation (Ukrainetz, 2009). The H1N1

pandemic of 2009 has produced a more surprising at-risk group: the very young.

Is Pandemic Inevitable?

Based on historical patterns, experts suggest a pandemic resulting from a new virus subtype within the next decade. This new strain will have little immunity in the current population, most likely because there has been no prior exposure to the new virus. Because this virus can replicate in humans, transmitting efficiently from one human to another, it can cause community-wide outbreaks (WHO, 2009). The current H1N1 pandemic might not become this long-dreaded outbreak because current death rates are much lower than feared. Taubenberger and Morens (2006) cautioned that:

> Even with modern antiviral and antibacterial drugs, vaccines, and prevention knowledge, the return of a pandemic virus equivalent in pathogenicity to the virus of 1918 would likely kill [greater than] 100 million people worldwide. A pandemic virus with the (alleged) pathogenic potential of some recent H5N1 outbreaks could cause substantially more deaths (p. 21).

Avian Flu (H5N1) Remains a Threat

Avian flu produced sporadic epidemics in migratory birds and poultry in Asia in 1997 and has remained active. Bird-to-human infection has been confirmed in the following countries where people live in close proximity to poultry: Vietnam, Cambodia, Thailand, Indonesia, Russia, Azerbaijan, Egypt, India, Iraq, Laos, Nigeria, and Turkey. It is not known whether human-to-human transmission has occurred.

Although the number of individuals infected with H5N1 is small, nearly half of those infected die from it. Globalsecurity.org (2009) projected that 200 million United States citizens, 15% to 35% of the population, could become infected with 87,000–207,000 deaths and 314,400–733,800 individuals hospitalized.

Pandemic's Impact

Unlike previous pandemics that spread slowly through sea travel, the frequent use of air travel increases the probability of reaching all continents within 3 months. Also, the world's population has increased, and the majority of people live in densely populated cities. In New Jersey, the most densely populated state in the nation, where nearly half the population lives in one-third of the state (near New York City), there could be 8,000 deaths, with 5,700 occurring in hospitals, and 41,000 hospital admissions. (See Chapter 38).

When the perceived threat is greater than the actual threat in a health crisis, fear and anxiety are common reactions. Storming a vaccination or medication point-of-distribution site or a government building where supplies are believed to be stored can threaten to undermine governmental authority. In general, stress and fear lead to somatic complaints; more healthcare is sought, taxing resources and leading to the perception that the outbreak is worse than it is.

COUNSELOR ROLE STRESS

While helping the general public, counselors also will be needed to help people cope with illness, death, mistrust, and scarcity. Counselors may simultaneously serve as caregivers to family members and others outside of the family, leading to role conflict. Working with death may lead to vicarious traumatization when counselors begin to experience the same symptoms as their clients.

Altering the Delivery System for Counselors

In order to ensure the safety of those providing disaster response, new methods of delivering disaster first aid and general social support to victims and survivors will be needed. With possible closings of schools, senior centers, or disabled programs and the canceling of social, religious, or cultural gatherings, social support could crumble. People will need help in other ways as social distancing, isolation, quarantine, and travel restrictions occur. These methods must ensure the "perceived" safety of counselors, while at the same time provide access to mental health services because there may be no way of knowing if vaccinated providers are safe. These delivery methods may include telephone counseling, home visits with face-to-face sessions outdoors at a safe distance, Internet sessions, drive-in window counseling using banks or similar facilities, or door-to-door delivery of psychiatric medication.

Lessons Learned from SARS

As we look back to SARS, the first epidemic of the 21st century, we learned that first responders experienced role conflict because they were torn between protecting property and maintaining order and remaining at home with their family, while at the same time experiencing personal loss or illness (LeDuc & Barry, 2004). Unlike with fires and terrorist attacks, healthcare workers were the first responders to respond to the Hong Kong

and Toronto SARS outbreaks. Studies of these workers found a higher degree of emotional distress than that of the public, although they were dying at same rate during the outbreak. Mackler, Wilkerson, and Cinti (2007) found that these workers stayed away from home to protect their family, refused work assignments, and avoided patients. Counselors may be faced with similar challenges in a pandemic.

A report by the Central Intelligence Agency (2003) following the SARS epidemic warned that "...understanding and managing the public's psychological and behavioral reactions to an unexpected outbreak of infectious disease are integral to successful response and containment." Counselors may be a key factor in how well the nation handles the next pandemic and the challenges unique to a disease.

Ambiguous Loss

A number of human factors will complicate the successful management of a pandemic:

- Ambiguous loss, the process of losing a loved one without cultural funeral rituals or the ability to see or care for the dying person
- A *psychological presence* with a *physical absence*, when family members are hospitalized or quarantined, disconnected from relatives, and experiencing profound uncertainty
- Overwhelmed funeral homes and the potential for mass graves or mass cremation
- Inability to travel to funerals leading to bereavement without closure

UNCHARTED TERRITORY

Most of what we know about pandemics is from history. The good news is that unlike the 1600s or 1918, medicine, public health, and our understanding of disease have evolved. Equally significant is the fact that governments, WHO, the Red Cross, and the Council for the Accreditation of Counseling and Related Educational Programs (2009) (with its infusion of the new disaster standards) suggest that counselors and the public health system in general are better prepared to respond to a pandemic. Still, diseases offer unique challenges that have yet to be tested in a large-scale 21st century pandemic. We now know that in addition to arming themselves with disaster and trauma skills, counselors who anticipate being on the front lines are advised to read more about pandemic and public health procedures to ensure they know what they may be facing.

J. Barry Mascari EdD, LPC, LCADC, is chair of the Counselor Education Department at Kean University, Union, New Jersey and holds New Jersey Disaster Response Crisis Counselor certification (NJDRCC).

Jane Webber PhD, LPC, is associate professor and coordinator of the Counseling Program at New Jersey City University. She is a counselor in private practice and holds New Jersey Disaster Response Crisis Counselor certification (NJDRCC).

REFERENCES

Billings, M. (2005). *The influenza pandemic of 1918.* Retrieved from http://virus.stanford.edu/uda/

Camus, A. (1947). *The plague.* New York: Random House.

Centers for Disease Control and Prevention. (2009). *CDC resources for pandemic flu.* Retrieved from www.cdc.gov/flu/pandemic

Central Intelligence Agency. (2003). *SARS: Lessons learned from the first epidemic of the 21st Century.* Washington, DC: Author.

Council for the Accreditation of Counseling & Related Educational Programs. (2009). *2009 Standards.* Alexandria, VA: Author.

Crawford, R. (1995). The Spanish Flu. *Stranger than fiction: Vignettes of San Diego history.* San Diego, CA: San Diego Historical Society.

GlobalSecurity.org (2009). Flu pandemic morbidity/mortality. Retrieved from http://www.globalsecurity.org/security/ops/hsc-scen-3_flu-pandemic-deaths.htm

LeDuc, J. W., & Barry, M. A., (2004, November). *SARS, the first pandemic of the 21st century. Emerging Infectious Diseases.* Retrieved from http://www.cdc.gov/ncidod/EID/vol10no11/04-0797_02.htm

Mackler, N., Wilkerson, W., & Cinti, S. (2007). Will first-responders show up for work during a pandemic? Lessons from a smallpox vaccination survey of paramedics. *Disaster Management and Response 5*(2), 45–48.

MSNBC.com. (2009). *Kids Tamiflu in short supply.* Retrieved from http://www.msnbc.msn.com/id/32989141/ns/health-swine_flu/

Taubenberger, J., & Morens, D. (2006). 1918 Influenza: The mother of all pandemics. *Emerging Infectious Diseases, 12*(1), 15–22.

Ukrainetz, G. (2009). *Swine flu and the cytokine storm.* Retrieved from http://ezinearticles.com/?Swine-Flu-and-the-Cytokine-Storm&id=3163281

U.S. Department of Health & Human Services (2009). HHS pandemic influenza plan. Retrieved from http://www.hhs.gov/pandemicflu/plan/appendixb.html

Webber, J., Mascari, J. B., & Dubi, M. (2007, March). Responding to pandemic flu: What counselors need to know. Presentation at ACA Annual Conference. Detroit, MI.

World Health Organization. (2009). *Pandemic 2009.* Retrieved from http://www.who.int/csr/disease/influenza/pandemic/en/

COPING WITH FINANCIAL CRISIS 39

Steven M. Crimando and Cynthia L. Simeone

The 2008 annual survey, *Stress in America* (American Psychological Association, 2008) revealed that 8 out of 10 Americans identified money matters as the leading source of daily stress. Since the survey was released, the economic climate has darkened substantially. With the consumer confidence level at an all-time low (The Conference Board, 2009), people feel stressed and anxious about their financial future. Many are unsure how they will handle a recession or more economic bad news about foreclosures and layoffs.

ECONOMIC CRISIS: PANDEMIC-LITE

The global economic crisis that started in 2007 with the collapse of the housing bubble may be viewed as *pandemic-lite:* there is pain and psychosocial disruption without deaths. Both economic crisis and pandemic will likely result in the closures of many businesses, lost earnings, and other hardships. In both instances, individuals and households may suffer great financial distress and difficulties such as reduced household income, depleted savings, increased dependence on credit cards, default on loans or mortgages, and crisis-related financial scams.

The arrival of a pandemic influenza in the midst of the global financial crisis would represent a "perfect storm" scenario resulting in potentially unimaginable consequences for the global economy, as well as individuals, families, communities and organizations. If an organization is forced to layoff a substantial number of employees and it is already operating with a depleted workforce in a down economy, further diminishing the remaining workforce by another 30%-40% during a pandemic may have a paralytic—if not fatal—effect on the organization.

The national strategy for surviving an economic crisis or a pandemic hinges on three key actions: (a) stopping, slowing, or limiting the spread of crisis; (b) mitigating the impact, suffering, and permanent damage (or death); and (c) sustaining the infrastructure/economy and functioning of society. Comparing the economic crisis to a pandemic shows many interesting similarities of event dynamics, impact, response, planning, and recovery (see Table 1).

Table I. Event dynamics common to both an economic crisis and a pandemic.

- Global reach—few, if any, are immune
- Contributing factors identified long in advance of the onset of crisis
- Small pool of experts warned of impending doom
- Threat not fully recognized until reaching dramatic, irreversible levels
- General public had little awareness of the risk
- Highly technical/exotic factors triggered onset
- Slow-moving but unstoppable once in motion with long, complex crises
- Progresses in waves or cascading sequence
- Disagreement among experts about best way to handle the situation
- Remedy or vaccine is not readily available and must be developed quickly
- Initial attempts to "treat" the problem prove to be insufficient
- Intensity and duration of crisis exhausts resources
- Distinct social, economic, and emotional consequences
- Raises many ethical dilemmas
- Characterized by loss
- Contains aspects of both "sudden" and "smoldering" crises
- Increases distrust of authorities
- Creates a sense of helplessness or powerlessness

THE HUMAN RESPONSE

Sudden and Smoldering Crises

A *sudden crisis* tends to produce acute stress reactions in individuals, families, communities, and organizations. These events have "bookends"—it is clear when the event began, when it ended, and whether one was affected directly. A *smoldering crisis* often lacks these clear markers; it may begin slowly with many of the early warning signs remaining below the radar. Once the crisis begins, it is difficult to know exactly when it will end or how badly someone is affected because sudden crises are dynamic and shifting in severity over time.

Smoldering crises tend to result in chronic stress reactions. They can exhaust individual, organizational, and national resources. A pandemic that circles the globe in waves over the course of 12 months or longer would generally be considered a smoldering crisis. Likewise, the economic crisis, though beginning with the initial subprime calamity, reached the sudden crisis phase on one specific weekend in September 2008, but it will most likely be remembered as a long, complex, smoldering crisis.

Impact

The impact and response to sudden and smoldering crises differ. A sudden crisis has a definitive beginning and end, and, although shocking, the human impact is more easily compartmentalized because of the definitive timeline. With smoldering crises, the effects are usually more insidious and difficult to overcome because the emotional and behavioral cycles associated with the crises repeat over a sustained period of time. Recovery from a smoldering crisis is often more complicated than recovering from a sudden one.

However, both types of crises are characterized by loss and dread. Although loss of life is more likely in a catastrophic disease outbreak, other losses associated with the financial crisis may result in similar emotional and behavioral reactions, possibly further complicating response and recovery. These losses include, but are not limited to, the loss of identity, sense of community and belonging, status and role, control, security, trust, confidence, beliefs or faith (i.e., patriotism, religious beliefs), and future and purpose.

Dread. In the book, *The Unthinkable: Who Survives When Disaster Strikes and Why*, Ripley (2009) isolated dread as a significant factor influencing the human response to threatening events. She developed a *dread formula* to explain these dynamics: uncontrollability + unfamiliarity + unimaginability + suffering + scale of destruction + unfairness = dread. Each element can be assigned to an aspect present in both the economic crisis and most pandemic scenarios. Many commentators have used the terms "unimaginable" and "unthinkable" in their descriptions of the financial meltdown and the potential pandemic because the impact of both events can potentially reach all corners of the globe and all spheres of our personal and professional lives.

Trauma and Grief. Grief has been described as our reaction to something (or someone) "good" leaving our lives, and trauma is our response to something "bad" coming into our lives. In the instances of a worker losing a job, baby boomers losing 40% or more of their retirement savings, or a family losing their home, loss is loss and our minds and bodies do not necessarily distinguish between a health crisis or an economic disaster. Behavioral reactions tied to our appraisal of the situation can lead to social isolation, withdrawal, increased irritability and change in sleep patterns, emotional eating (especially sweet, salty, and high-fat foods), alcohol and drug use, risk-taking, and difficulty in concentrating, problem solving, and decision-making.

Many behavioral reactions affect interpersonal relationships in the home and workplace. These can be manifested as increased conflict, diminished communications, difficulty parenting or supervising workplace subordinates, and poor spousal/partner or peer relations.

TRACKING AND BENCHMARKING THROUGH A SMOLDERING CRISIS

There is very little, if any, empirical research from the Great Influenza Pandemic or the Great Depression that can be applied to predicting human behavior in a smoldering health crisis or financial crisis. So what else can be done by organizations to utilize the lessons learned from the past to address the financial pandemic at hand?

Tracking can help leaders gain a better understanding of how prolonged adversity affects the "worried well" (those who are still employed or not otherwise derailed by the crisis); this would help to inform organizational policies and practices. Organizational benchmarking of human factor issues can be invaluable in making plans for sustaining productivity and the bottom line during a pandemic or other smoldering crisis. Organizations have begun to track the impact that employee benefit or wellness programs (weight reduction, smoking cessation, and exercise programs) have on an organization's bottom line. It would be beneficial to also document other human factors issues (absenteeism, performance, morale, conflict, etc.) in the home, business, and community as we move through the various phases of the financial crisis.

The likely psychosocial challenges of long-term recovery from both a pandemic and economic crisis are similar. In a typical disaster, as fear escalates, the behavioral response cycle can quickly shift from *neighbor-helps-neighbor* to *neighbor-fears-neighbor* to *neighbor-competes-with-neighbor*. During the recovery period, the cycle gradually returns from self-preservation back toward community cohesion and support. In fact, one of the lessons learned from other smoldering crises is that the natural support systems within the home, business, or community become the most important and dominant source of help. Families, businesses, and communities should take every opportunity to bolster and promote cohesion in the early phases of a crisis because it will become increasingly important as time goes on.

Other challenges that need to be addressed in a crisis include:

- Overcoming loss or guilt from having survived
- Taking inventory of one's current state of personal and professional affairs
- Addressing both the physical and psychological consequences
- Developing a reconstruction plan to rebuild or recoup losses
- Reaching out to friends and the community to give and get support

Emotional responses can range from simple distress to diagnosable mental health conditions including extreme fear and anxiety, sadness and depression, anger, blame, helplessness, hopelessness, increased suicide risk, traumatic stress reactions, and complicated grief and bereavement.

Personal and organizational resilience is essential to recovery from a smoldering crisis. Resilience often is defined as "the human capacity and ability to face, overcome, be strengthened by, and even be transformed by experiences of adversity" (ResilienceNet). Resilience can and should be nurtured. Smoldering crises are best approached through applying the discipline and strategy of the marathon runner, not the sprinter. Everyone wants out of a tough situation sooner rather than later, but both financial crises and pandemics are challenges of endurance.

Those who have survived and thrived through smoldering crises in the past identify three common tactics: facing the sources of their stress directly, learning from past experiences, and reaching out for and using resources.

WORKPLACE PLANNING

Much can be done to reduce or mitigate the impact of a financial crisis or pandemic through conscientious planning in the home, workplace, and community. In planning, it is important to ensure that critical work can continue with a reduction of workforce and that the remaining workforce retains the core skills and knowledge (corporate memory) to continue operating. Successful consequence management through the financial crisis will require attention to many of the same concerns in a pandemic: communications, physical and mental health of employees, the ability to travel to or attend to work, and developing organizational resilience. If, during the economic crisis, workforce reduction is necessary, ensure the remaining workforce still retains the core skills and knowledge (corporate memory) to carry out essential business functions or make sure critical processes are documented so unskilled laborers can perform the required function.

Crisis-sizing or temporarily adjusting the size and configuration of an organization's workforce due to economic pressures rather than illness may be a necessary part of a survival strategy. Pandemic planning guides suggest that leaders explore creative workforce restructuring for survival. In the recent economic crisis, businesses have implemented creative alternatives to layoffs, including reduced hours for all. Cost-saving alternatives include working from home and job sharing to reduce office space requirements and overhead costs. If the organization is reliant on external resources or services, leaders should conduct business risk and impact assessments to identify critical suppliers, identify alternative sources, and negotiate contract terms in advance of any potential disruption.

A great deal of time, effort, and money has been spent in the United States and abroad developing plans and procedures to mitigate the effects of a pandemic on the workplace. The financial crisis has triggered many of the same workplace dynamics anticipated by pandemic planners, including high levels of stress and fear; diminished or depleted workforce; decline in retail, travel, entertainment, construction, and many other economic sectors; escalating unemployment; and disruption or closure of financial institutions.

Many organizations active in pandemic planning had initiated training programs for executives and supervisors, as well as internal crisis management and first responder teams, to raise awareness of the unique physical and mental health challenges associated with an influenza outbreak. These training programs were designed to help decision-makers predict and prepare for a pandemic using accurate information about the disease and its likely impact on society, as well as the organization. Specialized training focused on the unique challenges associated with a financial crisis is equally important.

In the workplace, survival is a shared responsibility. Organizations can provide the greatest value to employees by communicating their priorities and survival strategies, particularly in a financial crisis. Clarity regarding roles and responsibilities during a crisis is crucial. To reduce anxiety, leaders should provide employees with two-way communication vehicles.

From an ethical standpoint, it is much better to communicate these challenges, but there is also a legal obligation; the Worker Adjustment and Retraining Notification (WARN) Act (1988) requires companies to provide 90 days notice prior to plant closure or mass layoffs so that affected employees can prepare financially and emotionally. Proactive, pre-approved communications as well as a hotline can empower employees and help stabilize the workplace environment.

SOURCES OF EMOTIONAL SUPPORT

With economic losses, there will be an increased need for psychological support programs for workers and their families. A lesson learned from pandemic is that natural support systems in the home, community, and workplace tend to be the most helpful in other smoldering crises. Employee assistance programs (EAPs) or community outreach programs can help employees with financial planning. Promoting peer support programs for employees to both give and get emotional support from each other may prove invaluable.

The emotional demands of both a pandemic and a financial crisis can erode relationships in the home during a time when the support of loved ones is needed most. Providing family members with information goes a long way toward an effective response and recovery. Communicating about the effects of smoldering crises on homes and families may help individuals anticipate the likely emotional traps that characterize long-term stress situations.

Employers also can provide additional assistance in financial planning and household money management.

Those not yet seriously affected by the financial crisis can modify the household budget and identify ways to curtail unnecessary spending. It is helpful to enlist all family members in the process; even young children can understand the concept of saving for future benefit.

CONCLUSION

Both financial collapse and pandemics are smoldering crises with similar human and economic consequences. Although a catastrophic disease outbreak could result in a tremendous loss of life, there are enough similarities between the two crises to allow one to inform the other. In fact, a weakened global economy may leave nations, businesses, communities, and families much more at risk to a public health disaster.

Steven M. Crimando is a Board Certified Expert in Traumatic Stress and is the Director of Training for the Disaster and Terrorism Branch of the New Jersey Department of Human Services' Division of Mental Health Services. He is Managing Director of Extreme Behavioral Risk Management.

Cynthia L. Simeone, a management consultant, is a Certified Business Continuity Professional, and is a member of the Disaster Recovery Institute International as well as the Association of Contingency Planners.

This chapter was adapted from A Special Report from *Extreme Behavioral Risk Management* (A Division of ALLSector Technology Group Inc.) and used with permission.

REFERENCES

American Psychological Association. (2008). *Stress in America.* Retrieved from http://apahelpcenter.mediaroom.com/file.php/173/APA%2BStress%2Bin%2BAmerica%2BRelease%2BFINAL%2BNO%2BEmbargo.pdf

ResilienceNet. (2009). About ResilienceNet. Retrieved from http://resilnet.uiuc.edu/abtrnet.html

Ripley, A. (2009). *The unthinkable: Who survives when disaster strikes and why.* New York: Random House.

The Conference Board. (2009). *Consumer confidence press release.* Retrieved from http://www.conference-board.org/utilities/pressDetail.cfm?press_ID=3567

U.S. Department of Labor. (1988). Worker Adjustment and Retraining Notification Act. Retrieved from http://www.doleta.gov/layoff/pdf/WorkerWARN2003.pdf

General Standards for Disaster Crisis Counselors

Karin Jordan

40

Since the 1970s, numerous disasters worldwide have increased the demand for crisis counseling, often provided by volunteer crisis counselors with relief agencies. Crisis counselors frequently provide limited services to survivors who are lacking essential needs such as water, food, shelter, safety, and security and those who are struggling with multiple losses and displacement. Natural disasters, acts of terrorism, plane accidents, or any other type of tragedy can occur anywhere in the world; therefore, general standards are needed for responding to people in ways that are sensitive to the broad range of social, economic, political, cultural, religious, and family factors.

General Standards

The six general standards proposed below have been specifically designed for crisis counselors to use in responding to disaster-affected people and countries. The standards are rooted in the belief that all trauma-affected persons, families, and countries have the right to be treated with dignity and respect. Crisis counselors should understand the philosophical principles underlying the six general standards in order to: practice from an ecological perspective, provide services that are fitting for the disaster-affected population and country, treat the affected population with dignity and respect, inform them, and be non-discriminatory. Although the standards do not provide answers to all the unique challenges crisis counselors face, they offer broad guidelines for planning and carrying out decisions. The examples provided for each standard are from the 2004 tsunami in Sri Lanka.

General Standard 1: Need and Capacity

The need for crisis counseling is dependent on: (a) the severity (loss of life, injuries, destruction of personal and community property, displacement) and duration of the disaster (ranging from minutes to hours, days, months, or years); (b) the relief organization's capacity (funding as well as availability of qualified crisis counselor volunteers); and (c) the local capacity (available mental health facilities and mental health professionals, and hospitals). Crisis counselors should be deployed to assist in a disaster event only at the invitation of a local organization so that they are organized in collaboration with others for the well-being of the affected people and country. They should follow guidelines set by government officials of the disaster-affected community/region.

Example. In 2004, a magnitude 9.0 earthquake in the Indian Ocean resulted in a tsunami with waves up to 100 feet, hitting 11 Indian Ocean countries. Sri Lanka was the second most affected country with a death toll of 35,322 as well as untold injuries and vast destruction of personal and community property. This resulted in displacement to refugee camps, the devastation of fishing boats, and the accompanying loss of livelihoods. Family and community support systems and a place of belonging, safety, and security were lost.

The local capacity for mental health services in Sri Lanka was limited, with 39 psychiatrists in the entire country. Non–governmental organizations (NGOs) and other committed groups provided mental health services without adequate coordination or oversight. A local mental health organization that had previously worked with an American relief organization requested that a mental health team be sent to assist them in the training of their organizations and other mental health professionals to help tsunami survivors.

The Sri Lanka Minister of Health was asked to provide clearance for a team of disaster crisis counselor volunteers to come to the country; the Minister made it clear that no direct crisis counseling should be provided by the team. Rather, they should only train local mental health professionals and teacher counselors (school counselors) in disaster mental health, with a special focus on school-age children and adolescents.

General Standard 2: Information Gathering and Initial Assessment

Crisis counselors need to gain a clear understanding of the disaster/trauma event and its impact, including the loss of life, injury, destruction of property and community, displacement, and separation of family and community. They should understand the impact that the disaster has on the affected people and country, as well as the capacity of the local community, available resources, and relevant authorities.

The information gathering and assessment process includes the most vulnerable, at-risk population (children, women, elderly, disabled, physically ill, poor, displaced, those with previous trauma histories) with a focus on people's ethnic origins and religious or political affiliations while taking into account local authorities, standards, and laws. Some information might be sensitive and should be treated confidentially. The process is done on two levels:

Pre-deployment: seeking information through secondary sources including literature, reports about important historical events, cultural information and pre-disaster data (disaster preparedness plans/efforts, underlying political, security, economic, demographic, and environmental issues).

Post-deployment: seeking information through primary sources such as all sectors of the disaster-affected people, community leaders, local authorities, health staff, and teachers; this should occur within a couple of days (or sometimes weeks) after the disaster in order to design a plan that is disaster, population, and country specific.

Example. The tsunami hit the southern and eastern coasts of Sri Lanka with the people who lived at the beach (often fishermen) having a high death toll and the most severe destruction of homes and community. Many survivors initially moved into crowded refugee camps where there were shortages of food and water; however, more than 100,000 left the camps within 2 weeks. Some moved in with relatives and friends; others moved back to their partially destroyed homes and worked on rebuilding their homes.

The crisis counselors had gathered pre-deployment information indicating that the country had a history of civil war between the Sinhalese who hold a Buddhist belief system, and the Tamils who hold a Hindu belief system. Additional belief systems in Sri Lanka are Roman Catholic, Protestant Christian, and Muslim. Fathers are seen as the head of the family, whereas mothers are often in charge of the family finances. Children learn obedience and family loyalty early in life, as well as control over their emotions.

When the crisis counselors were in-country, they gathered additional information by meeting with representatives of the mental health organization with whom they partnered, as well as traveling to the south and east coasts seeing first-hand the level of destruction caused by the tsunami. They then interviewed tsunami-affected adults and collected drawings from nearly 100 tsunami-affected children. They also visited several government organizations and met with other NGOs.

General Standard 3: Service Delivery

Participation in the services provided for disaster-affected people is voluntary, and the goals are to reinforce the survivor's sense of dignity, hope, resiliency, and decision-making, and to strengthen their own coping strategies. Crisis counselors are respectful of the culture, religious/spiritual values and beliefs, socioeconomic status, and history of the people with whom they working. They should not simply use Western (often white middle-class) methods and techniques that may undermine the rights of others.

Crisis counselors provide equal and impartial nondiscriminatory services according to the needs of the disaster-affected people. Services need to be available to all disaster-affected persons, including the most vulnerable at-risk populations. Efficient services minimize dependency with an understanding of available resources and coping capacity. It is important to make decisions in concert with local officials and mental health professionals, as well as the disaster-affected people themselves. In countries and regions embroiled in conflict, war, or terrorism, it is also important to understand the nature and source of the conflict, which might influence how to serve individuals and the country.

Example. The training provided for the mental health professionals and teacher counselors was based on the information gathered from volunteers of the Peace Corps who had lived in Sri Lanka pre-deployment, from the literature, and from post-deployment, in collaboration with the partnering mental health organizations in Sri Lanka. Focus was placed on the diverse cultural and religious/spiritual beliefs and practices as a source of conflict that needed to be addressed sensitively because they were important in grief and loss issues. The civil war was addressed from a historical point of view because many of the tsunami-affected adults, as well as children and adolescents, had a history of previous trauma from their war experiences.

The crisis counselors developed a curriculum that was disaster and population specific, designed to provide general information about the effects of trauma across the lifespan with a special focus on children and adolescents, which had been requested by Sri Lanka's Minister of Health. The training addressed techniques and methods to be used with children and adolescents affected by both Type I (single trauma event: the tsunami) and Type II (multiple trauma events: the civil war and the tsunami) traumas.

General Standard 4: Process and Outcome Assessment

Crisis counselors should assess the crisis counseling services or psychoeducational training programs in order to determine whether any should be continued or made more relevant and effective for the disaster-affected people. This includes eliciting feedback throughout the process of providing services or training, as well as an assessment at the end of delivery.

Process and outcome assessment helps crisis counselors identify emerging issues, and both should be done not only within the context of the local culture, values, beliefs, and practices, but also the larger ecological perspective (historical, socioeconomic status). Crisis counselors should share their assessment findings with their relief organization and their replacement team, as well as partnering local agencies and other NGOs with whom they might work.

Example. After the team of crisis counselors had completed the psychoeducational training, they met with the training participants and received feedback. The training participants were interested in applying the skills learned by going to the refugee camps and getting supervision or consultation in case of questions and/or difficulties. This information was passed on to the relief organization and partnering Sri Lankan mental health organizations, creating an opportunity to determine how to respond to the identified need.

General Standard 5: Crisis Counselor Evaluation

To ensure accountability and to improve practice, relief organizations should evaluate crisis counselors. Evaluation ensures that they follow standards, are non-discriminatory,

and perform crisis counseling or psychoeducational training that is appropriate and meets needs.

The evaluation should be done impartially, in writing or through interviews involving those served and affected, local organizations/agencies, other officials, and the crisis counselor's team members. Results are "lessons learned" for crisis counselors and help for the relief organization in assessing what training, skills, and knowledge their crisis counselors should have.

Example. After the crisis counselors completed their psychoeducational training, the partnering mental health organization communicated with the relief organization directly, reporting the crisis counselors' effectiveness and skills in working with organizations involved, the local individuals affected by the tsunami, and the training participants. They found that the training was very comprehensive, despite the crisis counselors' varied knowledge. The relief organization also met separately with crisis counselors on the team to solicit their perceptions as to their own and other team members' training effectiveness, skill/knowledge level, professional behavior, and ability to operate from an ecological perspective and work effectively as part of a team.

General Standard 6: Crisis Counselor Skills and Responsibility

Crisis counselors require appropriate training, skills, and experience in traumatology, disaster mental health, and crisis counseling, as well as psychoeducational program delivery. Through training and supervision with a seasoned crisis counselor, they learn how to assess their ability to function effectively in disaster-affected areas. Crisis counselors are aware of the signs of compassion fatigue by looking at their own coping skills, resiliency, stress buffers, and previous history of trauma or present life cycle transitions. They know the importance of regularly assessing their own capacity for working with disaster-affected people and countries and seeking appropriate consultation, supervision, and continuing education.

To address the unique challenges they face, crisis counselors follow their professional code of ethics, as well as these six general standards, and do not practice beyond their skill level and scope of practice. When they volunteer, they represent themselves and their skill level accurately and do not misrepresent their credentials. Crisis counselors respect the rights and dignity of all trauma-affected people. They are also aware of the importance of attending to the most vulnerable, at-risk populations as well as the increased risk of exploitation and violence after a disaster. Crisis counselors recognize and do not engage in discriminatory, abusive, or illegal activities, and appropriately seek out consultation to explore possible actions that should be taken.

Example. The team sent to Sri Lanka had previous training in traumatology and disaster mental health and had good insight into their coping skills. One team member found journaling to be an effective coping skill, and another used humor. They followed their professional code of ethics and consulted with each other when ethical issues arose. They trained mental health professionals and teacher counselors, as was requested by the Sri Lankan Minister of Health, to assist children and adolescents (one of the vulnerable populations) to cope effectively with the impact of the tsunami.

Karin Jordan, PhD, is professor and chair of the Department of Counseling, The University of Akron, Ohio. She facilitates the ACA Traumatology Interest Network.

The Uniform Emergency Volunteer Health Practitioners Act and What It Means to Counselors

41

Jackson R. Schonberg

Many mental health volunteers responding to a major disaster give little thought to possible legal ramifications of the assignment. If a volunteer enters another state, will the license be honored? Typically, the answer is no. There is also a clear risk of financial liability through a lawsuit, and, in some rare instances, criminal prosecution for practicing without a valid license, as well as the possibility of personal injury or even death of a volunteer given that many disasters by definition create unsafe environments.

Historically, these issues have prevented prospective volunteer practitioners—including counselors—from providing their valuable services at a major disaster effectively.

Organized Disaster Response Units

The preferred model for all volunteer disaster responders is to become part of an organized response unit prior to an event. This process facilitates recruiting, selecting, and screening volunteers and their credentials. Some personality types—such as those who need structure and order—are not a good match for disaster service. Belonging to an organized unit also facilitates advanced training in role-specific disaster mental health (DMH) skills and agency culture, as well as in the National Incident Management System (NIMS) and Incident Command System (ICS), both of which are essential for safe and appropriate conduct in a disaster setting. (See list of websites at end of chapter.)

Comprehensively checking credentials at an active disaster is nearly impossible due to the inherent chaos, long lines, and lack of resources such as internet access, personnel, equipment, and in the absence of "official" documents. Congress cannot address these prob-

lems by passing a federal licensing act that would be valid throughout the United States because it is considered a "police power" specifically left to the states by the 10th Amendment of the U. S. Constitution. A solution was needed before another disaster such as Hurricane Katrina struck. Thus, the Uniform Emergency Volunteer Health Practitioners Act (UEVHPA) was developed. The intent was to:

> … fill the tragic gap so that in future years health practitioners will be able to be quickly deployed to health care facilities and disaster relief organizations pursuant to clear and well-understood rules that will both meet the needs of volunteers and relief agencies and provide an effective framework to ensure the delivery of high quality care to disaster victims. (National Conference of Commissioners on Uniform State Laws, 2006, p. 1)

Spontaneous vs. Formal Volunteers

Spontaneous volunteers often create problems at disaster sites. *Spontaneous volunteers* are defined as those frequently well-meaning individuals who appear at the scene of a disaster offering to help. Typically, they are not part of a recognized disaster response unit and may have little if any understanding of federal disaster response protocol such as the NIMS and ICS. Spontaneous volunteers may not understand the culture or disaster mental health services (DMHS) protocol of the onsite formal response unit they are attempting to join.

Because of extraordinary demands for service during the 2004 and 2005 hurricanes, particularly with Katrina, Rita, and Wilma, volunteers were recruited through the professional organizations of the various mental health and health disciplines. Frequently, this was accomplished directly from the clinic/office to the disaster site, bypassing the local American Red Cross (ARC) chapter and creating problems with validation of credentials and competencies.

During the 2004 hurricanes, I served with the ARC in Florida as a site supervisor of mental health services. At one site, the arrival of a new health services volunteer created a problem. It was discovered that the volunteer was a fully qualified neonatal intensive care unit (NICU) nurse who had arrived with deep expectations of saving and rescuing critically ill infants. If this individual had direct experience with the ARC's health services, as well as knowledge of response timing (several weeks into the disaster response operation), the volunteer would have understood that there was no role for a NICU nurse. After intensive de-escalation and educational intervention, the volunteer agreed to reframe her role expectations and she became a contributing member of the team.

Disaster Mental Health Volunteers

The Red Cross DMHS is the oldest, largest, and best-known volunteer service with which professional counselors are likely to be associated, and their standards are similar to those of most volunteer organizations that are active in disasters. Eligible volunteers include counselors, marriage and family therapists, psychiatrists, psychologists, registered nurses with documented psychiatric training and experience, social workers, and as of June 2008, school psychologists and school counselors, as well as some graduate students working with their supervisor (American Red Cross, 2008). Established in the 1990s primarily in response to the San Francisco earthquake, the ARC DMHS mission is to provide:

> ... mental health support to those affected by disasters, whether they have disaster-caused damage, reside in the disaster-affected area, are relatives of those affected or have disaster-related emotional difficulties created by mass media exposure, as well as to Red Cross Disaster Services staff assigned to a disaster relief operation, and to their families. (American Red Cross, 1998, p. 1)

> ARC DMHS volunteers provide a range of services including: psychological triage, crisis intervention, psychological support, instrumental support, advocacy, problem solving; education, referrals, supervision, support to Red Cross workers providing psychological first aid, monitoring and alleviating organizational stress, and casualty support. (American Red Cross, 2006, p.1)

THE UNIFORM EMERGENCY VOLUNTEER HEALTH PRACTITIONERS ACT (UEVHPA)

The National Conference of Commissioners on Uniform State Laws (NCCUSL), also known as the Uniform Law Commission, is the 118-year-old organization that facilitates consistent legislation in all states on a wide variety of issues including the movement of licensed health professionals across state lines during disasters. Following the 2005 Gulf Coast hurricanes, the NCCUSL moved rapidly to address problems and deficiencies in the system. With lessons learned from past mistakes and the desire to improve the situation for future disasters, the NCCUSL expedited the development of a model legislative act, completing the document in 1 year, rather than the anticipated 3 years. The UEVHPA resulted from the work of NCCUSL Drafting Committee with input from many government and non-governmental organizations (e.g., the ARC) as well as legal, and mental health representatives involved in disaster response. The Act created "a system for health professionals to register as volunteers in advance of, or during an emergency in an enacting state" that included the following improvements:

1. Establishes a system for the use of volunteer health practitioners capable of functioning autonomously, even when routine methods of communication are disrupted;

2. Provides reasonable safeguards to assure that volunteer health practitioners are appropriately licensed and regulated to protect the public's health;

3. Allows states to regulate, direct, and restrict the scope and extent of services provided by volunteer health practitioners to promote disaster recovery operations;

4. Provides limitations on the exposure of volunteer health practitioners to civil liability to create a legal environment conducive to volunteerism; and

5. Allows volunteer health practitioners who suffer injury or death while providing services pursuant to this act the option to elect workers' compensation benefits from the host state if such coverage is not otherwise available. (National Conference, 2007, p. 1)

Benefits of the UEVHPA

In addition to the broad improvements it made in the disaster response system, the UEVHPA also now includes:

- All medical professions: medical doctors, nurses, mental health, veterinary, pharmacy, and mortuary personnel
- Advance planning, especially through use of pre-registration of licensed professionals
- Pre-registration of professionals through use of Emergency System for Advanced Registration of Volunteer Health Professionals, ARC-DSHR, and state associations
- Alignment with the National Response Framework concept of "layering" local, county/region, state, multi-state, federal levels
- Application to multiple levels of emergencies, not just large events
- Ability to be invoked by multiple emergency management authorities
- Volunteers in addition to state employees and those paid outside of their regular employment responsibilities
- Control retained by host states so that volunteers can do only what they are permitted to do in their home state
- Professional, tort, and sponsoring agency liability
- The provision for workers compensation by the host state for responders functioning under the Act
- Oversight and discipline of professionals by respective licensing boards with reporting to home states
- Reciprocity time limited by event

As of August 24, 2009, 10 states (Arkansas, Colorado, Indiana, Kentucky, Louisiana, New Mexico, North Dakota, Oklahoma, Tennessee, and Utah) enacted the UEVHPA; many others are at some stage of the legislative process.

The Emergency Management Assistance Compact (EMAC)

Disaster mental health counselors should be aware of another legal system, limited to state employees and those temporarily "seconded" to state service, but not covering volunteers outside of state employment. The Emergency Management Assistance Compact (Emergency Management, 2009), adopted by all 50 states and territories, is designed to address these problems directly and generally does a fine job. EMAC recognizes the need for states to utilize personnel and resources provided from other states to respond to governor-declared emergencies --usually high-level events and frequently invoked following major disasters. There is a provision for oversight of professionals or limitation of practice, unless specifically formulated by individual states.

The Emergency Volunteer Action Project (EVAN)

A major attempt is underway by the University of North Carolina School of Public Health (North Carolina, 2008) to improve emergency legal preparedness for volunteers who cooperate with state agencies in responding to disasters. This initiative, the Emergency Volunteer Action Project (EVAN), aims to modify Good Samaritan laws to be more inclusive through entity vs. individual emergency liability protection. The EVAN Project would extend Good Samaritan protection to business and nonprofit entities acting in good faith during an emergency declared by the Governor.

Coverage would apply only to emergency activities conducted in coordination with the state. The liability protection would not extend to businesses and nonprofits acting unilaterally and without coordination with the state government. It would require the activity to be conducted pursuant to the order or request of the state government or any political subdivision of the state (North Carolina, 2008).

The issue of inter-state license reciprocity is unclear and workers' compensation is not addressed. In addition to state activities, liability coverage would also include pre-event planning and training activities. North Carolina, Georgia, Washington, Iowa, and Virginia have passed legislation based on the EVAN principles.

What Counselors Need to Know and Do

The DMHS has improved dramatically since the early 1990s, but many problems still exist. The following recommendations may help counselors avoid the remaining problems and do their part to improve the quality and responsiveness of the system:

1. *Keep your license up to date and on record with your sponsor agency.* When criminalized, the unlicensed practice of medicine or any other healing art is usually considered a strict liability crime; that is, there may not be the need to demonstrate criminal intent to find a violation. Thus, the mere engagement in practice without a license would be criminal regardless of the intent or justification (Hodge, 2006). Generally, the state licensure board is responsible for

enforcing prohibitions against unauthorized practice by unlicensed health professionals. Practicing without a license will probably invalidate personal professional liability insurance and place one's responder's license at risk, thereby creating potential legal liability for the host agency.

2. *Plan to register in advance as a disaster mental health volunteer.* The U.S. Department of Health and Human Services developed the Emergency System for Advance Registration of Volunteer Health Professionals, which is implemented in the individual states under a variety of names. If a volunteer is a member of the ARC Disaster Services Human Resources System, their records are fully computerized and national in scope. The ARC online registry of volunteers, whose credentials are fully verified during the quiet times before disasters, is accessible to staff who select and validate volunteers.

3. *Educate DMHS responders as to why the UEVHPA is needed and how to support its enactment.* It is needed in all 50 states and territories because EMAC does not solve the problems volunteers face during disasters.

4. *Encourage potential DMHS responders to join recognized response units before a disaster.* Membership not only facilitates credentialing, training, and acculturation prior to a major event, but also permits participation in practice drills and responding to local disaster events.

5. *Take DMHS and other relevant training courses and participate in drills offered.*

6. *Learn the culture of your response unit.*

Jackson R. Schonberg, EdD, is co-chair of disaster services, Central Vermont–New Hampshire Valley Chapter, American Red Cross, and a Disaster Mental Health Manager in the ARC DSHR system.

REFERENCES

American Red Cross. (1998). *Disaster mental health services ARC 3043.* Washington, DC: Author.

American Red Cross. (2006). *ARC disaster services program guidance manual-Individual client services: Disaster mental health services.* Washington, DC: Author.

American Red Cross. (2008). *Disaster mental health expands eligibility criteria.* Retrieved from CrossNet (Internal website). Washington, DC: Author.

Emergency Management Assistance Compact. (2009). *An Act to ratify the Emergency Management Assistance Compact.* Retrieved from http://www.emacweb.org

Hodge, J. (2006). *Emergency System for Advance Registration of Volunteer Health Professionals (ESAR-VHP): Legal and regulatory issues.* Washington, DC: Department of Health and Human Services, Health Resources and Services Administration.

National Conference of Commissioners on Uniform State Laws. (2006). *Uniform Emergency Volunteer Health Practitioners Act-Summary.* Retrieved from http://www.nccusl.org/Update/uniformact_summaries/uniformacts-s-uevhpa.asp

National Conference of Commissioners on Uniform State Laws. (2007). *Uniform Emergency Volunteer Health Practitioners Act with Prefatory Note and Comments.* Retrieved from http://www.law.upenn.edu/bll/archives/ulc/uiehsa/2007act_final.pdf

North Carolina Institute of Public Health. (2008). *Emergency Volunteer Action Network.* Retrieved from http://nciph.sph.unc.edu/law/

ADDITIONAL RESOURCES/WEBSITES

FEMA NIMS Resource Center
http://www.fema.gov/emergency/nims/

FEMA National Response Framework
http://www.fema.gov/emergency/nrf/aboutNRF.htm

FEMA Incident Control System
http://www.fema.gov/emergency/nims/IncidentCommandSystem.shtm

PSYCHOLOGICAL FIRST AID: A NEW PARADIGM FOR DISASTER MENTAL HEALTH

42

Jane Webber, J. Barry Mascari, and Julia Runte

Following September 11, counselors struggled to find resources and information about responding to disaster. The need for disaster mental health (DMH) skills led to the publication in 2002 of the first edition of this book, *Terrorism, Trauma and Tragedies: A Counselor's Guide to Preparing and Responding.* Smith (2002) cautioned in the first edition, "Providing mental health services in a disaster environment requires an additional set of skills that are noticeably lacking in counselor education programs" (p. 37). In recent years, trauma research has rapidly expanded, significantly influencing the nature of DMH response and how individuals cope with trauma (Dass-Brailford, 2009; Courtois & Gold, 2009). Webber, Mascari, Dubi, and Gentry (2006) proposed an agenda to promote evidence-informed disaster mental health practice following the 2005 hurricanes; to date, several of those goals have been accomplished. Since then, new research and practice have changed the nature of DMH response. The 2009 CACREP standards now require every graduate of a CACREP-accredited program to have a foundation of awareness, knowledge, and skills for disaster, trauma, and crisis counseling. Although curriculum and training approaches have yet to be developed and validated through research to ensure best practices, six guidelines for developing curricula were identified (Webber & Mascari, 2009):

1. Know the organizations and government agencies and their purposes.
2. Understand the major principles of disaster response, trauma counseling, and crisis intervention and their differences.
3. Ensure that students understand their ethical responsibility to practice disaster response only to the extent of their competence.
4. Develop knowledge and practice competencies in disaster response, trauma counseling, and crisis intervention when planning to teach this specialty in classes.
5. Establish relationships with credentialed disaster and trauma specialists with field experience who are willing to be guest trainers for specialized course components.
6. Recognize that disaster and trauma counseling is a growing specialty that needs research and study to ensure outcome-based practices. (pp. 128–132)

UNDERSTANDING TRAUMA: A NEW PARADIGM

Since the first edition, this publication has emphasized that individuals exposed to disasters experience normal reactions to an abnormal event. Trauma response had little empirical evidence and largely was informed by personal experience and clinical observation. Gold (2009) suggested, "The entire field of trauma psychology is based on theory. The assertion—or assumption—that catastrophic events can have appreciable adverse impact on psychological functioning is itself a theoretical position" (p. 1). In the last 30 years, findings of empirical studies on trauma have changed our beliefs about how trauma affects people and how counseling professionals should intervene. We now know that:

- Most posttraumatic stressors (PTS) appearing immediately following a mass disaster are normal and expected responses to an abnormal event.
- Following a disaster, the majority of individuals will not develop posttraumatic stress disorder (PTSD) or severe mental health problems.
- Most survivors of mass disasters return to a level of normal functioning within a few days or weeks without mental health treatment.

- Trauma is not an unusual occurrence and the majority of people experience one or more traumatic events.
- Not all persons who are exposed to traumatic events show shock or distress or become traumatized.
- Actively involving and empowering survivors facilitates the return to normalcy.
- Many people experience psychological growth as a result of traumatic events.
- "Neighbor helping neighbor" provides support and promotes family and community resiliency immediately following a disaster.

Psychological First Aid

Psychological first aid (PFA) is now considered the primary evidence-informed practice in promoting recovery after a disaster. In the immediate aftermath of a traumatic event, DMH volunteers become "a supportive and compassionate presence designed to reduce acute psychological distress" (Everly & Flynn, 2005, p. 80). They promote individual and family coping skills for survivors through, supportive personal connections, social support, psychoeducation, and ongoing care (Institute of Medicine, 2003). This is often provided through active reflective listening and empathic responding while distributing bottles of water, food, information, and handouts, or helping individuals find family members.

The purpose of PFA is not to solicit or discuss details of the individual's traumatic experience or provide debriefing or counseling. Mental health counseling skills are not required to provide PFA; in fact, this model is effectively used by paraprofessionals and nonprofessionals from the community (Everly & Flynn, 2006). However, formal training and practice in PFA skills are essential to serve and protect survivors from emotional harm or retraumatization.

The Field Operations Guide for Psychological First Aid developed by The National Child Traumatic Stress Network and the National Center for PTSD is considered state-of-the-art, evidence-informed practice. PFA skills and techniques have been tested in the field and shown to reduce the immediate distress following a traumatic event and facilitate individual and group adaptive behavior. Among the fundamental goals of PFA are to:

- Establish a human connection in a non-intrusive, compassionate manner.
- Enhance immediate and ongoing safety and provide physical and emotional comfort.
- Calm and orient emotionally overwhelmed or distraught survivors.

- Help survivors to tell you specifically what their immediate needs and concerns are and gather additional information as appropriate.
- Offer practical assistance and information to help survivors address those needs and concerns.
- Connect survivors as soon as possible to social support networks, including family members, friends, neighbors, and community helping resources.
- Support adaptive coping, acknowledge coping efforts and strengths, and empower survivors; encourage adults, children, and families to take an active role in their recovery.
- Provide information that may help survivors cope effectively with the psychological impact of disasters. (NTCSN, 2006, p. 2)

Responders are deployed by an authorized community agency or disaster response system and operate only within their scope of practice and competence. The Incident Command System provides a uniform structure for response operations. Roles, responsibilities, and the chain of command are consistent in any field location (U.S. Department of Homeland Security Federal Emergency Management Agency, 2010).

Guidelines for Delivering Psychological First Aid

The process of PFA (NTCSN, 2006) involves seven core actions: (a) contact and engagement, (b) safety and comfort, (c) stabilization, (d) information gathering on current needs and concerns, (e) practical assistance, (f) connection with social supports, and (g) information on coping and linkage with collaborative services. To facilitate self-efficacy in survivors and encourage them to meet their own needs, responders should follow three basic principles in providing PFA: protect from further exposure and media; direct in a gentle and clear manner; and connect with loved ones, information, and support (Crimando, 2009). Several techniques to facilitate contact, engagement, and stabilization follow.

Contact and Engagement

Compassionate loitering. Providers of PFA engage in a behavioral approach called "active lurking" or "compassionate loitering" (see Chapter 16), emphasizing careful observation, a nonintrusive presence and caring, respectful contact. Immediately after a traumatic event, as survivors gather in shelters, points of distribution, or family centers, responders make themselves available with a warm, approachable presence.

Responders also encourage natural connections and

support networks in the community as "neighbor helping neighbor" helps to reduce isolation and rebuild social groups. Of particular importance for responders is providing comfort and safety to children and older adults who have been separated from parents and caregivers, and helping them reconnect as soon as possible. (The American Red Cross Safe and Well System website helps locate family and loved ones during and after disasters.) The PFA Guide (NCTSN & NCPTSD, 2006) describes several scenarios with children and adults illustrating these principles. Here is one example for counselors: "Here's what's going to happen next. You and your mom are going together soon to a place called a shelter, which really is just a safe building with food, clean clothing, and a place to rest. Stay here close to your mom until it's time to go." (p. 29)

PFA contact. Responders should initiate contacts in a non-intrusive and compassionate manner. First, observe the individual's behavior and determine that your contact would not be perceived as intrusive and then approach the individual saying, "Hi, I'm Rosa. I'm part of the county disaster team. I'm checking with people here at the shelter to see how they're doing after the floor and to see if I can help in any way. Is it ok if we can talk for a few minutes? Can I ask you name? Can I call you Keesha, or would you prefer Mrs. Jackson? Before we talk, is there anything you need right now, Mrs. Jackson? Juice or water? Have you had a chance to eat since you arrived at the shelter? (Keesha responds). Good. Well, let's sit for a few minutes and talk" (adapted from NTCSN, 2006, p. 3).

Stabilization

TV coverage of Haiti showed DMH providers employing stabilization techniques to calm and orient anxious, disoriented, or confused victims. Grounding, relaxation, and entrainment are three helpful techniques for victims when acute stress symptoms affect their functioning. These techniques should not be used until DMH volunteers receive formal training as well as practice in tabletop exercises. State and county agencies and professional associations frequently provide training, and in New Jersey, PFA training is a requirement for Disaster Response Crisis Counselor certification. Practice skills in a calm training environment before you need to respond during a real disaster. Dass-Brailsford (2010) reminded us, "A disaster site should not be the place where helping professionals test their skills for the first time" (p. 58).

Grounding. This technique helps individuals re-orient themselves when they appear to be losing touch with their environment. Begin to orient the individual by describing the grounding process. "After a frightening experience, you can find yourself overwhelmed with emotions or unable to stop thinking about or imagining what happened. You can use a method called 'grounding' to feel less overwhelmed. Grounding works by turning your attention back to the outside word. Here's what you do."

As the individual sits in a comfortable position, ask them to breathe deeply and slowly. Then continue, "Look around you and name five non-distressing objects that you can see. For example you could say, 'I see the floor, I see a shoe, I see a table, I see a chair, I see a person.' Breathe in and out again slowly" (NTCSN, 2006, p. 51).

The next two steps to the grounding technique, strengthen and confirm sensory connections in auditory and kinesthetic channels. "Name five non-distressing sounds that you can hear. For example, 'I hear a woman talking, I hear myself breathing, I hear someone typing, I hear a door closing. I hear a cell phone ringing.' Breathe slowly and deeply. Then continue to speak in a slow, calm voice. "Name five non-distressing things that you can feel. For example, 'I can feel the wooden armrest of this chair, I can feel my toes inside my shoes, I can feel my back pressing against my chair, I can feel the blanket I am holding, I can feel my lips pressing together.' Breathe slowly and deeply." (p. 56)

Relaxation. Most counselors have been trained in relaxation techniques using deep breathing or progressive muscle relaxation. Competency is important to be comfortable teaching these techniques to distressed individuals. Responders are most effective using active reflective listening and speaking in a slow, calm voice. Trauma survivors may find closing their eyes to picture a calming image a difficult task with images of the disaster floating in their mind.

The PFA Guide provides several exercises to teach deep breathing to distressed individuals. For example, while inhaling, individuals can visualize and say silently, "My body is filling with calm," and "My body is releasing tension" while exhaling (p. 83). Children can visualize their bodies like a balloon filling up with air and slowly letting the air out. In the "box breathing" technique, individuals picture themselves going around each side of a square, counting slowly while you direct them to: (a) breathe in (b) hold (c) breathe out, and (d) wait (Crimando, 2009, p. 22). While you count out loud, individuals count silently, distracting them from immediate stressors and empowering them to self-monitor their breathing.

Entrainment. The PFA provider can use entrainment techniques to calm agitated individuals who are speaking loudly or rapidly. Entrainment involves adapting the volume and tone of your voice in small increments to subtly influence the individual's next response to resonate more with yours. Start speaking a little more loudly than you usually do, but not as loudly as the individual is speaking. Then slowly lower the volume of your voice, thus influencing the individual to lower his or her voice to be more synchronous with yours. If the individual is speaking very fast, start by speaking a little more quickly than you normally do, then gradually slow your rhythm and pace to influence the individual to slow down (Crimando, 2009).

STOP. Remember the steps of the STOP technique when approaching distressed individuals: (a) Sit, (b) Think, (c) Observe, and (d) Plan. Sitting down first influences the individual to take action and follow your behavior, or begin walking slowly in the direction of assistance to guide the individual as you encourage them to follow. Guide your eye contact, personal distance, and touch by the norms of the culture and the community prior to the traumatic event. Observe the individual's body language, and before touching, ask, "Would you like a hug?"

SOLER. The SOLER technique uses body language and position to convey your interest, openness, and compassion. Five steps to remember are: (a) Sit squarely, (b) Open posture, (c) Lean forward, (d) Eye contact, and (e) Relax. Responders should be "low and slow" but always remain aware of the situation around you. Standing to the side of an anxious individual shows respect and reduces the potential for confrontation. Avoid asking several questions in succession, and most importantly, never tell the individual to calm down. Even if you are able to remain calm and confident, there are times that you may need assistance with highly distressed individuals. Maintaining an open position and personal space also provides you an opportunity to move quickly toward safety.

Responding to Trauma in Haiti

PFA's evidence-informed practice focuses on integrating multisensory approaches in connecting with distressed individuals. In this way, you talk less and integrate more physical action into your approach. Although this chapter focuses on disaster first aid, these principles and practices also inform trauma counseling. Disaster mental health cannot be adequately addressed without understanding the impact of trauma. Most survivors of mass

natural disasters such as floods or earthquakes return to a level of normal functioning quickly without mental health interventions while a small number (12% –15%) may go on to develop symptoms of PTSD. Recent advances in understanding the roles of the brain and body in trauma help integrate PFA with kinesthetic approaches for those times when talking is not effective. According to van der Kolk (2009),

> Our research showed that talking about traumatic events does not necessarily allow mind and brain to integrate the dissociated images and sensations into a coherent whole. Techniques other than figuring out, talking, and understanding have proven to be enormously helpful in the integration of these fragments of the traumatic past. (p. 463)

Indigenous cultural traditions empower individuals to reconnect with their families and community. Rituals such as chanting, singing, yoga, meditation, breathing, movement, drumming, tapping pressure points, and theater reduce stress and promote healing. The world watched as Haiti's children sang *Frère Jacques* and clapped their hands in tents in the devastated city of Port-au-Prince, and adults and families danced in the street. Tapping the strength and resiliency of individuals, families, and community is essential for recovery.

The traumatization extends to family members and friends who do not live in Haiti. For example, our Haitian friends living here lost relatives and friends, their high school was leveled, their vice principal killed, and the hospital where their mother had worked as a pediatrician was damaged. These images are indelibly marked in their minds and ours. (See the ACA podcast *Stress and Haitian Americans, After the Earthquake* at www.counseling.org.) The grave need for DMH responders in the first days following the earthquake in Haiti helps to underscore that disasters require more than individual help. Gold (2009) warned that response to trauma:

> …is inextricably tied to politics and policy. We cannot dispassionately conceptualize trauma, study trauma, or intervene to assist trauma survivors, while ignoring the conditions that rise to and perpetuate traumatic events. (p. 26)

Thus, as trauma providers, we are deeply moved and changed by the experience of those with whom we work. It is the fervent hope of all those involved with this book that in some significant way, you, our readers will also be moved and changed as a result.

MOVING FORWARD

If you read the full text of this new edition of *Terrorism, Trauma, and Tragedies: A Counselor's Guide to Preparing and Responding*, you will see strong themes emerging in the growing field of disaster mental health. You will note similar conclusions are drawn by many of the authors in this book and by researchers in the field whose work is cited in this edition. Best practices are now part of counselor training and are used by counseling professionals in their disaster and trauma work.

The second edition emphasized, "Trauma healing takes place through the process of telling one's story in order to reconstruct the experience" (Webber & Mascari, 2005). This edition continues that tradition and reflects the movement forward as evidenced by the enormous growth in research and practice.

Predominant themes agreed upon by both field traumatologists and disaster mental health counselors referenced in this final chapter reflect the professionalization of the field and the progress from evidence-informed toward evidence-based practice. These themes include: psychological first aid, standards of practice, cultural competence, compassion fatigue, posttraumatic growth, natural capacities for healing, neighbor-helping-neighbor, approaches for specific populations and settings, and stage-specific treatment for both disaster and trauma recovery.

The fourth edition will take these themes to the next level as we continue to shape best practices for counseling professionals. Please email your thoughts and suggestions to jwebber@ncju.com or dbass@counseling.org

Jane Webber, PhD, LPC, is associate professor and coordinator of the Counseling Program at New Jersey City University. She is a counselor in private practice and holds New Jersey Disaster Response Crisis Counselor certification (NJDRCC).

J. Barry Mascari, EdD, LPC, LCADC, is chair of the Counselor Education Department at Kean University, Union, New Jersey and holds New Jersey Disaster Response Crisis Counselor certification (NJDRCC).

Julia Runte is a graduate student in the Multicultural Education Department at New Jersey City University.

We are indebted to Steven Crimando, Director of Training at New Jersey Division of Mental Health Services-Disaster and Terrorism Branch, for training us in psychological first aid and disaster mental health.

REFERENCES

Courtois, C. A., & Gold, S. N. (2009).The need for inclusion of psychological trauma in the professional curriculum: A call to action. *Psychological trauma: Theory, research, practice and policy, 1*(1), 3–23.

Crimando, S. (April, 2009). Psychological first aid: Skills training for practical frontline assistance. Presentation to Disaster Response Crisis Counselors, Montclair, NJ.

Dass-Brailsford, P. A. (2010). *Crisis and disaster counseling: Lessons learned from Hurricane Katrina.* New York: Sage.

Everly, G. S., & Flynn, B. W. (2005). Principles and practice of acute psychological first aid after disasters. In G. S. Everly & C. L. Parker (Eds.), *Mental health aspects of disasters: Public health preparedness and respond, Revised* (pp. 79–89). Baltimore, MD: Johns Hopkins Center for Public Health Preparedness.

Everly, G. S., & Flynn, B. W. (2006). Principles and practical procedures for acute psychological first aid training for personnel without mental health experience. *International Journal of Emergency Mental Health, 8*(2), 93–100.

Gold, S. (2009, Fall). Keeping it real: The four pillars of trauma. *Trauma Psychology Newsletter. 4*(3), 1, 24–27.

Institute of Medicine. (2003). *Preparing for the psychological consequences of terrorism.* Washington, DC: National Academies Press.

National Child Traumatic Stress Network and National Center for PTSD (NCTSN/NCPTSD). (2006). *Psychological first aid: Field operations guide* (2nd ed.). Retrieved from www.nctsn.org and www.ncptsd.va.gov and http://www.nctsn.org/nctsn_assets/pdfs/pfa/2/PsyFirstAid.pdf

Smith, H. (2002). The American Red Cross: How to be part of the solution, rather than part of the problem. In D. Bass & R. Yep (Eds.), *Terrorism, trauma and tragedies: A counselor's guide to preparing and responding* (pp. 37-38). Alexandria, VA: American Counseling Association Foundation.

U.S. Department of Homeland Security Federal Emergency Management Agency. (2010). NIMS Resource Center. Retrieved from fema.gov/emergency/nims

van der Kolk, B. A. (2009). Afterword. In C. Courtois & J. Ford (Eds.), *Treating complex traumatic stress disorders: An evidence-based guide* (pp. 456-466). New York: Guilford Press.

Webber, J., & Mascari, J. B. (2009). Critical issues in implementing the new CACREP Standards for disaster, trauma, and crisis counseling. In G. Walz, J. C. Bleuer, & R. K. Yep (Eds.), *Compelling counseling interventions: VISTAS 2009* (pp.125–138). Alexandria, VA: American Counseling Association Foundation.

Webber, J., Mascari, J. B., Dubi, M., & Gentry, E. (2006). Moving forward: Issues in trauma response and treatment. In G. Walz, J. C. Bleuer, & R. K. Yep (Eds.), *VISTAS: Compelling perspectives on counseling 2006* (pp. 17-21). Alexandria, VA: American Counseling Association Foundation.